ISLAM IN THE BALANCE

ISLAM IN THE BALANCE

Ideational Threats in Arab Politics

Lawrence Rubin

Stanford Security Studies
An Imprint of Stanford University Press
Stanford, California

Stanford University Press
Stanford, California

Printed in the United States of America on acid-free, archival-quality paper

Library of Congress Cataloging-in-Publication Data

Rubin, Lawrence, 1973– author.
Islam in the balance : ideational threats in Arab politics / Lawrence Rubin.
pages cm—(Stanford security studies)
Includes bibliographical references and index.
ISBN 978-0-8047-9079-6 (cloth : alk. paper)
ISBN 978-1-5036-0065-2 (pbk. : alk. paper)
1. Islam and politics—Middle East. 2. National security—Middle East. 3. Egypt—Politics and government—1981– 4. Saudi Arabia—Politics and government—1982– 5. Iran—Foreign public opinion, Arab. 6. Sudan—Foreign public opinion, Arab. 7. Middle East—Foreign relations—1979– 8. Middle East—Politics and government—1979– 9. Threat (Psychology)—Political aspects—Middle East. 10. International relations—Psychological aspects. I. Title.
BP173.7.R82 2014
320.55'70956—dc23
2013044156

Contents

Acknowledgments

ISLAM IN THE BALANCE GREW OUT OF AN EFFORT TO reconcile international relations theories with the realities of Middle East politics. The inspiration and material in the pages that follow came from a collection of interactions and experiences over the years. Throughout the course of the 2000s when I lived for periods of time in Morocco, Yemen, and Egypt, I was confronted with a reality far different from the classical international relations theories I had learned. These diverse experiences provided unique insights into how different actors perceive the same threat and in what ways. Moreover, leaders seemed to respond to and be alarmed by words and ideas—forces that were difficult to measure by traditional means. Thus, my initial research agenda to understand the impact of Iran's nuclear proliferation efforts on Arab threat perceptions soon evolved into something much larger.

This book is an analysis of how ideas, or political ideology, can threaten states and how states react to ideational threats. More specifically, it examines the threat perception and policies of two influential Arab Muslim-majority states, Egypt and Saudi Arabia, in response to the rise and activities of two "Islamic states," established in Iran (1979) and Sudan (1989). My aim in this book is to provide important insight about the role of religious ideology in international and domestic politics of the Middle East and, in doing so, advance our understanding of how, why, and when ideology affects threat perception and state policy.

The major theme running through the book is that transnational ideologies may present a greater and more immediate national security threat than shifts in the military balance of power. There are two main components of this theme. First, ideology, or ideational power, triggers threat perception and affects state policy because it can undermine domestic political stability and regime survival in other states. Second, states engage in ideational balancing in response to an ideological threat. The analytical framework for understanding strategic interaction in this realm of international politics is referred to as an "ideational security dilemma."

In this work, I aim to combine a study of international relations with an in-depth regional focus on the Middle East. While the book examines the threat perception and policies of two Arab Muslim-majority states, Egypt and Saudi Arabia, it has broader implications for the region and lessons for the future of the Middle East. My objective is to provide a clearer understanding of these issues and relate why they are relevant for academics and policymakers alike. Because the region is changing so rapidly, I conclude with the fall of the Morsi regime in Egypt, two-and-a-half years after the beginning of the Arab uprisings. I am confident that my main arguments will continue to be relevant in the future.

This book has evolved over a long period of time and I have many debts to acknowledge. Leonard Binder and Deborah Larson were instrumental in my professional and academic development, as were Barry O'Neill, Bertram Raven, and David Rapoport. David in particular has served as an informal mentor. I also benefited from my interactions with Marc Trachtenberg and Steven Spiegel while I was at UCLA.

While my language training and experience in other parts of the Arab world had a profound effect on my intellectual development, the majority of my field research took place in Cairo over a period of many years. I wish to thank the many individuals who gave of their time to talk to me. Only a portion of the interviews I conducted over the years are cited in the book. In some cases, the interviews gave me important background information not found in the media. When the interviews are cited, I did not refer to the interviewee by name if the interviewee requested that his/her name not be used. Nonetheless, I would like to mention a few individuals who were generous with their time or pointed me to others that could help me: Albadr Alshateri, Gehad Auda, Mohammed Abdel Salaam, Mohammed Abu Dhahab, David Dumke, Mohammed Habib, Theodore Karasik, and Moheb Zaki. I would also like to thank Andreas Jacobs, the former head of the Konrad Adenauer Stiftung in Cairo, for providing me with a place to work and Dan Ross for his hospitality.

I received support both institutionally and financially from many sources. These include: multiple Foreign Language Area Studies Fellowships for Arabic, which were administered by the UCLA Von Grunebaum Center for Near East Studies; the Institute of Global Cooperation and Conflict; and the Horowitz Foundation for Social Policy.

Outside of UCLA, I would like to thank Shai Feldman and Kristina Cherniahivsky for my year as a visiting lecturer on the Myra and Robert Kraft Chair in Arab Politics at the Crown Center for Middle East Studies, Brandeis University (2008–2009). I would also like to thank the Belfer Center for Science and International Affairs at the Harvard Kennedy School of Government where I was a research fellow (2009–2010) with the Dubai Initiative. The interactions I had during these two years in Boston were instrumental in shaping this project. Lastly, the Ivan Allen College for Liberal Arts at the Georgia Institute of Technology provided me with teaching relief to complete the book.

My debts also extend to my colleagues and friends from a variety of capacities over the years: Lisa Blaydes, Eric Bordenkircher, Dan Byman, Udi Eiran, Sarah Feuer, Jarrod Hayes, Ron Hassner, Justin Hastings, Patrick James, David Karol, Joshua Karsh, Megan Kroll, David Palkki, Norrin Ripsman, Dane Swango, Fred Wehrey, Melissa Willard-Foster, Stacey Philbrick Yadav, and Vikash Yadav. I am particularly grateful to Ilai Saltzman and Jenna Jordan for reading multiple chapters and multiple drafts of chapters. I thank the anonymous reviewers who provided critical feedback. Editor Geoffrey Burn, Assistant Editor James Holt, and Senior Production Editor Tim Roberts were instrumental in shepherding this book through the process.

Lastly, I owe my family a great deal of thanks. My love goes to my parents, siblings, and my two children, Elie and Matan, who always help me with their smiles and endless laughter. And finally, my greatest appreciation goes to my wife, Adi, who has been with me from the beginning and has been my biggest source of support.

1   Introduction

"**Y**A AKHI [MY BROTHER], YOU KNOW, THE SHI'A ARE really just interested in dominating the whole Middle East. Their religion is a deviation from Islam." This was the response I got from a retired Egyptian military officer in 2005 when I asked if Iran's nuclear program presented a threat to Egyptian national security. This former career soldier continued: "After 30 years, Iran still wants to export the revolution." Later that week, I asked another official what he thought was Egypt's greatest national security threat. He responded, "Iran. They spread extremism and violence wherever they go."[1] At the time of these comments, Iran's brazen noncompliance with the International Atomic Energy Agency's requests was well underway.

The broader regional context is important here. In the run-up to Iraq's first democratic elections, Jordan's King Abdullah warned that a "Shi'a crescent" would emerge if Shi'a pro-Iranian parties came to dominate Iraq's new government. King Abdullah's warning went beyond Iran's influence in Iraq's domestic politics and even a purely sectarian religious issue. He claimed that the emergence of a Shi'a crescent could "alter the traditional balance of power between the two main Islamic sects and pose new challenges to US interests and allies."[2] At the core of this statement was a fear that Iran's regional ambitions sought to marshal an arc of ideological allies aimed at destabilizing Arab Sunni regimes. Over the next few years, a number of other Sunni Arab leaders followed suit and warned of Iranian "meddling" in domestic politics in even harsher terms.

Regional responses since the Arab uprisings raise similar questions about the role of ideas, threats, and power in international politics. Populations overthrew highly entrenched authoritarian regimes backed by powerful coercive apparatuses, supported by the most powerful military on the planet, the United States. A generation frustrated by the lack of economic or political opportunity and human dignity used new and old media technologies to mobilize and protest en masse against their authoritarian rulers. Beginning with the self-immolation of a Tunisian fruit seller in December 2010, "the Arab uprising unfolded as a single unified Arab narrative of protest with shared heroes and villains, common stakes, and a deeply felt sense of shared destiny."[3]

In response, conservative monarchies in the Gulf dedicated vast resources—economic, ideational and military—to preventing revolutionary contagion and the spread of ideas that pushed for political reform. Then, after Islamists came to power in Egypt, Saudi Arabia and the United Arab Emirates (UAE) mobilized ideational resources at home and abroad to balance against the Muslim Brotherhood's influence. These massive information and disinformation campaigns were accompanied by repressive measures against supporters of the Brotherhood in their own countries. Riyadh and Abu Dhabi quickly welcomed the Egyptian military's overthrow of the Islamist-led Morsi regime in July 2013, pledging billions in aid. The Morsi regime was overthrown in 2013 but it is too early to dismiss the importance of Islamist ideologies, or other political ideologies, for the international politics of the region.

These events should give international relations scholars pause when thinking about what role military power and ideas will play in the future Middle East and how the rise of Islamist regimes may affect regional relations. Thus, understanding the implications of these events for regional peace and security can be encompassed in a few key questions that lie at the heart of international relations theory: Can ideas threaten? If so, how and why? How have states responded to these threats? The story of how Islamist regimes have affected international relations provides the necessary insight.

The Islamist regimes that seized power in Iran (1979) and Sudan (1989) were regarded by neighboring states, including Muslim-majority countries, as national security threats even though these "Islamic states" did not have significant military capabilities when they came to power and in some cases never acquired them.[4] For example, Iran's military capabilities actually decreased immediately after the revolution that brought Islamists to power, yet many of Iran's former Arab allies, including Egypt and Saudi Arabia, came to consider the Islamic Republic one of their most serious national security threats for the next three decades. The resulting hostility led to hard balancing, including allying with Iraq against Iran during the Iran-Iraq War; opposing regionally popular Iranian proxies; engaging in arms racing; and soft balancing, including political opposition and domestic policies.

A similar pattern of events occurred after Islamists seized power in Sudan in 1989. Militarily weak and wartorn Sudan became a national security threat to its former allies Egypt and Saudi Arabia. But after hostilities peaked in the mid-1990s, including armed border clashes, Egypt and Saudi Arabia's relations with the first Sunni Islamic state normalized. Not only are we left with the puzzle of why Egypt and Saudi Arabia feared this militarily weak state, we must also ask why the threat subsided.

These cases raise a number of intriguing questions and provocative puzzles with direct relevance for understanding the future of the Middle East. Why did these Arab Muslim-majority states fear the rise of Islamist regimes, and how did these states respond? If military power was not the primary determinant of threat perception, can ideas threaten a state? If so, how and why?

Recent changes in the political and social landscape of the region as a result of the Arab uprisings, as well as the transformation in communication technologies, make answers to these questions even timelier and more relevant for policymakers. Domestic politics may once again become a fierce battleground for states to compete by projecting transnational political ideology as they did in the 1950s and 1960s when Egyptian president Gamal Abdel Nasser's speeches were a greater security threat than his state's military power. During the height of Nasser's regional influence, his most effective power projection capability was his ability to mobilize foreign domestic audiences as a threat to regime security against other states.[5]

Wars of words and ideas have been destabilizing in the past, contributing to regime change or even war. Nasser is credited or blamed for his role in overthrowing the Iraqi monarchy in 1958. It was the fierce symbolic competition between Arab states over their commitment to Arabism that compelled Arab leaders to make decisions that contributed to Israel's decision to attack preemptively on June 5, 1967. These decisions may have turned out to be unwise strategically, but they were necessary politically at the time.[6]

Scholars have written extensively about the role of military power and ideational variables in international relations theory. Yet the history of Islamic states in the modern Middle East demonstrates that conventional approaches do not necessarily explain threat perception and state policy, and few scholars have addressed this subject of regional and global importance. This book seeks to fill these empirical and theoretical gaps. First, it analyzes the threat perception and policy responses of Egypt and Saudi Arabia. Then it moves on to discuss the rise and activities of two "Islamic states," Iran and Sudan, as a way to contribute to our understanding of international relations and at the same time use international relations to better understand important dynamics in Middle East politics.

The Argument

This book is an analysis of how and why ideas, or political ideology, can threaten states and also how and why states respond to nonmilitary, ideational threats. More specifically, it examines the threat perception and policy responses of Egypt and Saudi Arabia to the rise and activities of two "Islamic states," Iran and Sudan. Four dyads that examine changes in threat perception before and after Islamists come to power form the empirical body of this work. The findings will help us make sense of the regional system that may emerge in the future.

The major theme running through the book—that transnational ideologies may present a greater and more immediate national security threat than shifts in the military balance of power—has two main components.[7] First, ideology, or ideational power, triggers threat perception and affects state policy because it can undermine domestic political stability and regime survival in another state. The sociopolitical logic of this external political threat is that the projection of domestic ideology through culturally resonant symbols could alter commonly held beliefs about the targeted regime's legitimacy and facilitate social unrest. Second, states engage in *ideational balancing* in response to an ideological threat. This nonmilitary response aims to mitigate an ideational threat's political-symbolic power through resource mobilization and counterframing. Consisting of domestic and foreign policies, this state behavior aims to bolster commonly held beliefs about its own legitimacy and seeks to undermine the credibility of the source of the ideational threat.

How and when a state utilizes an ideology affects threat perception and the type of policy response. An ideology must be *projected* for it to be considered a national security threat. The extent of this threat, as well as the response, is conditioned by the political environment. Islamist regimes became threats when they projected their ideologies *directly* through statements, including aggressive rhetoric, or *indirectly* through alliances, financial and military aid, and international institutions. This projection of power is not subject to a loss of strength gradient.[8] Periods of societal crisis in which state-society relations were strained made the regime particularly vulnerable to external threats. These conditions explain why Egypt and Saudi Arabia did not immediately consider the rise of these Islamist regimes as threats, why there is variation in a targeted state's policy response, and why other Arab states in similar situations did not consider Islamist regimes as threats. Turkey, although successfully ruled since 2003 by what has been called a liberal Islamist party, the Justice and Development Party (AKP), has not been considered a threat in the same manner because it has not projected its ideology.

In other words, this book is not saying that a change in ideological nature, however inimical to another state, immediately leads to change in threat perception or policy. Threat perception does not increase when the ideological distance of the elites increases.[9] Instead, this book argues that the ideas and symbols that express the projected ideological threat must resonate with a foreign domestic audience. Targeted regimes fear this foreign ideational projection more during periods of societal unrest. The potential for the resonance of symbols and ideas is heightened during periods of societal crisis in which the legitimacy of the ruling order is under strain and scrutiny.

The analytical framework for understanding strategic interaction in this realm of international politics is called an "ideational security dilemma." The logic of this framework is similar to the traditional security dilemma: one state's move in pursuit of security generates insecurity in another state. The uncertainty about intentions drives states to balance or bandwagon to achieve security, thus increasing the potential for conflict. Indeed, this concept has been used to understand ethnic conflict, interstate relations, and energy politics. Following this tradition, the currency of the threat is nonmilitary and ideological, and regime survival, not state survival, is what needs to be secured. Lastly, since transnational identity linkages in the Middle East play a role in connecting national security with international security concerns, this focus on regime security and transnational ideology recognizes the overlap between domestic and foreign policies.[10]

To be sure, the purpose behind this framework is not to argue that military power or the state is unimportant. Rather, this framework aims to capture dynamics at play that may be overlooked using more conventional approaches. Most observe and assess threat by examining alliance formation. But these indicators of threat are only part of the picture to get a sense of what really threatens a state. Domestic as well as foreign policies may be indicators and responses to an ideational threat that aims to undermine regime legitimacy and domestic stability. In addition, alliance formation may be motivated by, or even take on, a political value as a way to bolster a state's domestic legitimacy.

The ideational security dilemma can also be destabilizing, resulting in outbidding wars, misperception of intentions, and military confrontation. The escalation of rhetoric between the leaders of Jordan, Syria, and Egypt over who really represented Arab interests contributed to Israel's decision to launch a preemptive strike that launched the Six Day War (also known as the June War). The ideational security dilemma represents a dynamic that captures the ideational game, which can be destabilizing itself because regime survival is at stake in these strategic interactions. The approach in this book focuses on how ideas are national security threats outside of military conflict. Thus, this framework helps us understand how and why ideas threaten as well as why states engage in ideational balancing. It focuses on the notion that security should be conceived more broadly: states may balance for reasons other than increasing their military power and military power is not the only form of threat.

Through this framework we are also able to identify the mechanism by which ideas threaten. This is done largely through looking at the role of symbols as both a vehicle of ideational power and a heuristic to understand this type of nonconventional power and threat. A symbol is a powerful and efficient way to communicate information in a language that is easily understood by a particular audience within a particular cultural environment.[11] This information package, however, has the capacity to do more than just transmit information; political actors use symbols as a shorthand to communicate information about themselves, their opponents, and strategic settings in an effort to guide social action. When linked to a shared transnational identity, culturally resonant symbols can be used as effective tools to project an ideology and mobilize supporters abroad. But just as a shared identity across one identity category may be an asset for one actor, it can also be a liability. For example, during periods in which Iran's regional influence has grown, Sunni Arab leaders have pursued policies that promoted their sectarian and ethnic identities in an effort to undermine Iran's ideological, pan-Islamic appeals to

Arab publics. The domestic political environment affects the ways in which these threats are understood and the means to combat them.

In sum, ideas threaten when they are projected during periods of domestic crisis. Ideational factors, such as political ideologies, constitute a form of power and a means to threaten a regime's survival. States respond to this threat through ideational balancing. The ideational security dilemma helps us understand this phenomenon. The book's findings suggest that domestic and foreign policies, including but not limited to alliance formation, are crucial for understanding the nature and mechanism of an ideational threat.

Limitations of Previous Approaches

Why do states regard an ideologically oriented regime with limited power projection capability as a security threat? Why do Arab Muslim-majority states in the Middle East fear the rise of an Islamist regime? How do these incumbent Arab regimes manage transnational ideational threats posed by Islamist regimes? How and why do ideas threaten states? These questions cut across a broad range of literatures in both comparative politics and international relations, but at their core they are about how states assess threat.

Threat perception is important for understanding domestic and international politics: decision makers must be able to assess threats accurately to formulate policies that ensure their survival.[12] Threat perception is defined as expectations about the future behavior of another actor based on some combination of perceived intentions and capabilities.[13] The arguments about how states assess threats and how observers can measure them are subject to debate. Indeed, the idea that threat perception is based on some combination of capability and intent highlights the lack of consensus among international relations scholars about the relative weight that decision makers give a particular element in assessing threats. Whereas realism posits that capability is the most reliable indicator of threat, others, including some constructivists and those who favor political psychology approaches, emphasize the importance of intent. Other questions emerge: What types of threat are important? Who perceives and assesses the threat? Does threat perception necessarily translate to certain types of foreign policy outcomes, such as alliance formation? Lastly, how do factors such as regime type, state identity, and domestic politics affect how states assess threat?

The realist tradition, the paradigmatic approach to threat perception, provides an important starting point for this discussion. It posits that systemic factors, such as shifts in the relative balance of power, cause security concerns, and states are expected to respond to external military threats by balancing through alliance formation. In neorealist formulations, asymmetries of power alone (military and economic) can create perceptions of threat and interstate conflict.[14] This view dismisses altogether the role of intentions for assessing threat because intentions are too difficult to discern and states must assume the worst case scenario.[15] Domestic politics, ideology, regime type, and identity are unimportant and considered "reductionist."

The security dilemma exemplifies the structural approach to international politics. One state's moves to ensure its security in an anarchic system in which intentions are unknown cause insecurity for another state. The uncertainty about intentions and each state's quest for security drives arms racing and alliance formation, and through a spiral model this uncertainty can lead to conflict even if neither side intended it. Security is defined as the survival of the nation-state.

By way of stark contrast, the constructivist approach sees this dilemma and threat perception very differently. To begin, threats are not objective, materially based facts; threats are social constructions. This difference stems from an approach that emphasizes the role of ideas in creating social facts, such as identities and interests. Identity and the social actions of states play a central role in international politics for constructivists. Identity is a source of state interest, and this interest is a product of state interaction. These interests and social processes have been used to explain international conflict as well as cooperation.[16]

State identity is also considered a motive for security-seeking behavior. Challenging the assumption held by realists and mainstream constructivists that nation-states pursue survival and physical security, proponents of ontological security argue that states pursue other forms of security, such as self-identity, even when they compromise physical security.[17] Meanwhile, the literature on the "securitization" of nonmilitary threats suggests that issues related to identity may become security issues.[18]

These approaches to international politics differ over what factors determine foreign policy and, more broadly, war and peace. Stephen M. Walt's *The Origins of Alliances* represents a foundational work for a limited literature that engages these broader international relations questions by focusing on the Middle East. Walt marshals evidence from the Middle East to argue that neither ideological explanations nor balance of power theories alone explain alliance choice. Instead, Walt asserts that his balance of threat theory is the best explanation.[19] As a refinement of neorealism's heavy reliance on relative capability as the determinant of threat perception, this theory argues that states assess threats according to three additional factors: geographic proximity, the offense/defense balance, and aggressive intent.

Scholars have challenged this theory from a number of different angles revolving around the source of the threat and the type of threat that leads to foreign policy outcomes. Steven David's argument that states, particularly in the third world, "omnibalance" against systemic and domestic threats underscores the role of domestic politics in alliance formation. In particular, David suggests Egypt's realignment from the Soviet Union to the United States was driven by domestic threats to President Sadat's political survival.[20] Malik Mufti also highlights the role of domestic politics and regime security, not ideological commitment or balance of power/threat, as the crucial determinant of alliance behavior in his examination of pan-Arab unification efforts by Syria and Iraq in the 1950s and 1960s.[21] Michael Barnett and Marc Lynch's constructivist works on the Middle East focus on the importance of the domestic level in which state identity is central.[22] While Lynch emphasizes the role of the international public space, Barnett shows how nonmaterial interests, such as identity, have affected interstate cooperation and conflict. In his constructivist critique of Walt's neorealist characterization of Middle East politics, Barnett asserts it was the Arab states' competition over the shared identity and norm of Arabism that precipitated conflict.[23] Arab politics was essentially symbolic politics over who could define the regional order, and these debates were connected to the regime's legitimacy.

Other scholars have suggested that ideology does play an important role in threat perception and alliance choice. While Mark Haas's *Ideological Origins of Alliances* uses a broad set of cases to show that ideology, as an independent variable, affects alliance formation,[24] F. Gregory Gause III offers an important corrective of both realist and constructivist approaches. Using cases from the Middle East, Gause shows that alliance choice was driven by a state's decision to balance against the greatest ideological threat.[25] Taken together, these works, without dismissing the importance of material power, suggest that military capabilities are not always the primary determinants of state behavior and that domestic perceptual variables can affect foreign policy.

Foreign policies are affected by domestic politics and transnational ideologies, and states may not balance against the greatest external military threat.

These ideas highlight the salience of regime security over state security as a unit of analysis. As Curtis Ryan observes in his study of Jordanian foreign policy, "the preoccupation with system-level and structural explanations for alliances have too often led scholars to overlook the critical variables found within the domestic political realm."[26] In this way, regime security is both an assumption about decision makers' interests and an approach to foreign-policy analysis that examines opportunities and constraints imposed by the international and domestic spheres.[27]

This approach underscores the notion that security has been broadened in two directions: what threatens security and who is threatened. The point here is that a nontraditional force, ideational power, threatens domestic political stability and regime survival. National security is thus connected to the international system through transnational identities that have played an important role in Middle East politics. These ideational factors have been the source of threat and caused state balancing against the most threatening political challenge to regime survival.[28]

Ideology, Regime Security, and Domestic Symbolic Threats

The recent scholarship on regime security has incorporated domestic as well as systemic variables, including internal and external threats as well as nonmilitary threats. Whereas Gause highlights ideational political threats to regime security to explain foreign policy, particularly alliance formation, Ryan emphasizes economic and normative factors.[29] Ryan in particular argues that domestic regime security is the key explanatory factor in Jordanian foreign policy in which states face multiple security dilemmas. Barnett, coming from a constructivist perspective, also emphasizes the salience of regime security and survival as what motivates the "game of Arab politics."[30]

I extend these crucial insights about threat perception, regime security, and security dilemmas. Like Barnett, my argument suggests these symbolic political struggles are about regime legitimacy. The battlefield is the domestic public sphere embedded in the international public sphere of an Arab state system.[31] But the argument goes beyond these constructivist approaches as well as Gause's and Ryan's regime security approaches to illustrate the mechanism and sociopolitical logic by which these types of ideas and symbols in international politics become a perceived threat at the domestic level.

Moreover, my argument also explicitly identifies that project, in the presence of relevant domestic conditions, trigger the threat.

These crucial insights from threat perception and regime security lead to a new conceptualization of identity and security found in the ideational security dilemma and articulated by ideational balancing. The cases show that state-society relations affect a regime's perception of its security and this dynamic is influenced by international, particularly regional, politics.[32] This means that perception is not just a discrete event but a process of interactions among states, between state and society, and between the perceived connection between a foreign state and a local state's society. Ideological factors and domestic politics play an important role in understanding threat perception and its link to foreign policy.

This study differs from the way the previous literature, including regime security, has characterized threat perception and the way ideological threats have been examined. The heavy focus on alliance behavior by international relations scholars across the epistemological divide overlooks other types of state responses at domestic and international levels that identify the type and source of threat. Using alliance formation as an indicator of threat perception treats it as a dichotomous variable and cannot capture the intensity or change in intensity of a threat, especially if an alliance is already in place. This focus also obscures other types of foreign policies, including soft balancing, as well as domestic policies that are responses to external threats. Thus, as a departure from much of the traditional literature, I examine domestic and other types of foreign policy behaviors that have communicative-political value. This state behavior, ideational balancing, consists of resource mobilization and counterframing efforts at domestic and international levels.

Why study ideas and ideologies in the Middle East?

There is no better region than the Middle East to understand how ideas can threaten. The Middle East can be considered a subsystem and regional security complex that contains other overlapping systems in which global systemic pressures may affect, but not determine, regional politics.[33] Broadly speaking, the region is connected by geography, the intensity of security interactions, and transnational identities. The military weakness of states in this region, the existence of overlapping and competing transnational identities incongruous with political boundaries, and the establishment of ruling regimes with limited local support have elevated the salience of other forms of power and made regime survival, not just state survival, the primary national security concern. Thus, the regime, which determines domestic and foreign policies in these authoritarian settings, and political and transnational political ideology, is the focus of my analysis.

Nonetheless, there are many challenges in emphasizing the importance of ideational factors when studying this region. Stephen Walt, in fact, justified his case selection to develop his "Balance of Threat" because the Middle East was "dripping" with identity politics. These debates have only intensified since the events of 9/11, the Iraq War, Iran's pursuit of nuclear capability, and the Arab uprisings. While some downplay the significance of these factors, others overemphasize them by describing regional conflicts as "ancient hatreds" between Islam and the West, Sunnis and Shi'a, Arabs and Jews, Persians and Arabs, and Kurds and Arabs.

On the other hand, the complexities of this region provide tremendous analytical opportunities. This domain offers necessary nuance and vital clarity about policy debates and problems in international relations. By focusing on four dyads of interstate relations within one geopolitical domain, there is both similarity and difference across identity categories, such as ethnicity and religion, as well as variation in military capability. The threat perceptions and policies of Egypt and Saudi Arabia, the two most important Arab states in the region, are crucial windows for understanding broader trends and regional dynamics.

While all of the cases deal with the intersection of religion and politics, this book is not just about religion or Islam. Islamism, the most important force in Arab political discourse during the periods examined, is treated as a subset of other political ideologies. As such, readers should be struck by the similarities to other political ideologies, such as pan-Arabism in the Middle East during the 1950s and 1960s and Marxism during the Cold War.

The Islamist regimes established in Iran and Sudan should also be considered within a broader context of "ideological states." This type of state defines security as an expansion of its domestic system, which may come at the expense of traditional forms of security.[34] This security motive—to project its political ideology—means that these states, under certain conditions, could also be categorized as revolutionary and revisionist. But what distinguishes ideological states is that their ultimate goal is not necessarily to increase their relative power in the international system or to acquire territory; rather, they seek to transform the members of the system.[35]

While Islamism shares many similarities with other political ideologies, it is also somewhat unique because its basis is religion.[36] Religion is broadly defined as a belief in a supernatural being and its associated practices. It is often an "imagined community" that transcends political boundaries and contains divinely mandated norms that can justify self-sacrifice.[37] This means that the boundaries of a potential political community are not limited by territory and may increase through conversion. As a set of beliefs about a shared history and destiny, religion can serve as the source of a rich set of "cultural tools" for collective political behavior by connecting believers' ancient past with the present and future. Thus, these factors, particularly the potential to communicate and mobilize across borders, make religion a powerful social force and basis for a political ideology.

Because our interest is in understanding how perceptions affect strategic interaction, perhaps the most striking feature of religion is its association with "irrational" political behavior and violence. Religious norms can justify and reward violence and also demand self-sacrifice, such as martyrdom, in pursuit of a particular goal. In some cases, religious violence may even be the goal and not just the means to an end. Religion can act as a "force-multiplier" to strengthen assumptions about ideological actors' inflexibility, pursuit of values over strategic interests, risk acceptance, and aggressiveness.

Past and present trends in the Middle East make a compelling case for the importance of religion in contemporary politics. The Iranian revolution, the pinnacle of the Islamic resurgence, inspired many Islamic movements across the region that formed the backbone of violent and nonviolent opposition to authoritarian rule for the last three decades. The increased religiosity of society associated with the Islamic resurgence has enhanced the meaning, relevance, and political utility of religious symbols and ideology. During the 1990s, there was a growing challenge to authoritarian regimes from moderate and violent Islamic opposition movements. Islamist movements benefited from authoritarian regimes' experimentations with political liberalism and still continued to grow after incumbent authoritarian regimes tightened the political space. Radical Islamic groups targeted the "near enemy," their local, "un-Islamic" repressive regimes, until their defeat in the late 1990s led many of them to join al-Qaeda in its fight against the "far enemy."[38] This violence from "Islam's bloody borders" prompted broader debates about the clash of civilizations in which religion was the defining characteristic of a civilization or group.[39]

In the last decade, religion has mattered for threat perception in new ways. It has not simply been about clashes between Islam and the West or religious versus secular states; rather, sectarianism has played a major role as prism through which to view regional politics. The overthrow of Saddam Hussein's Sunni-minority regime had implications not just for the sectarian balance of power in Iraq but also for other parts of the region.[40] The Shi'a revival and the rise of Iran have meant that Arab leaders of countries with little or no Shi'a populations have framed threats that emanate from Iran in sectarian and even ethnic terms—at times intentionally blurring the distinction. King Abdullah of Jordan's warning of the "Shi'a crescent" became a coordinating symbol for Sunni cooperation and a justification for domestic and international policies. These changes have caused states such as Saudi Arabia to view Iran increasingly through a sectarian prism, including conflicts in Yemen, Lebanon, Palestine, and Bahrain.[41] Thus, the role of sectarianism in regional politics is important for how we think about threat perception, religion, and ideology. While Samuel Huntington's famous thesis on the clash of civilizations may have oversimplified the cohesiveness of Islam found within its "bloody borders," he correctly identified religion as the basis of a political ideological threat.[42]

Research Design

This book is organized around a series of bilateral relationships between a state in which an Islamist regime comes to power and a former ally (such as Iran/Egypt and Iran/Saudi Arabia or Sudan/Egypt and Sudan/Saudi Arabia). These dyads represents a subset of a larger set of cases, Islamist regimes and their relationship to other Arab states or, at an even broader level, ideologically orientated regimes and their neighbors. This research design allows us to pick the most appropriate cases for an in-depth analysis.[43] The point is to examine a state's threat perception and its policy toward another state in which an Islamist regime comes to power as a sound basis for evaluating the role of power and ideology in determining how states react to perceived threats. Therefore, these relationships are analyzed both before and after Islamists come to power marking "breakpoints" or "critical junctures." This provides the basis for a before-and-after design of process tracing so the fewest number of variables will change.[44] The case studies, which contain geographic, ethnic, and religious variation, help identify the extent to which certain variables matter.

These dyads as a whole exhibit both within-case and cross-case variation to test alternative hypotheses and explore interesting theoretical and empirical puzzles.[45] The within-case studies focus on the changes in threat perception (intervening variable) and state policy (dependent variable) before and after an Islamist regime comes to power. The within-case variation of an Islamist regime (Iran or Sudan) and another state (Egypt or Saudi Arabia) is examined alongside the within-case variation of the same Islamist regime's relationship to a second state. Policies and statements as indicators of threat should therefore be consistent with a change in threat perception.

Change in threat perception and state policy is assessed using a variety of methods. The empirical evidence for this book is drawn largely from extensive fieldwork in the Middle East (Egypt, UAE, Yemen, Jordan, Israel, and Qatar) over a six-year period (2004–2010). The sources of the data are interviews with current and former government officials, academics, and other local analysts as well as reports in the local Arabic press and media. A good example of a valuable source I obtained from my fieldwork was a parliamentary report written on Egyptian-Sudanese relations.

Case selection

As a matter of both case selection and definitional clarity, it is necessary to begin by discussing the terms "Islamic state," "Islamist regime," and "Islamic republic." The term "Islamic state" in its contemporary political usage is an elusive and contested term that is often used loosely for political purposes both outside and within the Muslim world. What a true "Islamic state" is and which countries fall under that category will not be answered here. However, since the purpose of this work is to analyze how other states respond to the emergence of this type of state as an embodiment of a set of political-religious ideas, the term "Islamic state" is used in an effort to capture the notion that the state and political order is defined in Islamic terms. At a very basic level, it is understood as a type of government whose source is shari'a (Islamic law).

Nonetheless, the term "Islamic state" is used interchangeably throughout this text with the terms "Islamic republic" and "Islamist regime." Sudan and Iran are officially "Islamic republics" even though they or others also use the term "Islamic state."[46] This book uses the term "Islamist regime" to refer to the interaction of an Islamic state that uses ideational power.

Some might ask about other states that refer to themselves as Islamic republics (i.e., the Islamic Republic of Pakistan) or those that are often categorized as Islamic states, such as Saudi Arabia, which claims that shari'a is the source of its legislation. Since there is no way for this author or anyone else to determine what constitutes a true Islamic state, the present study focuses on a specific domain of cases within the Arab Muslim world in which Islamists come to power. For many Islamists, who believe it is a religious obligation to become politically active, the goal of this activism is to create an Islamic state and society.

More broadly, why are the Islamist regimes of Iran and Sudan the focus of this study and not the liberal Islamist regime of Turkey, for example? It would seem plausible that a democratically elected liberal Islamist regime in a well-functioning political system and strong economy should constitute more of a threat. The reason is that under Prime Minister Erdogan, Turkey, during the period covered in this book, did not try to aggressively project their ideology as a threat to other regimes in the region. However, toward the end of the 2000s, there were growing signs that some states interpreted Turkey's turn toward the Middle East as a soft projection of its ideational power.

The examination of Egypt's and Saudi Arabia's threat perceptions of Iran and Sudan is both policy-relevant and offers an extremely useful opportunity for theory building. Other differences include regime type. During the period of inquiry, the regime in Egypt represents a republican form of government whose legitimacy is not based on religion, whereas Saudi Arabia is a monarchy whose legitimacy is intimately tied to religion. Not only are Egypt and Saudi Arabia both Arab Sunni states, they are arguably the two most influential actors in the "Arab system."[47] They have different forms of both hard (material) and soft power. Egypt's material power is military and Saudi Arabia's is economic. Egypt's soft power has been based on its Arab leadership, and Saudi Arabia's soft power is linked to its Islamic heritage. These nonmaterial capabilities form the basis of their claims to regional leadership.

When paired with the states in which Islamist regimes have come to power, Iran and Sudan, the case studies contain similarity and difference along constants such as sectarian and ethnic identity, geography, and variation in domestic ideology and military capability (see table 1.1). There is considerable variance in the relative balance of power when Iran is part of the dyad and little variation or even military power in the cases involving Sudan. Ethnic and sectarian differences do not vary over time but they do vary across dyads. From this design, it is possible to generate hypotheses about the outcomes of ideological appeals and, in some cases, to show how the

TABLE 1.1 Characteristics of Cases

Dyad	Ethnicity	Sect	Geographic Proximity
Egypt-Iran	Arab-Persian	Sunni-Shi'a	Far
Egypt-Sudan	Arab-Arab	Sunni-Sunni	Near
Saudi Arabia-Iran	Arab-Persian	Sunni-Shi'a	Near
Saudi Arabia-Sudan	Arab-Arab	Sunni-Sunni	Far

outcomes are somewhat counterintuitive at the theoretical level. For example, why would Saudi Arabia, a majority of whose inhabitants adhere to a form of Islamic practice that is socially and politically conservative and staunchly anti-Shi'a, fear religious appeals from a regime that is not only non-Arab but also founded on a revolutionary Shi'a ideology? One would expect the vast differences between the Islamic Republic of Iran's Shi'a revolutionary ideology and the (conservative) Saudi regime's staunchly anti-Shi'a Wahhabi foundations to mitigate the mobilizing potential of religious symbols and messages coming from Shi'a Iran.

Although all the cases share the same dynamic where allies became enemies some time after Islamists came to power, the variations within the cases overcome the perceived selection bias. After all, the purpose is not to make a universal argument that Islamist regimes or ideology is threatening in all cases. Rather, the purpose is to use and test theories to explore an unexplained phenomenon. The idea is to show how ideas can threaten, focusing on a specific set of cases and a select domain to advance our understanding of this phenomenon.

Lastly, the cases themselves have "intrinsic importance."[48] Saudi Arabia's and Egypt's relations with Iran have been incredibly important for regional peace and security. These relationships during periods of cooperation and hostility have had a tremendous impact on regional politics and will do so for years to come.

Contributions

This book makes important theoretical and empirical contributions to the study of Middle East politics, international relations of the Middle East, and international relations theory. Leveraging regional expertise to make a broader academic and policy contribution, this book is the first of its kind in international relations to focus on how Islamic states affect the threat perception of Arab states. Within the small body of work on international relations of the Middle East, there is even less written about Islam and international politics that engages international relations theory. Most of the works that do focus on Islam, ideology, and international politics do so from a comparative politics, diplomatic history, or terrorism studies perspective.

This book has important implications for international relations theory. The main contribution is the introduction of the analytical framework of the ideational security dilemma and the concept of ideational balancing. These contributions capture a different way to think about the indicators, sources, and mechanisms of threat perception. While the existing literature devotes an overwhelming amount of attention to alliance formation as an indicator of threat, this approach only captures part of the picture. Domestic policies and foreign policies outside the realm of alliances in response to systemic ideological threats may fall under the radar. As a result, previous approaches fail to recognize that the most serious national security threat at a particular time concerns domestic political stability. This is why domestic politics and domestic policy responses must be taken into account.

Second, the book speaks to the question of how threats are defined and assessed by states. Paralleling the debates about ideas versus interests, most of the literature either over- or understates the importance of ideology. This book is an attempt to take ideology seriously and yet remain within a realist framework that accepts the centrality of states and their pursuit of security in an anarchic system. In doing so, the emphasis on cultural, perceptual variables at the domestic level engages the growing literature on neoclassical realism. On a broader level, it refocuses attention on the importance of ideas in international politics that does not focus on norms. It shows that ideas matter in how they threaten and can be a source of conflict.

Third, the engagement of religious symbols as a component of ideology will contribute to the study of religion and international relations. Although the burgeoning literature in this new field includes both interpretivist and rationalist accounts, this book bridges the gap by illustrating mechanisms for how, why, and when symbols and religious ideas connect domestic and international politics. The importance of sectarianism as a way to counterframe ideational threats and as a fear of ideational projection introduces something unique from religion to international affairs. It follows that states may also assess threats according to sectarian affinity as a category of identity.

Beyond international relations, the quest to answer why and how an incumbent regime perceives religious symbols and transnational ideology

(Islamism) as a threat to its political stability engages important debates in comparative politics about authoritarianism and Islamic activism. While most of this literature has focused on bottom-up (societal) pressures and top-down state policies, this work shows how external ideational pressures affect state-society relations. Indeed, the main contribution of this literature is that international forces affect Arab authoritarian regimes' perception of their vulnerability to Islamic political activism.

Road Map

Each chapter makes a unique contribution to my argument. Chapter 2 presents the argument and describes the mechanism for understanding why states fear transnational ideological threats by looking at the logic of states' responses. In particular, the chapter discusses the ideational security dilemma, what ideational power is, and how it threatens by examining the role of symbols in ideational threats. It also elaborates on types of ideational-balancing activities as a state's response to nonmilitary threats.

The rest of the book proceeds chronologically by examining relationships between Arab Muslim-majority states (Egypt and Saudi Arabia) and states in which an Islamist regime comes to power (Iran and Sudan). Chapter 3, "Ideational Projection and the Iranian Revolution," examines how Saudi Arabia and Egypt responded to the Iranian revolution. This chapter clearly shows how changes in Iranian military capabilities had little effect on Saudi Arabia's and Egypt's threat perception. Iran's military capabilities dramatically increased in the 1970s as relations with Egypt and Saudi Arabia strengthened. After the revolution, as Iran's military capabilities declined, it became a greater threat. Egypt and Saudi Arabia responded to Iran's ideational power projection through ideational balancing to mitigate the nonmilitary, national security threat.

Chapter 4, "The Power of a Weak State: Sudan's Relations with Saudi Arabia and Egypt," examines the threat perception of Sudan before and after Islamists came to power. This chapter makes the strongest case for threat perception changing in the absence of a military threat and illustrates how the actual *projection* of the ideology correlates with the intensity of the perceived threat. The dyad is significant because Egypt and Sudan share borders, as well as sectarian and ethnic identities, and their relative balance of power remained asymmetric in Egypt's favor. Comparing the other dyad, Saudi Arabia considered Islamist Sudan a threat not because it harbored bin Laden, supported terrorism, and allied with Iraq; rather, Sudan claimed a mantle of leadership that challenged Saudi legitimacy and could mobilize domestic opposition around important symbols. Sudan challenged Saudi Arabia through activities of the Popular Arab Islamic Conference (PAIC), which Khartoum created as a counterweight to the Organization of Islamic Conferences (OIC). This case also reveals how important context is: the shared sectarian identity, Sunni Islam, seems to have played a role in exacerbating tensions because the ideas could resonate instead of being a basis for cooperation.

Chapter 5, "Indirect Power Projection and Ideational Balancing after Khomeini," examines Saudi and Egyptian relations with Iran. It highlights how these Arab states feared Iran's indirect ideational power projection and how they responded in slightly different ways. Although they chose slightly different types of ideational balancing in the 1990s, during the 2000s, both states' ideational balancing took the form of "securitizing sectarianism" as a means to mitigate the ideational threat. Cairo's and Riyadh's promotion of sectarianism as a response to Iran's ideational power projection also served domestic and foreign policy interests. This dynamic is vital for a more nuanced understanding of Egypt's, and especially Saudi Arabia's, fear of Iran's growing regional role, spurred by its nuclear program. Overall, this chapter is a clear illustration of how the interplay of domestic and regional politics affects threat perception and state policy.

Chapter 6, "Balancing the Brotherhood," concludes the book by summarizing the findings within and across cases and by illustrating how these findings contribute to the study of international relations and Middle East politics. It examines the post–Arab Spring environment until the fall of the Morsi regime in Egypt in 2013 and also discusses why Turkey's liberal, Islamist-led government has not been a threat so far. In this new environment, there are signs that more unified Arab publics may play a greater role in conditioning the stability of states as they did in the 1950s and 1960s. Thus, the book and this chapter conclude by discussing how conservative Gulf monarchies of Saudi Arabia and the UAE have employed ideational balancing strategies.

2 The Ideational Security Dilemma, Ideational Power, and Ideational Balancing

THE PREVIOUS CHAPTER PRESENTED THE ARGUMENT for how and why ideational power triggers threat perception and affects state policy. The ideational security dilemma provides the analytical framework to understand how and why ideas can be national security threats. Targeted states fear this nonmilitary form of power because it could undermine their domestic political stability. More specifically, targeted regimes fear the projection of politically subversive ideas through culturally resonant symbols that could alter commonly held beliefs about their legitimacy and facilitate social unrest. In response, these targeted states engage in *ideational balancing* to mitigate an adversary's ideational power.

This chapter proceeds by elaborating upon the ideational security dilemma as an analytical framework for this study. I then move on to define ideational power, what its resources are, and how it has been employed as a tool of statecraft in the Middle East and elsewhere. These sections are followed by an in-depth discussion of symbols. A symbol is an information package, and it is both the most effective delivery vehicle of this form of power as well as a heuristic device to illustrate the sociopolitical logic of how ideas affect threat perception and policy.

The last part of this chapter describes the components and logic of ideational balancing—the targeted regime's response to an ideational threat. Ideational balancing aims to mitigate the domestic political threat from a projected transnational political ideology. Consisting of domestic and foreign policies, the goal of ideational balancing is to mitigate the threat of ideational power projection. States employ counterframing and resource allocation measures to undermine the credibility of the source of the ideational threat and to bolster commonly held beliefs about regime legitimacy. Examining the components and logic behind these responses further illuminates the source and mechanism of this nonmilitary, domestic symbolic threat.

The Ideational Security Dilemma

The security dilemma—the notion that one state's move in search of security can threaten another state—is one of the central concepts of international relations theory. "Striving to attain security from such attacks, they are driven to acquire more and more power in order to escape the effects of the power of others. This in turn renders the others more insecure and compels them to prepare for the worst." Herz, the scholar credited with coining the term "security dilemma," explains the way this uncertainty drives arms racing: "Because no state can ever feel entirely secure in such a world of competing units, competition ensues, and the vicious circle of security and power accumulation is on."[1]

A vast literature has developed around this concept. It is at the center of debates within realism, the dominant paradigm of international relations. This concept has been applied to understand "many of the most important questions of international relations theory and security policy."[2] It has been applied to interstate conflict, ethnic conflict, and energy politics. While some call for a refinement along structural lines, this book departs from the traditional usage in a number of ways and, at the same time, extends this concept to a different area—the ideational realm of international politics and regime security.[3] Similar to Ryan's work on security dilemmas in Arab politics, which highlights the salience of regime security, I use this analytical framework as a way to better understand the strategic interaction of two states and how and why ideas can threaten.[4]

There are a number of analytical advantages in using this framework. First, the empirical reality of the Middle East suggests a different dynamic from the conventional approaches in which states respond to external military threats through external alliance formation. This is not to say that the Middle East is exceptional or unique but rather that many of the concepts and theories based on a different set of empirical realities may not always apply to other regions. State-based external military power has not always been the most salient determinant of threat perception. In fact, within the Arab fold, power lay in the ability to mobilize foreign domestic audiences.[5] "Nasser's power derived not from Egypt's military capabilities but from his ability to impose a meaning on the events of his time, to establish the norms of Arabism, and to weave a compelling image of the future."[6] After "statism" increased from the 1970s after two decades of coups, internal challenges continued to be the biggest source of threat.[7] Even though the Arab state system became less permeable, it has still remained susceptible to transnational currents.[8] "Internal cleavages and instability make states vulnerable to outside intervention, penetration, or further destabilizing events."[9] Internal threats caused some states to form external alliances against internal threats, and external threats caused states to balance or bandwagon against the greatest ideological threat.[10] At a broader level, Ryan suggests that Arab states may actually face two security dilemmas: internal and external.[11]

These empirical realities have led some to suggest that the concept of security should be expanded. Buzan, Waever, and de Wilde argue that this concept of security for the state should be broken down in other areas and developed.[12] It follows that the state may not be the appropriate unit of analysis. The strong linkage between security and systemic security overlooks the role of internal threats.[13] These broader theoretical underpinnings form the basis of seeing regime security, not state security, as the driver of policy, particularly in the Arab world.[14] Therefore, we should look to other forms of power and state responses.

One manifestation of this type of dynamic is the "outbidding" wars between states that have based their legitimacy on maintaining a particular image. "Arab governments manipulated and deployed symbols that derived from their shared cultural foundations, persuaded their audience that their definition of events and proposed response was appropriate, legitimate, and consistent with Arabism and, second, control the foreign policies of their rivals."[15] This led to a "dangerous game of brinkmanship" in which Arab states would be drawn in to prove who was more committed to the Arab cause than another or face a loss of prestige.[16] The security motivation to project ideational power may be domestic to shore up the regime's legitimacy. Revolutionary regimes often face this pressure and look outward, especially when the ideology that drives the revolution has a universal component (whether the French Revolution, Bolshevik revolution, Islamic revolution, etc.). But this domestic source of foreign policy could be an outcome of a local political struggle as well. Moves to acquire ideational power through statements or actions in pursuit of regime security may challenge another regime, especially if it has similar political struggles over similar issues.

This two-level framework shows how this type of power threatens and how a state responds to this type of threat. States engage in ideational balancing in response to an ideological threat. This nonmilitary response aims to mitigate the communicative power of an ideational threat through resource mobilization and counterframing. Consisting of domestic and foreign policies, this state behavior focuses on bolstering beliefs about a targeted regime's legitimacy, defending against rhetorical attacks, or undermining the credibility of the source of the ideational threat. A more detailed discussion of ideational balancing is found at the end of this chapter.

The logic of this framework is similar to the traditional security dilemma: one state's move in pursuit of security generates insecurity in another state. The uncertainty about intentions drives states to balance or bandwagon to achieve security, increasing the chances of conflict. Yet, there are a number of key differences. First, the currency to acquire security is nonmilitary. Second, the threat is to regime survival and it is political. The ideational security dilemma suggests a way to capture a set of interactions that take place outside this realm of politics. The acquisition and use of this type of power is what can trigger insecurity in another state. The focus in this book is not whether and why the perceived ideational aggressor, an Islamist regime, projects this type of power. Instead, introducing this framework focuses attention on how this type of threat works and how states respond to it.

The point of this framework is also to emphasize that regime security drives interstate relations. Regimes are compelled to defend against potential challenges to societal beliefs about their legitimacy. The refinements form the basis of the ideational security dilemma as a way to understand the context in which a different type of power, ideational power, can be perceived as a threat. It highlights a different understanding of security that is based on a different type of threat using a different unit, the regime, as an effective guarantor and determinant of state security.

How Ideational Power Threatens

Traditional approaches to international politics have largely focused on the role that military power plays in driving war and peace in international politics. In addition, there is an underlying assumption in much of the international relations literature that the expected utility of conflict is material (alliances portfolios are part of this).[17] But a number of scholars have identified how nonphysical forms of power can influence foreign policy decision-making and international politics. These challenges raise important questions for how to think about power.[18] Social psychologists, for example, have developed categories of "social power" whose influence is related to the subjective qualities the actor possesses.[19] This form of power parallels nonmilitary power resources in international relations including moral authority, norms, and status.[20] And in the realist realm, proponents of soft balancing argue that states use nonmilitary forms of balancing, including normative power, to respond to a military threat.[21]

The most widely known and influential conceptualization of this nonphysical form of power is soft power. Coined by Joseph Nye, soft power is the ability to accomplish a foreign policy objective "through attraction rather than coercion or payments."[22] In contrast to hard power, which influences decisions through the use of carrots or sticks based on material capabilities (economic and military), soft power gets "others to want the outcomes that you want."[23] This type of power shapes preferences through attraction.[24]

The concept of ideational power incorporates these nonphysical or nonmaterial power assets that can influence decision making and political behavior. A country's culture, values, moral authority, and foreign policies are its ideational power resources. These elements are interconnected. Culture and values expressed through foreign policy can enhance moral authority as a form of social power.

Foreign policies are the way a state communicates its culture, values, and ideas as ideational power. Foreign policies include messages and statements, through official and nonofficial channels, about the regime's values; diplomatic support; membership in international organizations; economic aid and military support; and alliance formation. While some of these foreign policies may certainly enhance a state's hard power, these foreign policies communicate crucial information either directly or indirectly. For example, Iran's economic aid to Hamas communicates that Iran is committed to a pan-Islamic, anti-Western order in which it sees itself as the leader, but this act does not alter the balance of power with any of its adversaries.

The most recent example notwithstanding, there seems to be a fairly positive association with ideational power, particularly by the state that wields it.

For example, most Americans think that their values, which form a basis of its soft power, are a positive force in the world. But during the Cold War, the Soviets did not view U.S. soft-power activities that tried to spread democratic ideas and capitalism as anything but threatening to Soviet interests at home and abroad. Similarly, the United States viewed Soviet propaganda during the Cold War as evidence of an expansionist ideology.[25]

While ideology played a role in superpower competition during the Cold War, it played a greater role in the Middle East during what is known as the "Arab Cold War" of the 1950s and 1960s.[26] Egyptian President Gamal Abdel Nasser used pan-Arabism to mobilize domestic opposition in Western-aligned monarchies such as Saudi Arabia and Jordan as well as Iraq, whose monarchy was overthrown in 1958 due to this pressure. Saudi Arabia used Islam to counter these appeals. The outbidding war over who could be more anti-Zionist and anti-imperialist was motivated by a fear of appearing uncommitted to the Palestinian cause domestically and internationally, and it also contributed to the escalation spiral before the 1967 War that caused Israel to preempt. Other states such as Syria and Iraq, which swore their allegiance to pan-Arab ideals, also tried to use this type of foreign policy tool. After the Iranian revolution, Iran used pan-Islamism in a similar manner to pressure its adversaries.

The mechanism of ideational power's sociopolitical threat

These examples underscore the potential political threat of ideational power. This ideational threat is the danger that a particular set of ideas, a transnational political ideology, can challenge an adversary's domestic political stability and survival. This political threat can destabilize the domestic political order by challenging the legitimacy of the regime as well as its external legitimacy, an important part of its domestic legitimacy.[27] Moreover, the power of "attraction" to an external source of political authority is a challenge to the local political authority and state sovereignty. The force has the potential to facilitate social mobilization and alter commonly held beliefs about the targeted regime's legitimacy.

The idea-based threat drives the perception that the regime is unstable and the regime believes it is vulnerable to such a threat. In this way, the threat that ideational power poses for national security is both real and perceived, or objective and intersubjective.[28] The objective qualities are a state's policies, such as public pledges of aid, military or economic agreements, and statements. How targeted leaders perceive the impact of these policies on their society's beliefs is the intersubjective aspect. Lastly, the power of this threat does not take place in a vacuum. An ideational threat requires an environment of shared characteristics because it must have the potential to resonate due to some *shared* set of values or beliefs. Projected domestic ideologies are directed at the characteristics of other states.[29]

The ideological threat is thus highly dependent on domestic politics and, in particular, a regime's perception of its domestic legitimacy. But what is meant by "legitimacy"? This widely used term is generally understood to mean the public's acceptance of political authority. Political legitimacy is also referred to as popular consent and the public's belief in the "rightness" of the government. Some scholars see it as an important component of national security, particularly in the Arab world, as the center and target of internal threats. Mohammed Ayoob argues that political legitimacy is linked to "stateness," which is the product of state making and state building.[30] Others that do try to incorporate domestic variables into systemic-level analysis do so by equating political legitimacy implicitly or explicitly with regime security.

Rather than weigh in on this debate, it is more constructive to say something about how legitimacy functions. Legitimacy does two things: it increases the efficiency of the state's coercive capabilities and provides a "protective belt" during times of crisis.[31] It is also clear that governments without legitimacy may become unstable. Since traditional sources of legitimacy are scarce in the Arab world, most symbols of legitimacy are social, cultural, and religious.[32] These symbols draw on transnational identities. Therefore, Arab governments' legitimacy is dependent on what happens not only within their borders but also outside them.[33] "Regimes have gained power and legitimacy if they have been seen as loyal to accepted Arab goals, and they have lost these assets if they have appeared to stray outside the Arab consensus."[34]

It is also important to highlight another key aspect of this type of power: its relationship to geography. For a military threat, there is often assumed to be a loss of strength gradient.[35] In other words, the further away you are, the lower the ability to threaten because it is difficult to project military power at a sustained rate over distance. But for ideational power, geography does not cause the same type of loss of strength. Geography matters insofar as distance affects the extent to which cultural characteristics, such as identity, are shared. This is because ideational power and the spread of ideas can be projected by using a variety of nonterritorial communication devices, most notably radio, satellite television, and the Internet. Most recently, new social media technologies can help disseminate ideas that can largely transcend state boundaries as long as they can find ways to penetrate or seep into the local public space. Therefore, this external force can appeal to citizens of states over the heads of local political authorities for support against their own governments.[36] On a more basic level, regimes fear that public deliberation on a serious level can also affect a state's identity and interests.[37] This change can in turn threaten the legitimacy of the regime.

Let me summarize the argument and the mechanism so far. An ideational security dilemma captures the dynamic that ideational power, when projected, can trigger threat perception. Regime security is threatened when leaders fear that these projected ideas will change commonly held beliefs about their right to rule. Projection, not just the regime type, matters. The information has to be presented to a public to potentially alter beliefs and ideas.

An ideational threat marshals different resources and poses a different type of threat to a different actor in contrast to a military threat. An ideational threat targets the regime or, more crucially, the public space in which beliefs about legitimacy can be shaped. It has been a matter of national security to maintain an image that a particular regime adheres closely to its foundational ideology or national narrative because ideologies as well as national narratives have been crucial elements of regime legitimacy,

The Hardware of Ideational Power:
Media Technologies, Transnational Networks, and Symbols

The capacity to distribute a message or idea is a vital capability. "The participants of a square dance may all be thoroughly dissatisfied with the particular dances being called, but as long as the caller has the microphone, nobody can dance anything else."[38] Before the Internet and the explosion of new social media technologies, the playing field was limited. While the threshold may be much lower today, some political actors, such as states, have greater capabilities than others. And in this regard, the media and social networks play crucial roles.

This section will survey the hardware of how symbols are a component but also can be used as a heuristic to understand the mobilization mechanism. One of the ways that we can see this power in action is by identifying some its components and, in particular, tracing the role of symbols as a way to understand the mechanism. Because the spread of ideas is the only way a capability becomes a potential threat, we must examine these resources.

Media technologies

A state's media or informational apparatus can be one of the most effective ways to produce the necessary information to promote its image or undermine a rival. In the early part of the last century, radio broadcasts in foreign languages were used to promote "favorable images of their countries and ideologies to foreign publics."[39] The United States established the Voice of America during World War II to counter Nazi propaganda. In addition, during the Cold War, the Voice of America broadcast in Russian to counter Soviet propaganda. Print media, satellite television, and the Internet constitute other forms of information or communication used by states as well as nonstate actors.

Innovation in communication technologies has changed some of the players of the game but not necessarily the game itself. Satellite television and the Internet have become the new tools—as well as liabilities—for those political actors whose existence depends on controlling information. One of the oldest modern communication technologies, print, has had a powerful impact in the past and is still relevant. The two Saudi-owned international Arabic dailies, *al-Hayat* and *al-Sharq al-Awsat*, give the Saudi regime a measure of power to control debates and set the agenda. The Internet has increased the ability of foreign audiences to access these sources of news. Audio cassettes, although generally associated with religious sermons and not as official state instruments, were an effective political tool in the past. In fact, the cassette-sermon audition tape was an integral part of the Islamic revival since the 1960s[40] and has played a role in spreading Islamic fundamentalism.[41] The most famous example of mobilization against a political authority using cassettes is Ayatollah Khomeini's sermons, which were smuggled into Iran while he was in exile. Today, we might find CDs, MP3/4s, and YouTube videos as their replacements.

The most famous model of transnational media influence is Gamal Abdel Nasser's Voice of the Arabs (*Sawt al-Arab*), a transnational radio service, which he used to spread his ideology and in effect to undermine the legitimacy of his foes by appealing to pan-Arab sentiments. Decades after the Voice of the Arabs declined in importance, satellite television was able to penetrate the public spaces over which semi-authoritarian regimes sought to dominate. While Arab satellite channels were launched early in the decade, the establishment of al-Jazeera in 1996 had a transformative effect because it was a seen as a credible and accessible source of information that challenged state narratives.[42] The effect on public political discourse prompted Saudi Arabia to establish al-Arabiyya, al-Jazeera's primary competitor, to counteract some of the information deemed harmful to Saudi interests.[43]

The 2000s saw the intensification of these media wars over narratives about important regional crises with implications for domestic politics. The Iraq War was also a turning point.[44] And although the battle was largely between al-Arabiyya and al-Jazeera, other actors tried to engage the Arab public. The United States set up al-Hurra. And more significantly, just after the U.S. invasion of Iraq in 2003, Iran established al-Alam, a twenty-four-hour Arabic-language satellite news channel for the Arab world that Iraqis could access without a satellite dish.[45]

Transnational networks

Social networks are another vehicle for information distribution, serving as a potential medium for a state to exert its influence and to spread ideas. Social networks are seen by many as the most powerful means to spread ideas and information.[46] Indeed, this potential state or nonstate asset is an important resource not only because it can spread information but also because, if activated, it can serve as a basis for transnational collective action. In addition to providing social movements with legitimacy, money, prestige, and power, social networks can radicalize individuals and form the most important base for recruitment.[47] "Networks are not just umbilical cords that provide sustenance to movements through recruitment; they can be actively manipulated, and thus impacted and reshaped by formal organizations."[48] Much of the growing research on social networks investigates the links between information communication technologies and political mobilization as well as the role of social networks in terrorism and nuclear trafficking.

In the Muslim world, religious networks have and may continue to play a potential political role.[49] While many think of terrorism and al-Qaeda when this subject is mentioned, the idea that networks can be manipulated or serve as avenues to spread ideas and change identities in the Muslim world can be traced back to the neo-Sufi reform movements of the nineteenth and twentieth centuries.[50] Another variant of this type of mobilization was the Mahdist Jihad movement in Sudan in the latter half of the nineteenth century.[51] Shi'a communities also have important transnational networks because their religious authority may be located outside the community's political borders. Although the center of Shi'a Islam today is Iran (Qom), Iraq (Najaf) still remains an important center of Shi'a scholarship and religious authority and may, in fact, compete with Qom in the future. The fact that Shi'a Islamic groups have penetrated local societies through social (religious and political) networks concerns Arab Sunni regimes in Saudi Arabia, the UAE, and Bahrain greatly.[52] Although many Gulf Shi'a communities look to a *marja'* outside of Iran for religious authority, many Sunni leaders assume that Shi'a collective sectarian identity can be easily manipulated, thus trumping their loyalty to the state.[53]

The existence of these networks has been both a real and an imagined threat for some Arab incumbent regimes. Assessing the actual strength of the networks is difficult because both authoritarian regimes and Islamist oppositions face situations in which it is advantageous to either exaggerate or minimize the transnational linkages. An authoritarian regime may want to inflate the transnational linkages to use them as a pretext for repression, or they can minimize an indigenous linkage to show that the regime has complete control over society. Islamic activists may wish to inflate the image of their reach to attract recruits, or they may prefer to hide their transnational connections (usually financial resources) to avoid the glare of the regime and maintain a perception of loyalty. Islamic movements' preference to operate through informal networks may be a rational response to the repressive environment in which they have operated,[54] but it has also increased suspicion of their transnational links and ultimate intentions. Finally, the common ideological foundations of the movements and their goals contribute to the perception that Islamists cooperate transnationally.

Symbols: The vehicles of ideational power

Symbols constitute the most powerful delivery vehicle to communicate a transnational ideology as a political threat in two related ways. First, symbols are an effective way to promote a particular set of ideas about the strategic environment, and the actors themselves, to influence the audience's beliefs. Second, the symbol itself can be a focal point to facilitate collective political behavior. This means that in international affairs, the communicative function a symbol plays can be part of a game of strategic interaction between states and their domestic audiences as well as between states and foreign domestic audiences.[55]

A symbol is defined as an information package, which may stand for something else or communicate information in a language that is easily understood by a particular audience within a particular cultural environment.[56] Political actors use symbols as a shorthand to communicate information about themselves, their opponents, strategic settings, and social action.[57] Symbols can be used as both a weapon and a battleground over who has the authority to interpret the meaning of the events.[58]

Symbols are often used in an important process called "framing." Frames are "schemata of interpretation . . . to locate, perceive, identify, and label" to explain the world at large.[59] Frames also transmit information, but they do so by producing counternarratives to align preferences of actors. Drawn from the social movement theory literature, frames serve "to mobilize potential adherents and constituents, to garner bystander support, and to demobilize antagonists."[60] Moreover, a frame may use a symbol to interpret the world. They effectively do the same thing as a symbol, but a symbol is a sign or cultural cue that possesses meaning. The framing process is interactive between the framer and the audience as well as between the two political competitors.

The way symbols are expressed matters. Symbols, and the ideas they embody, can be expressed either directly or indirectly or through a reference or act, respectively. A direct symbolic attack, one that includes aggressive rhetoric with a compelling cultural reference that is easily understood by the audience, is the most contentious. Referring to an adversary as a reviled enemy from a shared cultural tradition is meant to convince or coerce supporters to change their beliefs on normative grounds. Ayatollah Khomeini labeled the Shah as "Yazid," the second caliph of the Umayyad Empire considered by many as a tyrant, to frame the political struggle as a religious-normative conflict between the forces of good and evil. This type of framing makes the political struggle part of a larger historical process, and when connected to religion it connects the individual to the past. In some cases, these references may suggest political violence or rebellion as a religious imperative, such as referring to the Egyptian leader as the Pharaoh. On a more general level, attacks may refer to the source of cultural symbols, such as the Quran, to make a political point. Ayatollah Khomeini, for example, attacked the Saudi monarchy by claiming it was not only despotic and morally corrupt but also an un-Islamic institution according to the Quran.

Less direct ways of using symbolic expressions are of equal importance. The context of an event can obviate the need for a direct reference to an adversary or to a specific symbol. For example, when Saudi Arabia hosts a meeting or reaches an agreement in the holy city of Mecca, it is meant to convey a sense of religious legitimacy and provide additional normative glue for the actors. In fact, in the case of the Mecca Agreement of 2007 between Hamas and Fatah, the setting was a way to assert Saudi authority over the Palestinian conflict in opposition to Iran's growing influence in the Arab Muslim world.

Specific policies, including alliance formation and membership in international institutions, are also indirect ways of communicating symbols and ideas. While these public agreements may be a statement about a state's interests, they also project the values that participants embody. When Iran and Sudan announced their cooperation agreements over mutual security interests, they invoked religious principles to communicate that they represent "true" Muslim interests and that other states, which oppose them and their policies, do not. Symbols or symbolic acts may convey a set of values about the beliefs and intentions of the messenger as well as another actor.[61]

International institutions, meanwhile, have an additional dimension. International institutions play an important role as vehicles and battlegrounds of ideational power. Control of the institution provides tremendous ideational power resources. Theories of international relations tell us that states join or establish international institutions for a variety of reasons: signaling, norm adherence, material benefit, affirming legitimacy and status, facilitating cooperation, security, and extending power and influence through agenda setting. Although various schools of international relations might argue otherwise, these motivations are not mutually exclusive. During the Arab Cold War, Saudi Arabia established the Muslim World League in 1962 to combat Gamal Abdel Nasser's secular, nationalist pan-Arab ideology by appealing to religious values. This act provided an institutional framework not only for enhancing cooperation but also providing Saudi Arabia with a formal mechanism to set or defend a political agenda for the Muslim world. This reinforced the regime's legitimacy by reaffirming its authority as a spokesman for the Muslim world. Saudi Arabia's role emphasized its religious identity alongside its Arab one to trump the secular ethnic identity, Arab nationalism, which republican Egypt used to undermine other monarchical, Western-aligned regimes such as Saudi Arabia.

These international institutions are also important as an effective way to generate commonly held beliefs or even *common knowledge* about the extent to which a regime's political authority is perceived to be legitimate.[62] The regular summits or conferences of international institutions function as *public rituals* to produce common knowledge, whereby everyone knows everyone who attended and what that participation means. Ritualization, or repetition, of the meeting of a particular group conveys a meaning to its participants and observers, and as a communicative act, rituals express and reinforce a social order.[63]

The Arab League summits and Organization of Islamic Conferences meetings had this effect at various times or at least tried to. With its headquarters located in Cairo, the Arab League's summits during the 1950s and 1960s reinforced the idea that Egypt was the leader and agenda-setter for the Arab world.[64] Similarly, Saudi Arabia's role in the establishment and sponsorship of the Mecca-based Organization of Islamic Conferences (OIC) in 1969 was intended to have the same effect.

Given the potential benefits of establishing international institutions, it is logical that the Islamic Republic of Iran and Islamist Sudan created alternative international Islamic institutions to disseminate their messages and challenge existing commonly held beliefs about the legitimacy of the regional order. In the Sudanese case, Hassan al-Turabi established the Popular Arab Islamic Conference (PAIC) as a counterweight to the Saudi sponsored OIC. The PAIC's first meeting took place at the same time as the OIC's summit and became a regular public ritual.[65] The PAIC did more than just provide a "legitimate" and "credible" internationally accepted form of statecraft to express alternative views about the political and social order; it also communicated that Sudan saw itself as the leader of powerful political trends within the Arab world. In doing so, the PAIC promoted a set of beliefs about the social and political order in the Arab world that countered the OIC's quietist (politically quiescent) interpretation of Islam.

How symbols can threaten regimes

Symbols are also important tools for coordinating political behavior. Symbols reveal information about the strategic setting and may act as a focal point for coordinated social action among actors who want the same thing but are only willing to act if they know others will.[66] The existence of this coordination problem is one of the explanations for why unpopular authoritarian regimes are not faced with constant protests.

This is where the environment, particularly culture, plays a crucial role when it comes to social mobilization. Culture is the characteristic of the environment that provides meaning, enabling these information packets to be communicated and understood. A culture provides a "toolkit" for constructing "strategies of action."[67] "People may have in readiness cultural capacities they rarely employ; and all people know more culture than they use."[68] This is why, for example, religion and, as discussed in this book, Islam, is so important for coordinating social action in the Arab world.

Shared culture plays an important role in facilitating social action and can fill information gaps. If a focal point is not directly communicated, or if public communication of expected behavior is difficult, common conditions of authoritarian rule—"who the parties are and what they know about each other"—helps determine the focal point.[69] For example, Tahrir is the most obvious place for Cairenes to stage a major protest, just as Times Square, as Thomas Schelling relates, is the most obvious place for New Yorkers to meet without communicating.

Second, events exogenous to a particular game can become a point of convergence of beliefs and translate to social action.[70] The Danish Cartoon Affair (2005) resulted in many protests outside of Denmark against Western interests and united at least temporarily many local opposition groups over this issue. Most recently, Mohammed Buazzizi's symbolic act of self-immolation to protest the Tunisian system's corruption and despotism, commonly referred to as the catalyst for the Arab uprisings of 2011, inspired others beyond his country's borders. Many countries had their own Mohammed Buazzizi, including Egypt's Khaled Said, a twenty-six-year-old Alexandrian, whose lethal beating in 2010 at the hands of corrupt police officials was caught on video. It is impossible to explain the exact timing of why one symbol could serve as a focal point, but it is clear why this event became a mobilizing symbol: Buazzizi's plight was easily understood across Arab countries.

The influence of Buazzizi and the Arab uprisings generally surprised many because a bottom-up process with little organized ideological direction drove these dramatic events. Local leaders had understandably focused their efforts on preventing a religious source from creating a focal point through the "power to make a dramatic suggestion."[71] This brings us full circle to why the projection of ideology through symbols can be a source of threat. The common denominator of the opposition groups was religion. This is why Islam is so important for coordinating social action in the Arab world during the period covered in this book. Symbols resonate because they are drawn from a shared history, language, and culture and linked to identity and political community.[72]

These discussions underscore the role symbols can play in affirming or challenging commonly held beliefs that form the basis of a regime's legitimacy.

Rulers of contested authoritarian regimes are concerned about controlling the meaning of symbols. National narratives must be maintained because regime survival is at least partially based on society's belief about its ruling regime's legitimacy. They tell the story of why subjects should accept the ruling regime and why they need to accept the type of social contract the leadership has made.[73]

There is an important logic in ensuring that the regime's subjects accept this narrative so it remains a widely held belief: "These narratives create consent without the need to continuously exert direct repression or regularly distribute handouts."[74] The key for regime stability is to find ways to create public consent about the regime's narrative and, more importantly, its symbols. The way a regime maintains authority is that it forces citizens to behave *as if* they accept the meaning of the symbols.[75] Public obedience, demonstrated by taking part in elections or parades, thus reinforces the coordination problem that ensures authoritarian rule by communicating information about the expected behaviors of others. "The more willing one is to support authority, the more others support it."[76] Therefore, since common knowledge is crucial for social order, it is no surprise that political opponents fight over the mechanisms for generating it.[77]

The preceding discussion means that an adversary's projection of subversive ideas may pose a national security threat to a targeted regime by promoting ideas that challenge commonly held beliefs about the regime. The shift in beliefs may then trigger a shift in the expected behaviors of other actors and encourage others to publicize, not falsify, their preferences.[78] This is what Arab regimes tried to guard against during the Arab Spring—some with greater success than others.

The danger of reaching a "tipping point" in which it becomes individuals' dominant strategy to protest is what these contested regimes fear even when the opposition is severely divided.[79] In Egypt, the Kefaya movement, which led protests for political reform in the mid-2000s, managed to attract supporters that came from competing, if not hostile, ideological camps: Islamists, nationalists, liberals, and secularists.[80] This movement was not immediately successful even though it may have laid some of the groundwork for the Egyptian revolution of 2011. Nonetheless, overcoming a coordination problem only requires that motivations change based on knowledge of others' expected behavior and not necessarily a commonality of interests.[81] For this reason, a fragmented opposition containing secularists, religious moderates, and radicals, who may all have different motivations and risk tolerance for political action, can still pose a potential threat. And herein lies how ideational power can affect threat perception: a regime perceives that an adversary's projection of ideas and symbols during a societal crisis will undermine beliefs about its legitimacy, facilitate social mobilization, and threaten its survival.

Countering Ideational Threat through Ideational Balancing

States employ a variety of strategies and tactics to combat ideational threats. Ideational balancing aims to mitigate the domestic political threat from a projected transnational ideology. These domestic and external responses are composed of two pillars: counterframing and resource mobilization.

The first pillar is counterframing, or efforts to "rebut, undermine, or neutralize" an opponent's "myths, versions of reality, or interpretative framework."[82] Counterframing involves four tactics: denial, defense, counterattack, and neutralization. Denial is a countermeasure to minimize the spread of the message and subversive ideas. There are two options for (authoritarian) states that control the media: cut off communication entirely or not allow discussion of the issue. Before the advent of satellite television, authoritarian regimes were able to minimize their society's exposure to subversive messages through their control of the public space. The Saudi media has often taken this approach by ignoring certain controversial issues.[83] Still, even in contexts of liberalizing regimes, it is significant that the state-run media outlets decide not to discuss the issue but that other media outlets do.

The second tactic of counterframing is defense. Defense is a rhetorical rebuttal to charges that involve positive statements or justifications of policies that are consistent with core and commonly held beliefs about normative values. For example, in response to Ayatollah Khomeini's religious attacks against President Sadat for granting the deposed shah asylum, Sadat justified granting the terminally ill shah asylum by stating that a core value of Islam is compassion.

The third tactic takes the form of a counterattack. This approach aims to undermine the source of the threat and thus deny the claim's validity. One example is the Egyptian media's association of Hassan al-Turabi with Ayatollah Khomeini's ideological extremism along with the jab that Turabi lacked his charisma. To undermine Turabi further, the media described Sudan as a failed or failing state to show that Turabi was a failure too.

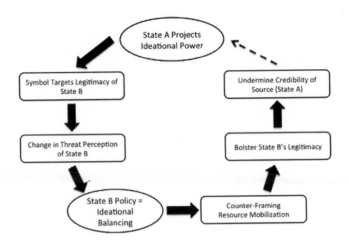

FIGURE 2.1 Mechanism of Ideational Power

The fourth tactic, neutralization, tries to recast the issue and change the environment to affect the resonance of a subversive idea. Pointing out the differences between the source of the threat and its intended audience is another way to undermine its credibility. Arab Sunni leaders have at various times referred to Iran as "Persian" or "Shi'a" to delegitimize its policies and ideas as well as those domestic actors that may support the policies. Two examples stand out. Arab leaders framed the Iran-Iraq War as an Arab-Persian war with tinges of sectarian framing as well, even though much of Iraq's army was composed of Shi'a soldiers. Second, during the 2000s, as Iran's popularity and regional influence grew, so did the rhetoric about a "Shi'a crescent" creeping over the Middle East.

The second pillar of ideational balancing involves resource mobilization. It is aimed largely to support efforts to mitigate the spread of subversive ideas and enhance the spread of favorable ideas. The state allocates resources for ideological apparatuses of the state, such as state-sponsored religious institutions or the "Official Islam."[84] The rationale for this type of resource allocation is to provide support for the most important societal source of moral authority. Policies are implemented to increase the number of clerics trained at state-sponsored religious institutions, aimed at creating more avenues of influence in society of ideas favorable to the regime's political survival. In the

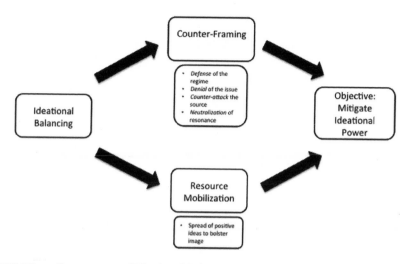

FIGURE 2.2 Components of Ideational Balancing

case of Saudi Arabia, these resources are allocated for institutions, scholarships, charities, and networks to enhance the regime's image abroad.

There may also be ideational benefits or even motivations for alliance formation. A group of states may respond to an ideational threat by reframing an issue. For example, during the 1990s many North African states, facing the same threat of Islamic fundamentalism and political violence, reaffirmed in public meetings that Islam was a religion of moderation and tolerance. Issuing these statements together was a way to show there was a consensus about what Islam is, and this definition naturally justified their political authority on religious grounds (see fig. 2.1).

Summary

This chapter has explained the key components and logic behind the argument for how and why ideational power triggers threat perception and affects state policy. The chapter has defined ideational power, what its resources are, and how it has been employed as a tool of statecraft in the Middle East and elsewhere. These sections were followed by a discussion of the role of symbols to illustrate the sociopolitical logic of how ideas affect threat perception and policy. The last part described the components and logic of "ideational balancing"—the targeted regime's response to an ideational threat. Ideational balancing aims to mitigate the domestic political threat from a projected transnational political ideology. To bring us full circle, the ideational balancing is a measure to combat the national security threat the regime fears and the precise mechanism of the ideational threat (see fig. 2.2).

The chapters that follow provide the empirical evidence and mechanisms that support these arguments. Egypt and Saudi Arabia feared this nonmilitary form of power because it could undermine their domestic political stability. More specifically, these regimes feared the projection of politically subversive ideas through culturally resonant symbols could alter commonly held beliefs about their legitimacy and facilitate social unrest. Each of these chapters shows how ideational balancing were responses to this nonmilitary external threat.

3 Ideational Projection after the Iranian Revolution

THE IRANIAN REVOLUTION STANDS OUT AS ONE OF the most important events of modern Middle Eastern history. It transformed the region's security architecture, affected state-society relations in many neighboring countries, and, on a global level, serves as an example of a successful social revolution. The establishment of the Islamic Republic of Iran in the wake of the Iranian revolution brought tense relations with many former regional allies. Arab Sunni states, particularly in the Gulf, balanced against Iran by forming such institutions as the Gulf Cooperation Council and supporting Iraq in its war against Iran.

Traditional realist explanations have trouble explaining this shift. Iran's military power actually declined during the revolution and immediately after. Moreover, the 1970s saw a drastic increase in Iranian military power projection capability yet relations between Iran and some Arab states, particularly Egypt and Saudi Arabia, improved. So why did threat perception decline when Iran's military power projection capability increased and threat perception increase when Iran's capabilities declined?

Many conventional explanations explain the shift in threat perception and relations through the fear of revolutionary contagion. The argument is that many Gulf monarchies feared the Iranian revolution as an inspiration for their own restive populations. This explanation does not fully explain how the revolutionary contagion is a threat and under what conditions. Why, for example, did Syria not fear this export of the revolution the way Egypt and Iran did?

This chapter argues that Egypt and Saudi Arabia perceived Iran's ideational power projection as a national security threat. The conflict was not a response to a military threat. The ideational security dilemma between Iran and its former allies, Egypt and Saudi Arabia, destabilized relations. In response to this situation, Egypt and Saudi Arabia pursued ideational balancing.

The chapter will proceed as follows. The focus is on Egyptian and Saudi responses to Islamists that came to power in Iran. The first part will separately cover the background of both relationships (Egypt-Iran, Saudi Arabia–Iran) to put them in perspective, highlighting the common theme that, particularly in the 1970s, relations improved despite the fact that Iran's power projection capabilities increased. The second part will examine how Egypt and Saudi Arabia perceived the Iranian ideational threat and what their response, ideational balancing, can tell us about the ideational threat they faced. The concluding section will briefly discuss why Syria, which we might have expected to fear Iran, did not.

Iran's Relations with Egypt and Saudi Arabia in Perspective

The most intense periods of ideological competition between Iran and Egypt for regional influence occurred after each country's respective modern revolutions. For Egypt, the 1952 Free Officer's Revolt brought Gamal Abdel Nasser and his secular pan-Arab, anticolonial ideology to power. Iran's Islamic revolution in 1979 challenged Egypt's regional status and political legitimacy. Both Iran and Egypt promoted ideology as a fundamental component of foreign policy and have used ideology as a strategic, rhetorical tool to undermine the political stability of other regimes. Each state sees itself as a regional leader seeking to maintain regional influence.

While ideological competition has often exacerbated tensions, Iranian-Egyptian competition for geopolitical influence has been a potential source of conflict. Iran sees the Gulf as vital to economic and military survival. Egypt sees the Gulf as its strategic reserve, for both military and economic purposes.[1] Gulf security, as a part of larger Arab security, is also part and parcel of Egyptian national security. Thus, it is natural that Iran and Egypt have wrestled not only over the naming of the Gulf, Persian versus Arab, but also over its political, and at times territorial, control.

Iran has had a long and complicated relationship with the Arab world. Empires based in Iran once controlled large swaths of territories inhabited by Arabs. The Arab conquests brought Islam to Iran. While the Ottomans ruled over Arab lands for six hundred years, the Persian Empire under different dynasties was its rival in Asia. In the twentieth century, Iran's relations with most of the Arab world grew stronger from the reinstatement of the shah in Iran in 1953 until his overthrow in 1979. During this period, Iran's relationship with the Arab world was entangled with the politics of the Cold War and, more importantly, the Arab Cold War. This conflict pitted Arab conservative, pro-Western countries against republics aligned with the Soviet Union and Egypt.[2]

Iran's pro-Western alignment ruled by a monarchy put it on a collision course with Egypt. From 1953 to 1970, relations between Egypt and Iran were fairly hostile. The CIA-sponsored coup, which overthrew Iranian Prime Minister Mohammed Mossadegh in 1953 and reinstalled the pro-Western shah, sparked a Cold War between Egypt and Iran. This hostility reached its peak in 1960 when Egypt cut diplomatic relations with Iran in response to Iran's refusal to renounce its de facto recognition of Israel.[3] Egypt perceived Iran as a threat because of its pro-Western orientation, its support for other monarchies, and its strategic partnership with Israel. Tensions increased during Egypt's war in Yemen (1962–1967), although Iran did not directly participate. Eventually relations improved between the two states following Egypt's defeat in 1967, and full diplomatic ties resumed after Gamal Abdel Nasser's death in 1970.

Saudi Arabia

Prior to the 1970s, Saudi-Iranian relations looked similar to Egyptian-Iranian relations. From the reinstatement of the shah in 1953 until the Iranian Revolution, Iran and Saudi Arabia cooperated on regional security issues and shared similar ideological beliefs about the norms of interstate relations. The overthrow of the Hashemite monarchy in Iraq in 1958 brought the fear of Nasserism close to home for Iran and Saudi Arabia.[4] From the announcement of the Baghdad Pact, Nasser lambasted the ruling Hashemite monarchy for joining this regional security organization backed by Western powers. This incitement against enemies of Arabism and the presence of other groups sympathetic to Nasser's pan-Arabism contributed to the perception that Nasser was involved in the military coup that overthrew the monarchy. Then, in 1962, Nasser formally expanded his military and political reach into Gulf affairs by backing the military coup that had overthrown the monarchy and by sending over 55,000 soldiers to fight with republican forces in the Yemeni Civil War

(1962–1970). Saudi Arabia and Iran supported the royalist forces with military and economic aid.[5]

These two Western-aligned monarchies formed the core of a bloc of states opposed to Nasserism (until its demise) and Soviet penetration. While Iran and Saudi Arabia perceived Soviet penetration as a threat for some of the same reasons, they feared Nasser's ideology and activities for slightly different reasons. For Saudi Arabia, Nasserism was an ideological threat both externally and internally. Riyadh feared Nasser's potential to subvert domestic politics through the mobilization of pan-Arab sympathies among local and foreign Arab publics (particularly the nascent Gulf States). In contrast, Tehran was more concerned about Egypt's activities in the Gulf and the stability of the Saudi regime; it was not concerned about domestic political subversion.[6]

Discounting Shifts in the Balance of Power: The Cairo-Tehran Axis and the "Twin Pillars" Policy

Iranian relations with Egypt and Saudi Arabia strengthened during the 1970s. The Cairo-Tehran axis developed as the "Twin Pillars" policy supported by the United States became the foundation of regional security.

This alliance between Egypt and Iran, two important U.S.-aligned regional powers, featured growing levels of diplomatic, economic, and political cooperation. While Iran benefited by continuing to improve its relations in the Arab world, Egypt benefited from Iran's investments and loans as well as Iran's political support for Sadat's unpopular peace initiative toward Israel. Finally, President Anwar Sadat and Shah Reza Pahlavi shared a very close personal relationship that complemented their strategic alliance. In his autobiography, Sadat describes a sense of loyalty to the shah for what he had done for Egypt: "I shall never forget the day when the Egyptian petroleum reserves fell to a dangerously low level, after the October 1973 War (due to the closure of our oilfields). I sent word to the shah of Iran and he immediately supplied us with more than 50,000 tons. He actually ordered Iranian oil tankers that were at sea to change course and go directly to Egypt to offer help. He said: 'El-Sadat is a brother to me; I shall respond to his request on the spot.'"[7]

Meanwhile, Iran's relationship with Saudi Arabia continually improved and became institutionalized. The end of Nasserism in the wake of the 1967 War brought the underlying and shared systemic-level threat of Soviet penetration to the forefront. During the 1970s, Saudi-Iran relations took on a greater strategic significance as these regional actors became part of the United States' Twin Pillars policy in the wake of the British withdrawal from the Gulf in 1971. Iran was concerned that the British withdrawal would allow extremists backed by Egypt and Iraq to fill the vacuum. Meanwhile, Saudi Arabia needed Iran to ensure a smooth power transition as the British left the Gulf sheikhdoms exposed. Cooperation between Iran and Saudi Arabia revolved around Gulf stability; King Fahd and the shah exchanged information on a regular basis concerning South Yemen, Soviet threats, and terrorism.[8]

These relationships peacefully coexisted. Iran's military and economic power grew exponentially. Iran used the dramatic rise in its oil revenues to purchase billions of dollars of U.S. military equipment. Iran's privileged position as the most important military power in President Nixon's Twin Pillars regional strategy gave Iran carte blanche to purchase military equipment.[9] These arms sales included F-4s and naval equipment, providing Iran with significant power projection capabilities. Many also suspected Iran's decision to build a peaceful nuclear program with U.S. assistance was motivated by a decision to acquire nuclear weapons.[10]

Iran's role as the Gulf policeman, as part of the Twin Pillars policy, along with its power projection capabilities enabled it to pursue an activist foreign policy role in the Gulf. The shah was committed to containing communist and radical influences. But the shah saw a greater role for Iran in the Gulf than just serving as a policeman. "We are thinking of a security perimeter and I am not speaking of it in terms of a few kilometers. Anyone versed in geo-politics understands this."[11] Iran periodically made irredentist claims to Bahrain and seized Abu Musa Island and the two larger Tunb Islands in December 1971, securing Iran an important strategic position in the Strait of Hormuz.[12] Iran also intervened militarily in the Dhofar rebellion in Oman by sending troops to defeat the Popular Front for the Liberation of Oman backed by the Soviet Union and China.

It should be noted that the Iranian-Saudi alliance and security cooperation wtihin the Iranian-Saudi alliance was not exactly equal. Iran had a much more powerful military. Also, during the 1970s, its vast increases in oil revenues enabled it to enhance its power projection capabilities dramatically.[13] The Nixon Doctrine and Twin Pillars policy, a system of cooperation to maintain regional stability, merely institutionalized the reality that Iran was the effective military power and real policeman.

These changes in the relative balance of power existed alongside indicators of greater Iranian ambitions. The shah's irredentist statements about Bahrain, although retracted, were consistent with its occupation of Abu Tunbs in 1971.[14] Saudi Arabia was aware that the shah wanted the United States to declare "that Iran was the only regional power capable of defending the Arab Sheikhdoms."[15] Moreover, Iran's activities as the Gulf policeman, including its dispatch of troops to Oman to put down an anti-Saudi Marxist group, must have also enhanced Saudi Arabia's suspicions of Iran even though Saudi Arabia benefited from Iran's regional activities.[16] Okruhlik summarizes these considerations: "And even though both were under the U.S. defense umbrella, Saudi Arabia was never close to Iran, as it feared the loss of its national autonomy. The House of Saud was always suspicious of the shah and never endorsed any formal security system with him but understood Iran's foreign policies guaranteed its stability by protecting the status quo.[17]

Nonetheless, Iran's increase in relative power and indicators of greater regional ambitions did not cause a shift in the Saudi threat perception of Iran. These factors were discounted in favor of balancing against the Soviet threat. This would all change with the outbreak of the Iranian revolution.

Egypt did not perceive Iran as a threat despite this massive military buildup and indicators of regional ambitions in a sphere of Egyptian influence. On a structural level, Egypt, like Iran, was aligned with the United States against the Soviet threat and its proxies. More importantly, however, Sadat was focused on consolidating political power and finding a way to regain the Sinai and eventually Egypt's power.

Egyptian and Saudi Responses to Iranian Ideational Power Projection

After many months of escalating violent protests against his rule, the cancer-stricken shah left Iran for good in January 1979. Less than a month later, Ayatollah Khomeini returned to Iran from exile. Khomeini's activities outside of Iran had been a mobilizing symbol during the revolution, and his return helped coordinate the social unrest. Less than a year later, Ayatollah Khomeini established the Islamic Republic of Iran.

The Iranian revolution sent shockwaves throughout the Gulf countries and the Middle East. It transformed regional relations and added pressure on state-society relations due to Iran's export of the revolution. While Gulf leaders with significant Shi'a populations faced mounting unrest, many Sunni regimes without Shi'a populations were concerned that their growing domestic opposition would try to emulate the Iranian model of social revolution. After all, Iranian clerics could claim that Islam had just mobilized opposition to overthrow a powerful, repressive autocrat backed by the United States and replaced it with a just, Islamic form of government.

The effects of the revolution and the establishment of the Islamic Republic of Iran shattered a cornerstone of U.S. security architecture in the region. And for both Egypt and Saudi Arabia, the cooperative relations that characterized the 1970s and the lack of threat perception came to a dramatic halt as Islamists established the Islamic Republic of Iran. The following section will deal with how Egypt and Saudi Arabia responded to Iranian ideational threats through ideational balancing.

Egypt

When the shah left Iran, initially Egyptian officials were concerned that a communist-Shiite government or ayatollahs would run its former ally.[18] However, when clerics began escalating their rhetorical attacks against President Sadat's policies as un-Islamic, pro-imperialist, and pro-Zionist, one of Egypt's two biggest fears was realized. Iranian leaders assailed President Sadat for granting asylum to the terminally ill shah. This hostility became official policy when the newly established Islamic Republic of Iran broke diplomatic relations with Egypt over its peace treaty with Israel.

The rhetorical attacks by Iran's clerics were more than just words. Clerics launched a "war of takfir" against the Sadat regime to undermine its legitimacy through religious symbols. This ideational threat consisted of three interconnected symbolic offensives. First, Khomeini called Sadat a *pharaoh*, the way Khomeini assailed the shah as a *Yazid*—a mobilizing symbol of Iran's own revolution.[19] Both religious-historical figures are known in Islamic history as tyrants.[20] This message connected President Sadat's fate with the fate of the shah, to whom Sadat had granted asylum, an act that infuriated Ayatollah Khomeini. The second offensive was Khomeini's charge that Sadat had acted against the interests of the *umma* by aligning with the West and making peace with the Zionist entity, the "little Satan," which occupied *al-Quds* (Jerusalem). One of Ayatollah Khomeini's messages was to present the Islamic Republic as the champion of the Palestinian cause. He reappropriated the language of liberation from a secular, nationalist Arab context into a religious context. The powerful symbolic dimension of this transfer was giving the building of the Israeli embassy to the Palestine Liberation Organization (PLO). It was, in a sense, the first territorial victory against the Israelis; Iran's agency helped give the Palestinian question an Islamic tone, and this small, symbolic victory was not accomplished by a secular Arab power.

Third, and most importantly, Iran's ideational offensive deemed Sadat's actions as *kufr* and thus, as a *kafir*, or infidel, he could be killed for his actions. The spiritual leader of the revolution, Ayatollah Khomeini, called President Sadat a purveyor of "false Islam." Khomeini's attacks served to "dehumanize" Sadat and shifted the discourse to further mobilize religious resentment against him.[21]

The projection of this ideology targeted Egypt's tenuous state-society relations. These symbols projected an anti-imperialist, pan-Islamic revolutionary ideology and framed the Egyptian regime as one that not only acted against Muslim interests but also violated Islamic law. These charges tried to expose the fact that the very foundational legitimacy of the Arab Republic of Egypt was not at all based on Islam.

*Domestic conditions and the potential
for transnational mobilization*

The Egyptian regime feared that these symbols and ideas would resonate with large segments of the Egyptian population in a highly charged domestic environment. Despite Sadat's celebrated military accomplishment in the 1973 Arab-Israeli War, other foreign and domestic policies had become objects of growing societal pressure and discontent. Sadat's *infitah* (opening to the West) raised fears of Western cultural, political, and economic penetration. More specifically, as a condition for accepting International Monetary Fund loans in an effort to advance his economic development programs for Egypt, Sadat implemented policies to increase efficiency and reduce government expenditures. These policies included ending subsidies for staples, such as bread, and resulted in violent riots in January 1977. The bread riots, as they became known, resulted in the deaths of nearly eighty people and thousands of injuries.

In addition to the socioeconomic discontent caused by these economic reforms, opposition to the Sadat regime grew within the Islamist camp. The very Islamists that Sadat had courted to combat Nasserist and leftist political challengers in the early 1970s became increasingly frustrated by Sadat's failure to implement shari'a as he had pledged. The frustration of these Islamists grew even stronger with the news of Sadat's highly unpopular peace initiatives toward Israel, culminating in the Camp David accords in 1978. Radical Islamists, inspired by the teachings of Sayyid Qutb among others, viewed the lack of progress toward an Islamic state, economic distress, the permeation of Western culture, and the Arab-Israeli peace process as a call to arms.[22]

Given these domestic conditions, how did the most important source of opposition, the Islamists, react to the Iranian revolution? Although the revolution in Iran was a social revolution and included many parts of society, religious elements played the most important role by providing a set of mobilizing symbols and organizing protests. In Egypt, Islamists such as the Muslim Brotherhood were generally inspired by the activism but were not necessarily willing to confront the Egyptian state. After an initial burst of enthusiasm, their spirits were slightly tempered by internal and external factors.[23] Similar to the Muslim Brotherhood, radical Islamists may have admired the Iranian revolution from a political perspective, but they found Khomeini's views to be a distortion of Islam and any association with it a distortion of their vision.[24]

The heightened domestic pressure and radicalization came to a climax with the assassination of President Anwar El-Sadat on October 6, 1981. Members of al-Jihad organization, who had infiltrated the military, killed the Egyptian president while he was reviewing a military parade commemorating Egypt's historic achievement in the October 1973 War.[25] But Sadat's assassination did not end this story, and it certainly did not temper Khomeini's attacks.[26] In fact, Khomeini later named a street after one of the assassins, Khalid Islambouli, and in 1982 commissioned a postal stamp in his honor. This symbolic act infuriated Mubarak and has long been an obstacle in any attempt at rapprochement between the two countries.

Egypt's ideational balancing

The Sadat and Mubarak regimes responded to the new geopolitical environment and the Iranian challenge through both domestic and foreign policies. President Sadat (and later Mubarak) responded through a mix of counterframing, resource mobilization, and foreign policies aimed at affecting the public space and society. President Sadat defended his policies in Islamic terms in an effort to recast Islamic values as being consistent with his policies. For example, Sadat framed his decision to grant the shah asylum as an expression of *authentic* Islamic values, which represented a tolerant and moderate

Islam, in contrast to Khomeini's version. "Khomeini is preaching vengeance and hatred which is not true Islam . . . I am a Muslim, a true Muslim. That is why the Shah will be living here among us with his family as brothers. This is the true spirit of Islam."[27] And on the more controversial subject of peace with Israel, Sadat mostly allowed al-Azhar's fatwas to speak for themselves.[28]

The regime allocated material resources to spread ideas that supported its political authority and legitimacy.[29] As early as February 1979, Sadat announced his plan to "face up to imported ideologies and to inculcate into the spirit of our youth the Islamic values and principles" by increasing the number of state-funded mosques and state-trained religious clerics.[30]

The state-led spread of ideas that recast Sadat's contested policies in a more positive light also included another tactic to decrease the attractiveness of subversive ideas. The Egyptian regime drew attention to the source of the ideas as a way to undermine the credibility of the messenger. One way Sadat did this was by emphasizing the foreignness of the Islam espoused by Ayatollah Khomeini. This neutralization tactic of ideational balancing sought to combat the spread of revolutionary political ideas that encouraged overturning the social and political order. It was meant to reinforce the sense that these ideas were foreign to the quiescent political culture found in Sunni Islam. What became increasingly more effective, however, was the emphasis on the non-Arab and non-Sunni source of the ideas.

This tactic of counterframing to undermine the credibility of the source received its greatest boost at the outbreak of the Iran-Iraq War through Egypt's "hard balancing" efforts against Iran on the side of Iraq. Fearing internal subversion from Iran's export of its Islamic revolution and seizing the opportunity of a weakened Iran, Iraq invaded Iran.[31] This brutal war, which lasted eight years, involved many Gulf states, directly or indirectly, and turned out to be a blessing in disguise for Egypt. Egypt's support of Iraq, or "hard balancing" against Iran, actually began before Iraq's invasion. Egypt signed an arms deal with Iraq in March 1980 and made a series of statements reaffirming its commitment to the Arab Gulf states.[32] Egypt's involvement in the war grew after Iraq's invasion of Iran in fall 1980. By spring 1982, approximately 30,000 Egyptians were serving in the Iraqi army and Egypt had agreed to double the amount of war materiel it sold Iraq under the previous deal.[33] Egypt's efforts paid off diplomatically and led to its gradual rehabilitation. In 1984, Egypt was readmitted to the Organization of Islamic Conferences. After the war

Egypt was readmitted to the Arab League, and the League's headquarters moved back to Cairo in 1990. This structural change provided political opportunities for the Egyptian regime to contain Iran's regional and domestic influence, minimize the destabilizing effects of Iran's ideational projection, neutralize Egypt's isolation in the Arab world, and temper its own Islamists. Egypt's human and material contribution to the war provided credibility to officials' claims that the real struggle was not between Islamists and the secularist republics they opposed but a civilizational one between Arab-Sunni and Persian-Shi'a civilizations.

What makes Cairo's hard balancing against Iran even more striking is the fact that it was now supporting Iraq, its long-standing rival for Arab leadership, in response to an ideational threat. In fact, Iraq was not just a rival for Arab leadership; it also initiated the suspension of Egypt from the Arab League for making peace with Israel. This tremendous blow to Egypt's prestige and status, which included the moving of the Arab League headquarters from Cairo to Tunis, cannot be underestimated, and neither can the fact that Baghdad directly benefited from Cairo's loss.

Egypt's participation in the war also had crucial domestic benefits, and in particular enabled the regime to recast the Iranian threat in more stark religious and ethnic terms, mitigating the attractiveness of the ideas and shrinking the political space for opposition groups to oppose the regime. Even without publicly identifying the extent of Egypt's human and material contribution to the war effort, Egypt's official responses recast the struggle as an ethno-religious one—Arab (Sunni) versus Persian (Shi'a) civilizations—that was being led by Iran.

The Egyptian regime's strategy of framing domestic dissent as an issue of Arab/Sunni national identity seems to have paid off. This frame forced local domestic opposition to weigh both the practical and ideological implications of supporting a Shi'a/Persian state however pan-Islamic it claimed to be. The Muslim Brotherhood, for example, after initially praising the revolution, paid less attention to Iran by the start of the Iran-Iraq War.[34] Aided by an internal shift of attitudes toward the revolution, the Brotherhood could be seen as choosing a transnational loyalty over Egyptian national identity. This type of constraint also affected the radical camp's attitudes, although to a lesser extent.[35] The Egyptian regime exploited this fearsome image of Khomeini's political and religious excesses to isolate extreme elements of Egypt's radical camp as well.

Saudi Arabia

Similar to Egyptian-Iranian relations, the close security cooperation that characterized Saudi-Iranian relations during the 1970s ended with the Iranian revolution. Amid the chaos of the Iranian revolution, Saudi leaders initially feared that communists would take over or that Soviets might move in. In fact, a year into the revolution and just before the shah left Iran, Saudi Crown Prince Fahd even tried to bolster the religious legitimacy of the Iranian regime by claiming the shah's rule was based on Islamic law.[36] Similar to other Western and Middle Eastern countries, Saudi Arabia misdiagnosed the threat and underestimated the gravity of the Iranian revolutionary situation.[37] King Khalid even congratulated Khomeini the day after he established the Islamic Republic:

> It gives me great pleasure that the new republic is based on Islamic principles which are a powerful bulwark for Islam and Muslim peoples who aspire to prosperity, dignity, and well-being. I pray the Almighty to guide you to the forefront of those who strive for the upholding of Islam and Muslims, and I wish the Iranian people progress, prosperity, and stability.[38]

These perceptions and the official pronouncements began to change after the fall of the Bazargan government.[39] While it is unclear exactly why Saudi Arabia misunderstood the trajectory of Iran's revolutionary clerics now in charge of the state, the level of Iranian hostility clearly shocked the Saudi regime.[40] Saudi officials could no longer ignore the virulent attacks against the House of Saud—statements aimed to incite rebellion among the Shi'a and Sunni populations of Saudi Arabia.

These attacks were threatening because they challenged the basis of legitimacy of the House of Saud in a language that was easily understood. The combination of Islamic symbols with anti-Western/anti-imperialist discourse that attacked the institution of the monarchy, its moral corruption, and the state's relationship with the West were central themes in this campaign. For example, Iranian broadcasts in Arabic projected into the kingdom condemned the idea of kingship, citing the Quran: "Kings despoil a country when they enter it and make the noblest of its people its meanest."[41] The Saudi *ulama* were also attacked. Iranian clerics assailed the lack of the *ulama*'s independence because of its political arrangement with the House of Saud whereby the *ulama* receives resources in exchange for political quietism and religious cover for the ruling family. This meant that the *ulama* supported a morally corrupt royal family that relied on Western protection for its survival, leading to the Western cultural and political penetration of a Muslim society.

In assailing Saudi Arabia, Ayatollah Khomeini went beyond the message that the House of Saud's un-Islamic behavior made it an unfit protector of Islam's holiest sites; they explicitly described the mechanism through which domestic instability (and regime change) would be triggered. "When the people have self-confidence and high morale, they will begin to demand their rights and oppose the authorities' policy and conduct. Indeed it is this which the corrupt monarchies fear most."[42] While statements such as these connected the fate of the shah with the fate of Saudi leadership,[43] they also aimed to bolster the credibility of the source of the message—the Islamic regime in Iran led by Ayatollah Khomeini. These statements drew attention to the fact that the clerics in Iran led a successful social revolution under similar conditions.

One of the most provocative and powerful symbolic threats was Iran's support of demonstrations, often violent, against the House of Saud during the annual Hajj. Iranian demonstrations against the Saudi regime began in 1979 when their pilgrims spread political propaganda among Saudi groups.[44] Continuing through the 1980s, the demonstrations involved provocative chants assailing the House of Saud, burning American and Israeli flags, and distributing propaganda attacking the leadership of the kingdom and Wahhabism.[45] The demonstrations took an exceedingly violent turn in 1987 when four hundred Iranian pilgrims and nearly a hundred Saudi security forces were killed.[46]

The reason why these provocations were so threatening is that they challenged a cornerstone of the Saudi regime's legitimacy—its administration of the Hajj. The attacks undermined the House of Saud's authority over this sacred space for the Muslim *umma*, while suggesting why it is morally incumbent on Muslims to overthrow this regime. The importance of the administration of the Hajj for the House of Saud and for Saudi claims of Islamic leadership cannot be understated. The pilgrimage is an opportunity to "demonstrate its paramount commitment to Islam and thus to certify its legitimacy."[47] By managing and controlling the Hajj, the Saudi state asserts its authority and leadership over the *umma*. Saudi authorities essentially determine the ability of all Muslims to perform one of Islam's five pillars, reminding the *umma* where the birthplace of Islam is and who controls this sacred space. Furthermore, the Hajj season is an institutionalized public ritual. It occurs every year, demonstrating to all participants and also to those who watch news reports or have relatives that embark on the journey the religious significance of the regime, the House of Saud, which is entrusted with protecting this sacred space. Iran's symbolic acts communicated important information about Iran and Saudi Arabia in front of a sacred audience at a sacred time and place.

This context is a good opportunity to explain a little more about how the House of Saud has remained in power and what role religion plays. The House of Saud has remained in power by maintaining stability through payoffs, co-optation, external agreements, and constructing a sacred narrative about the regime.[48] This historical narrative claims that the House of Saud helped bring *tawhid* (monotheism and unification) in a religious and political sense to Saudi Arabia.[49] Religiously, the regime enforces the Wahhabi approach of purifying Islam from innovation (*bida*), including "saint worship" (*ziyara*) practiced by Sufis and Shi'a. The state narrative claims that through Ibn Saud's leadership of jihad against a blasphemous population, he has politically unified the large geographic territory.[50]

The House of Saud has had to unify a diverse population across tribal, geographic, and sectarian lines to establish state authority, In doing so, the regime subordinated Islamic and tribal institutions.[51] The tribal component legitimates the king as the *Shaykh al-Masha`ikh*, the head of all the shaykhs, and in a sense also as a mediator. The religious aspect is arguably more important. The al-Saud family bases its religious legitimacy on the idea that it organizes the Hajj and is the guardian of Muslim holy places. Their right to this role is upheld by the *ulama*, who promote the sacred narrative of the historic alliance between Mohammed ibn Saud and Mohammed ibn Abdel Wahhab in 1745. The Wahhabi *ulama* are allowed to dictate the social agenda and the regime must enforce the strict Wahhabi interpretations (or delegate this duty). Oil, as a source of revenue for the state, has an important element because it provides the resources with which the regime is able to provide side-payments and payoffs.

Domestic unrest and regime vulnerability

Two events around the time of the Iranian revolution, the Qatif riots and the Siege of the Grand Mosque, demonstrate the vulnerabilities of the Saudi regime. The Saudi regime was naturally concerned about the Iranian Revolution's direct effect on its strategically sensitive Shi'a population. Insofar as the strength of Iran's ideological threat relied on Khomeini's ability to frame the revolution as a pan-Islamic and not a sectarian one, his message had particular resonance for the Shi'a population in Saudi Arabia and elsewhere. Khomeini used the Quranic term *mustazifin* (dispossessed), or those who were not treated as equal Muslims, to incite and inspire discontented Shi'a to challenge their *mustakbir* (arrogant) oppressors.[52]

Saudi intelligence services were extremely concerned about the possibility of subversion and incitement.[53] Although the Shi'a constitute only 10 to 15 percent of the Saudi population, the potential for mobilization among this marginalized population that faced unofficial and official discrimination was significant. The fact that Shi'a constitute 75 percent of the population in the oil-producing region of the country (Eastern province) made this an issue of national security. This rentier state could ill afford challenges to its control of oil production—the lifeline and currency with which Saudi Arabia is able to maintain stability through payoffs to various sectors of society. A journalist who covered Saudi Arabia for the *Financial Times* notes, "Even without the strident calls from Tehran radio, it was inevitable that the Iranian Revolution would produce a new consciousness among the Saudi Shi'as."[54]

The Shi'a uprisings in November 1979 and February 1980 in Qatif brought the threat home to the Saudi regime.[55] Rioting began after the Saudi National Guard tried to prevent Shi'a from publicly observing the day of 'Ashura, a holiday when Shi'a mourn the martyrdom of Hussein ibn Ali, the grandson of the Prophet Mohammed (it was banned by law). Many Shi'a were killed in these riots and in the others that took place a few months later. Shi'a criticisms echoed Khomeini's attacks on the Saudi regime for its dependence on the West, deviation from Islam, and moral corruption. These attacks also sounded similar to those of conservative *ulama* and radical Sunnis.

The most frightening aspect for the regime was not the political message from Tehran aimed at mobilizing Shi'a. The Shi'a were suppressed. Instead, Iran's message and use of symbols was framed to appeal to leftists as well as Islamists.[56] Toby Jones relates:

> Pamphlets circulated before and during the events of the fall of 1979 as well as what followed included various political groupings. Leftists who avoided specifically sectarian politics as well as Islamists mobilized and demonstrated in response to what they perceived to be years of neglect and to the course of events in November 1979 themselves.[57]

This was, in essence, a fragmented opposition united by anger and popular disaffection that "in many ways, transcended religious conviction."[58] In fact, the threat may have been even more severe. Had there been coordination similar to the Iranian Revolution, it is possible there may have been even greater social unrest.[59]

The second major event indicating an environment of social unrest, political opportunity, and vulnerability is the dramatic seizure of the Grand Mosque in Mecca. In November 1979, a group of armed Saudi messianists seized the Grand Mosque by force, took hostages, and proclaimed an end to the corrupt House of Saud rule in favor of their Mahdi, Juhayman al-Utaybi. The group occupied this sacred space for roughly two weeks until Saudi special forces with French assistance defeated them.[60]

The siege of the Grand Mosque represented a major crisis for the regime and an indicator of the vulnerability of the regime to ideational threats. The state was initially immobilized because of the political leadership's denial of the problem, the ineptitude of the Saudi security services, and the need for a religious ruling permitting armed forces to use violence in this sacred Muslim space. The fatwa that permitted violence inside the sacred space of the Grand Mosque as a necessary condition to remove the protesters was problematic. It exposed the political quiescence of the clergy—one of Utaybi and Qahtani's main grievances.[61] Moreover, despite Saudi attempts to keep foreign support quiet, French involvement proved the regime's dependence on the West to even protect Islam's holy sites. Thus, during this embarrassing crisis, Tehran took advantage of the situation to denounce the kingdom for their dependence on "foreigners to protect their hollow monarchies."[62]

This event shook the Saudi regime to its core for a number of reasons. Although there was limited popular support for the rebels, they had come from within Saudi society and their grievances found sympathetic ears within the religious establishment.[63] The rebels also represented a radical, militant challenge to the Sahwa, or awakening sheiks, and state-sponsored religious institutions.[64]

These local events provided good reason for the Saudi regime to feel vulnerable to external manipulation through the use of resonant symbols. While it is plausible that contagion may have contributed to the timing of the (Shi'a) Qatif revolts in 1979, Iran's incitement, which exploited preexisting Shi'a grievances against the Saudi state, was the catalyst. Finally, these events communicated that there were open challenges to the regime and that its ability to maintain order and protect the holy sites was in question. From the perspective of the Saudi leadership, Iran's capacity to destabilize events through its words, or even its subversive activities, likely generated a fear that there may be more incitement to come.

Saudi Arabia's ideational balancing

Saudi policy toward Iran consisted of both hard and soft responses at the domestic and international levels. Saudi Arabia (externally) balanced against Iran during the Iran-Iraq War (1980–1988) by providing military and economic aid to Iraq.[65] Saudi Arabia also spearheaded efforts to establish the Gulf Cooperation Council as a regional security regime in response to the Iranian Revolution, not as a response to the Iran-Iraq War.[66] Internal balancing took the form of arms procurements. Peaking in 1983, Saudi Arabia's defense expenditures were among the highest in the world in spite of its small size.[67] The Kingdom of Saudi Arabia enhanced its air defense system, a weak point against a potential Iranian attack, by initially deploying American AWACS (Airborne Warning and Control System) aircraft in September 1980 and purchasing these aircraft a year later.

Yet even these military responses in the context of the Iran-Iraq War had an important ideational component that often worked alongside or trumped the military threat. One way the Saudi regime responded to Iran's frontal rhetorical attacks was by engaging in defensive religious apologetics.[68] For example, to counter accusations that both the Shah and the Saudi Royal family treated issues of religion and state similarly, the Saudi leadership declared the following about its former ally: "Unlike the Shah, we adhere faithfully to our constitution, the holy Qur'an, whose law is being carried out in letter and spirit."[69] An example of a more assertive response was King Fahd's decision in 1986 to declare his title *Khadam al-Haramein al-Sharifein* (Guardian of the Two Noble Sanctuaries). This new, official title communicated Saudi Arabia and the House of Saud's sacred role as the leader of the Islamic world.

Other responses counterattacked Khomeini by aiming to discredit the source of the threatening messages and symbols. Saudi media portrayed Khomeini as an extremist whose beliefs and practices deviated from Islam. During the Iran-Iraq War, the Saudi regime tried to undermine Iran's pan-Islamic messages and symbols by emphasizing its ethnic and sectarian character. These counterframes won favor among the more extreme Wahhabi and Salafi elements within the kingdom and across the Sunni world.

The Saudi regime mobilized tremendous resources to support religious activities domestically and abroad. King Fahd sought to bolster the religious legitimacy of the regime that came under Utaybi's recent domestic attack by "appropriating the power of Islam."[70] Since recurrent domestic unrest could act as a force multiplier for ideational power, the regime needed to address these challenges. The regime combated domestic critics by co-opting them in some cases and "outbidding" them in others.[71] The state mobilized resources for these activities. It increased its allocation to religious activities (mosque construction, clerical training, etc.) by 900 percent from 1980 to 1985 compared to the previous five-year period.[72] The Sahwa were called upon as the religious group best able to mount a defense against Khomeinism.[73]

But this is only part of the story. The Soviet invasion of Afghanistan created a political opportunity for Saudi Arabia to reassert itself as the leader of the Islamic world while managing threats at home. Saudi Arabia's efforts to counteract Iran's challenges to its pan-Islamic legitimacy took the form of a "universalized" Salafi discourse.[74] Until that point, jihadi discourse was confined to the context of the state's foundation, but the confluence of Iranian challenges and the Afghan war enabled Riyadh to expand this discourse, its influence, and its networks beyond Saudi borders. The Saudi state provided unprecedented amounts of financial support, military aid, logistical support, supplies, and religious publications to the Afghan resistance through informal and formal channels, including international institutions such as the Muslim World League.[75] These volunteers were infused with vast amounts of anti-Shi'a and anti-Iranian propaganda in addition to classical jihadi works.

Saudi Arabia successfully outflanked Iran both geopolitically and in the competition for Islamic leadership. As Afghanistan moved from a battle between "Islam and communism to a contest between Saudi Wahhabism and Iranian Shi'ism,"[76] Iran's material assistance to Shi'a groups (including arms) and diplomacy at the UN could not keep up with Saudi Arabia.[77] Iran's limited resources were focused on the Iran-Iraq War, the Palestinians, and Lebanon; Iran's policy in Afghanistan was overtly sectarian.[78] Meanwhile, Saudi Arabia framed the instability in Afghanistan as an Iranian attempt to undermine Islam's great victory in which Saudi Arabia played the major role:

> We have to ask who is playing havoc in Afghanistan, and who is exploiting the situation in a country which has just emerged from a great jihad . . . . It is no secret that the first to be blamed are the sons of the Afghan people themselves,

and then the Tehran regime which kindled the fire in Afghanistan and came between the jihad brothers, divided them and tore them apart.[79]

Conclusion

This chapter has shown how and why Saudi Arabia and Egypt's threat perception changed in response to the transnational ideological threat posed by the Islamist regime in Iran. It highlighted the fact that changes in Iranian military power in the 1970s and the 1980s had little effect on Cairo and Riyadh's threat perception.

Iran's ideational power projection, however, did trigger threat perception. In this regard, the timing of the shift in threat perception helps illustrate that projection is a key condition. Saudi Arabia and Egypt did not immediately consider the nature of the regime; rather, the threat perception changed because of what Islamists did when they took power. Namely, the regime projected ideational power through culturally resonant symbols that could destabilize the targeted regimes.

This chapter also demonstrates why these regimes feared ideas—they feared the potential of domestic political mobilization. More specifically, there was a fear that a shift in commonly held beliefs about regime legitimacy could destabilize politics. As seen in the Saudi case, it was not just about the fear to mobilize a potential "fifth column" (i.e., the Shi'a). Instead, the Saudi regime was worried about different opposition forces uniting against them.

To guard against these nonmaterial threats, Cairo and Riyadh employed ideational balancing strategies. While both engaged in hard balancing, such as arms racing and alliance formation, the ideational aspects of these foreign policy behaviors complemented the intense activities in the ideational realm. Egypt counterframed these threats by redefining its image and using counterattack and neutralization tactics to undermine the credibility of the source. It also mobilized the source of support through state-sponsored religious institutions. Saudi Arabia's activities were similar. Resources to promote ideas about regime legitimacy were certainly much greater and more widespread at the domestic and international levels. At the domestic level, Saudi Arabia employed denial tactics in the public sphere more than anything else. The fact that the siege of the Grand Mosque, although not connected to Iran, was not even discussed in the media for days is but one example.

These cases and reactions all illustrate an important insight about the ideational security dilemma. The projection of ideational power generated ideological competition and an escalation in which the regimes perceived their security was threatened. In these cases, military conflict, though mostly indirect, also resulted. But the biggest fear was not the military aspect—it was the threat from an external ideational force that could challenge regime security.

Lastly, this chapter has emphasized how projection and domestic conditions mattered. In this regard, it is worth mentioning a case within this context that contains domestic instability but no change in threat perception even though the Islamist regime had just come to power. Syrian-Iranian relations represent this non-case of threat perception. Syria's threat perception actually declined as seen through its growing alliance with Iran over the next three decades. This is striking because Syria had many of the conditions that should trigger a fear. During the 1970s, Syria faced both secular and religious opposition. The latter form of opposition was in fact particularly violent at times resulting in an insurgency from 1976 to 1982, supported by Jordan and Iraq. President Hafez al-Assad eventually crushed the rebellion at Hama in 1982. But the Syrian regime, whose opposition was dominated by Islamists, did not consider an Iranian Islamist regime that took power a threat, despite the fact that elements of this religious opposition as well as some Iranian clerics saw the insurgency and unrest as an opportunity to overthrow the secular regime.

The conventional explanation is that both Iran and Syria shared mutual enemies, primarily Iraq, and other overlapping interests that brought them together. Moreover, they found ideological justifications for their cooperation that brought the avowedly secular, pan-Arab Baathist Syria that crushed its Islamists, together with an Islamic republic. These explanations help us understand this relationship but they miss one crucial factor—the lack of ideational power projection. The regime did not try to export this ideology. Had it tried and directed its ideology toward Syria, which it could make an argument for, this would have caused tremendous concern for the encircled Asad regime.

4   The Power of a Weak State: Sudan's Relations with Saudi Arabia and Egypt

O N JULY 30, 1989, A GROUP OF ISLAMIST MILITARY officers led by Brigadier General Omar al-Bashir seized power in Sudan. Backed by Sheikh Hassan al-Turabi's Islamist political party, the National Islamic Front, this new regime established an Islamic republic, took steps to impose Islamic law, and transformed Sudan's domestic institutions. A major deterioration with Sudan's former allies soon followed. Egypt and Sudan engaged in low-level armed clashes through the 1990s. An assassination attempt by Egyptian terrorists backed by Sudan against the Egyptian president almost brought the two states to war. Meanwhile, Sudan and Saudi Arabia engaged in a war of words, which started with Sudan's support for Iraq in the Persian Gulf War (1990–1991). Saudi Arabia cut off vital financial aid to Sudan, and Sudan hosted Osama bin Laden.

Yet, by the mid-1990s relations began to change; threat perceptions and tensions decreased. What explains this? Why did the threat perception increase in response to the rise of Sudan's Islamist regime and why did the threat subside? A number of puzzles follow: Why would these Arab states fear the militarily weak Sudan? Egypt had a vastly superior military to Sudan, and Sudan had no power-projection capabilities to threaten Saudi Arabia. If it is about the type of regime that came to power, an Islamic republic, why should Saudi Arabia, the most conservative Muslim state, consider Sudan an ideological competitor when Saudi Arabia had even supported the Islamists who seized power? Furthermore, how can we explain the fact that the Sudanese regime remained during the late 1990s as relations improved?

This chapter seeks to solve these complex puzzles by examining Sudan's relations with Egypt and Saudi Arabia from the 1970s through 2000, covering the periods before and after Islamists come to power in Sudan. The argument of the chapter is that military power played very little role in triggering threat perception. Instead, Egypt and Saudi Arabia feared Sudan's projection of its ideational power through culturally resonant symbols that aimed to undermine domestic political stability. In response, both Egypt and Saudi Arabia employed *ideational balancing,* consisting of resource mobilization and counterframing, to mitigate this nontraditional threat.

This chapter also illustrates how the ideational security dilemma was a source of instability. The most striking example comes from the escalation between Egypt and Sudan that resulted in low-level armed clashes. More generally, it was the structure of this strategic interaction around ideational power that serves as an important analytical framework to understand how ideational factors matter in interstate relations.

This chapter will proceed as follows. The first section will highlight some of the reasons for Sudan's warm relations with Egypt and Saudi Arabia before Islamists seized power. This period also shows that despite Sudan's Islamization efforts "from above" during the early 1980s under General Numeiri, these domestic efforts were not interpreted as a threat from Egypt or Saudi Arabia, and in fact they were encouraged by Riyadh. The second section will examine how and why Sudan's projections of its ideational power shifted the threat perceptions of Egypt and Saudi Arabia by affecting regime security, not state security. Cairo and Riyadh feared that Sudan's projection of ideas could alter commonly held beliefs about the domestic legitimacy of their regimes and serve as focal symbols for uniting disparate opposition groups. The responses to these measures and the fears are seen in their tactics of ideational balancing. Finally, the last section shows that threat perception declined because projection of the threat was absent. It is clear that domestic politics mattered but not as much as the act of projection.

Sudan's Relations with Egypt
and Saudi Arabia in Perspective

Egypt and Sudan have many historical and cultural links tied largely to the Nile River. This waterway has been the lifeblood of Egypt from the predynastic periods until the present. Successive Egyptian dynasties during ancient Egypt had great commercial, social, religious, and political influence over this area, and it was believed that they descended from a common ancestor.[1] Accordingly, Egypt has long regarded Nubia, and the areas around the lower Nile Valley, as an extension of Egypt.

The colonial experience also shaped Egyptian beliefs about Sudan. Sudan came under Egyptian administration when the viceroy of Egypt, Mohammed Ali, conquered Sudan in 1820. He aimed to restore Egypt's political role in Africa through reviving Egypt's ancient boundaries. Until Mohammed Ali, Egypt's influence in this area remained primarily relegated to religious and cultural realms.[2] After Mohammed Ali, Egypt was granted legal control of the area in 1841, and the Ottoman sultan recognized Egyptian rule in 1866.

Egyptian political dominance over Sudan grew as Cairo's importance for Great Britain's colonial policy increased. After the British occupied Egypt and Sudan in 1882, a cleric named Mohammed Ahmed ibn al-Sayyid Abdullah proclaimed himself the *Mahdi* (a redeemer figure or messiah) and led a religious and political rebellion against the Egyptian administration and Great Britain.[3] Mohammed Ahmed al-Mahdi and his followers waged a violent rebellion to expel the British and establish an Islamic state. Anglo-Egyptian forces finally put an end to the rebellion in 1898. The following year Britain established control over Sudan through the Egyptian administration as part of the Anglo-Egyptian Condominium of 1899.[4]

After Sudan gained its independence in 1956, Egyptian-Sudanese relations grew close despite Egypt's historic claims to the Sudan. Gamal Abdel Nasser took a different approach than his predecessors; he was less concerned with nationalist claims about Egyptian sovereignty over Sudan and more preoccupied by threats to Egyptian national security from foreign colonial powers. Nasser is reported to have said, "I do not fear an independent Sudan; I fear an occupied Sudan."[5] Gamal Abdel Nasser and the nonaligned movement influenced successive leaders who took power after coups in 1958, 1964, and 1969.

Warm relations between Egypt and Sudan peaked during the 1970s until the mid-1980s, an era known as al-ʿAsir al-Dhahabi (the Golden Age).[6]

Anchored in military cooperation and secured through a pro-Western alignment, the close relationship between Egypt and Sudan also included plans for economic and political integration.[7] Cooperation centered on security issues but also involved other matters. Security cooperation took the form of a mutual defense agreement between Egypt and Sudan, which was signed shortly after Egypt sent military forces to defeat a rebellion supported by Libya and Ethiopia against Jaafar al-Numeiri in 1976. Marking the apex of their friendship, this defense agreement committed Egypt and Sudan to come to each other's side in the event of an attack against one country.[8] On the diplomatic front, Numeiri was one of the very few Arab leaders to endorse President Sadat's peace initiative with Israel. In other nonmilitary affairs, Egypt and Sudan signed a charter of integration in 1982, and the following year they held the first Nile Valley Parliament that consisted of sixty Egyptian and sixty Sudanese members. This relationship was mutually beneficial and self-enforcing in many respects. At the regional level, this alliance meant that Egypt's gateway to Africa—an important arena of Egyptian foreign policy—was secure. Egypt was willing to help Numeiri maintain power insofar as Sudan remained a stable, pro-Egyptian, and Western-aligned state. Thus, this relationship earned Numeiri promises of external assistance to suppress internal and external threats.[9]

Despite Egypt's foreign policy to ensure the ruling regime's security in Sudan, Numeiri's domestic policies were a source of instability. Numeiri's enactment of the September Laws in 1983, which imposed shari'a over the non-Muslim population in the south, reignited ethnic and religious tensions and resulted in civil war. The imposition of these religious laws, which included Islamically mandated punishments such as floggings and amputations, known as *hudud*, seemed to mark a political turning-point in Numeiri's own turn to religion beginning in 1977.

Numeiri's turn toward Islam and his declarations of creating an "Islamic state" were troubling for Egypt but not because Numeiri's desire to Islamize Sudan directly affected Egypt. These policies undermined Egypt's perennial concern in Sudan, political instability, which could affect Egypt's leverage over the water supply from the Nile River basin. Egypt was also concerned that the Libyans would intervene. Egypt's disapproval of Numeiri's policies toward the rebels would remain a constant source of disagreement and tension.

Discontent over Numeiri's policies was not limited to Egypt. His conduct of the civil war and the deteriorating economic conditions caused discontent within his military and produced widespread popular dissent against the government.[10] Following weeks of public protests against bread and fuel price increases and shortages, Lieutenant General Siwar al-Dhahab led a bloodless coup in April 1985. On Sudanese radio al-Dhahab explained why he seized power and detailed the transitional nature of the new government: "In order to reduce bloodshed and to ensure the country's independence and unity the Sudanese armed forces have decided unanimously to stand by the people of Sudan and to respond to their demands by taking over power and transferring it to the people after a specified transitional period."[11]

Al-Dhahab did what he promised.[12] The following year he relinquished power to the democratically elected Sadiq al-Mahdi. Although this remarkable move by al-Dhahab ushered in a three-year period of democratic governance, polarization increased between those who favored a secular, pluralistic political system and the Islamists who called for a comprehensive religious system.[13]

Saudi Arabia

Sudanese-Saudi relations during the 1950s and 1960s followed the general pattern of Egyptian-Saudi relations. After General Jaafar al-Numeiri regained power in 1971 from the communist forces who overthrew him, Sudan aligned with Saudi Arabia as part of a bloc of Western-aligned Arab states opposed to Soviet or communist penetration through the 1980s. All three countries in this bloc protected an important strategic asset, the Red Sea.[14] While Egypt and Sudan faced internal challenges from leftists, Saudi Arabia's virulent ideological opposition to Communism was enhanced by the fear of Soviet penetration in the region and also the sponsorship of radical, revisionist political actors.

Saudi Arabia's interest in and relationship with Sudan went deeper than a commitment to protect the Red Sea. Saudi Arabia aimed to ensure Sudan remained in the Western-aligned, "moderate" Arab camp, which translated into Saudi efforts to prevent leftist opposition groups from gaining power in Sudan. Throughout this period, Saudi Arabia maintained influence through its economic aid to this extremely poor African country. During the 1970s and 1980s, Saudi Arabia was Sudan's largest creditor.[15]

Sudan's foreign and domestic policies during the 1970s and 1980s supported Saudi interests. After the Iranian revolution, Khartoum severed relations with Tehran and sent volunteers to fight against the Islamic Republic in the Iran-Iraq War (1980–1988). Subregionally, Sudan was seen as a bulwark against destabilizing influences from Libya and Marxist Ethiopia. Domestically, Numeiri's Islamization and his subsequent efforts to attract religious parties, which he believed would strengthen his rule, pleased Saudi Arabia. After Numeiri announced in September 1983 that he would impose shari'a in Sudan, Sheikh Abdel Aziz ibn Baz, president of the Administration of Scientific Research, Religious Scholarship and Guidance (Grand Mufti of Saudi Arabia 1993–1999), warmly congratulated Numeiri for this move.[16]

Ideational Projection and Threat Perception: From Cautious Optimism to Brinkmanship (1989–1995)

Saudi Arabia and Egypt watched closely as Sadiq al-Mahdi, who succeeded al-Dhahab, was unable to stabilize the country. The Sudanese military opposed the way the government was conducting the war in the south, economic conditions worsened, and political fights over religion reached a boiling point. Thus, on June 30, 1989, Brigadier Omar Hassan Ahmed al-Bashir together with a group of fourteen other young army officers overthrew Sadiq al-Mahdi's democratically elected government. The National Revolutionary Command Council (later known as the Revolution Command Council, or RCC), headed by al-Bashir, quickly implemented sweeping internal changes by dismissing all political parties, closing the parliament, and suspending the constitution.

Cairo initially welcomed the coup. Egyptian-Sudanese relations had not been particularly warm during Sadiq al-Mahdi's rule from 1986 to 1989.[17] Sudan objected to Egypt's involvement in its internal affairs, including Cairo's decision to grant asylum to Numeiri, and Khartoum resented Egypt's (and the United States') reluctance to provide military aid to Sudan to fight the rebellion in the south.[18] With al-Mahdi gone, Egypt hoped for more influence in Khartoum.[19] Thus, as a goodwill gesture and a way to gain favor, Egypt was the first country to extend diplomatic recognition to the RCC. Cairo sent 20,000 tons of gasoline and two planeloads of medical supplies within twenty-four hours of the regime change.[20] The Egyptian media reflected this cautious optimism by presenting a favorable attitude toward Bashir. The press described him as "pro-Egyptian" and "moderate" and emphasized the coup leaders' close connections to Cairo.[21] Despite the fact that an Islamist regime now ruled Sudan, Egyptian officials assumed the National Islamic Front (NIF)'s use of the Islamic card was simply for domestic political consumption.[22]

But Egypt's benign assessment did not last for long. Although the official public reaction was positive, troubling signs for Egypt appeared very early. Two days after the coup, Egypt's director of intelligence made a secret trip to Khartoum to assess the nature of the new regime and its implications for Egypt and possibly to curry favor with it.[23] He later discovered the extent of the Islamists' hostility to the Mubarak regime.[24]

Saudi Arabia also welcomed the military coup led by Omar al-Bashir that brought Islamists to power. During the rule of Sadiq al-Mahdi (1986–1989), Riyadh had been concerned Sudan would move closer toward Libya or the Soviet camp.[25] But within a month of the coup that brought him to power, Omar al-Bashir visited Saudi Arabia to boost bilateral relations.[26] Bashir did not stop at just an official visit and request for aid; he even praised Saudi Arabia's execution of sixteen Kuwaiti Shi'a accused of setting off bombs in Mecca during the Hajj.[27] These gestures may have encouraged Saudi Arabia to pledge economic assistance to Sudan as late as the first half of 1990.[28]

The timing of these interactions is significant because it was Sudan's support of Iraq during the Gulf War that first changed its relationship with Saudi Arabia. Sudanese political leaders joined Iranian and Iraqi clerics calling for a jihad against non-Muslim troops stationed there as Western and Arab military forces assembled in the Gulf to drive Iraq out of Kuwait. "Holy War and solidarity among Arabs and Moslems wherever they are to protect the Arab and Islamic holy places."[29]

Saudi leaders felt extremely betrayed for all of the support they had given Sudan over the years. According to a Saudi diplomat, "Betrayal is just not a strong enough word . . . . They took our money, then stabbed us in the back."[30] Several years later, Prince Naïf, Saudi Arabia's interior minister, attacked the Muslim Brotherhood and singled out the Sudanese branch, saying, "Whenever they got into difficulty or found their freedom restricted in their own countries, Brotherhood activists found refuge in the Kingdom which protected their lives . . . . But they later turned against the Kingdom."[31] Naïf also specifically criticized Turabi: "Hassan Al-Turabi lived and studied in the Kingdom. I personally consider him a friend . . . . But as soon as he came to power, he turned against the Kingdom."[32]

This feeling of betrayal stemmed from the fact that, since the 1970s, Saudi financial institutions had supported Islamists and their rise to positions of power in the Sudanese government. With the active assistance of Saudi Arabia, Turabi helped establish an extensive network of Islamic banks. This source of financial power enabled Turabi to mobilize and allocate resources to organizations and individuals, while strengthening the Muslim Brotherhood.[33] Saudi Arabia benefited from this process as well; Hassan al-Turabi's development of the Muslim Brotherhood's organizational capacities created opportunities for Saudi influence. Turabi was able to use his political strength drawn from Saudi financing to Islamize individuals in the military and the government bureaucracy.

Sudan's ideational threat

Sheikh Hassan al-Turabi was the spiritual leader and ideologue of the Islamic republic established in Sudan. Turabi began his program by transforming state institutions to bring his vision of an Islamic state to fruition. The institutional transformation began immediately after Bashir seized power and assigned three cabinet positions to members of Turabi's party, the NIF. Pursuant to Turabi's vision to turn Sudan into an Islamic republic, one of Bashir's first acts was to call for a referendum on the reinstatement of Islamic law. Although no referendum was held, *hudud* punishments were officially reintroduced as part of the Islamic Penal Code in March 1991. Public life visibly changed as the regime utilized and transformed state institutions to impose social order: decrees enforced the segregation of the sexes and the banning of alcohol.[34] Even though this coup, or revolution as the NIF claimed, could not be objectively described as having a massive backing, there were visible signs of domestic support for the new social and political order. Two million people demonstrated in Khartoum on June 30, 1990, in support of Bashir's regime while shouting, "Shari'a, shari'a now!" and "Shari'a or martyrdom!"[35]

The RCC transformed the character of the existing military institutions and created new ones that were consistent with the state's ideology. Bashir purged the army's leadership by replacing 600 officers with NIF supporters. These loyalists now accounted for roughly 40 percent of the army officer core.[36] The NIF also created the Popular Defense Forces (PDF), an Islamist army, to eventually replace the army and "eternalize Islamist rule as propagated by the NIF."[37] In addition to the domestic political benefits,[38] the immediate purpose of the PDF was to wage jihad against rebel forces, which were considered apostates and heathens by the state according to official propaganda. Students in higher education and future civil service employees were obligated to enlist in the PDF.[39]

In light of this state policy, it became clear that there was an additional purpose and motivation behind creating this military force: "Their indoctrination was more religious than military."[40] Although the PDF's activities were limited to the south, an official Egyptian report highlighted the ideological element of this military force and hinted at a future threat: the Iranian Revolutionary Guard was advising and training the PDF.[41] In addition to the symbolic value of creating an Islamic army fighting for ostensibly "Muslim" causes, the establishment of an Islamic military institution communicated the transformation of Sudan into an Islamic state. Al-Bashir's military coup backed by the NIF "maintained that Islam, the majority religion, and Arabic, the language of the Quran, represented the essential bases for the country's nationalism and should define its legal, political, and economic systems."[42]

Sudan's Islamic internationalism as a symbolic threat

Sheikh Hassan al-Turabi's political-religious ideology can be described as both revolutionary and expansionist. It was revolutionary in that the ideological program sought to replace, not just transform, society's values; and it was expansionist because the ultimate goal was to encourage the spread of the ideology that formed the basis of the Islamist regime's legitimacy. This political-religious ideology challenged the Westphalian order upon which the modern Arab state system was putatively established by promoting a political community based on religion that transcended territorial borders. "Final loyalty must be rendered to the umma—the whole community of Muslims," Turabi commanded.[43] Although the norm of state sovereignty and idea of *wataniyya* (local, state-based nationalism/patriotism) had strengthened considerably since decolonization in the Middle East, the incongruities among national, ethnic, class, and religious identities still remained a political liability.[44] This ideology claimed a political community beyond Sudan's borders. Turabi used his political-religious ideology to exploit these societal cleavages; he urged Islamic activism at the local level while uniting Islamic movements together under his leadership.

This ideological program, when turned toward Egypt and Saudi Arabia, targeted state-society and state-state relations in an attempt to undermine Egypt's legitimacy and status. As a popular Islamic reformer/renewer (*mujaddid*), Turabi challenged "establishment Islam" and the traditional religious institutions allied with the state in the Arab world. In Egypt and other countries, such as Saudi Arabia, the religious institutions provided the ruling regime with religious legitimacy in exchange for resources (nonmaterial and material) and a measured autonomy over society's norms.

The programmatic side of this political-religious ideology can be called *Islamic internationalism*.[45] Heavily infused with anti-imperialist rhetoric and religious symbolism, this ideology sought to change the way Arab Muslim-majority states related to each other through normative persuasion and coercion. This transnational ideology targeted state-society relations by combining religious symbols, institutions, and various tools of statecraft (rhetoric, support of nonstate groups, alliances) to pressure pro-Western regimes, such as Egypt and Saudi Arabia.

Sudan's status and position in the international system enhanced Turabi's credibility as an interpreter and messenger of Islamic symbols. As a "poor country but spiritually rich," Sudan's position as a have-not country, along with its pariah status in the eyes of the West and pro-Western Arab states, allowed Turabi to implicitly claim his regime's Islamic values had not been compromised or contaminated by the West. This claim of moral power and authenticity was used to argue that Sudan was the center of the Islamic revival. Stemming from this, Turabi suggested there would be a demonstration effect once Sudan became a full-fledged Islamic state:

> The model would radiate throughout the Muslim World. If the physical export of that model is subject to Islamic limitations in deference to international law, the reminiscence of the classical Caliphate and the deeply entrenched Islamic traditions of free migration (hijra) and fraternal solidarity would make any such state a focus of pan-Islamic attention and affection.[46]

Turabi is essentially claiming here that Sudan will develop the "power of attraction," or soft power, based on its values. Turabi draws on authentic symbols from Islamic history to project these values.

Hassan al-Turabi's leadership qualities were also an essential component of the ideological threat his regime posed. He was the éminence grise of the regime.[47] Turabi's ability to be an effective communicator and interpreter of these Islamic symbols was based on his leadership qualities, including his charisma, educational background (religious and secular), and path to power. Turabi's charismatic appeal was rooted in his ability to put a modern face on Islam while claiming it was both compatible with the modern world and authentic. Muslim audiences in the Middle East watched Turabi travel all over the West and converse freely in French and English about Islamic approaches to democracy, women's rights, and religious tolerance. While Arab leaders were angered at the West's courtship of this seemingly eloquent liberal

Islamist, Arab and Muslim publics saw Turabi as a *mujaddid* (renewer) who spoke about fulfilling the collective yearnings of the *umma* (Islamic community) to establish an Islamic order.[48] According to an astute scholar of Middle East politics:

> As an urbane intellectual, educated at the Sorbonne and the University of London, Turabi symbolizes the modern face of Islamism, a sharp contrast to the unsophisticated shaykhs of the Egyptian Brethren, the primitive rebels of the Saudi al-Ikhwan, or the turbaned mujtahids of Hizb Allah. A man of charisma, Hasan al-Turabi is a master of power politics.[49]

Part of Turabi's charismatic appeal was embedded in what he communicated about himself and his place in history. Turabi could be seen as following in the tradition of the nineteenth-century anticolonial Mahdist-revivalist movement.[50] At the same time, *New York Times* journalist Judith Miller writes, "Turabi thinks of himself, as Khomeini did, in far grander terms as a symbol of his country's revolution, an Islamic internationalist whose vision cannot be limited to his hopeless land, so isolated from regional and international power centers, that fate has designated as the site of militant Sunni Islam's first official experiment."[51]

The foundational ideology of Turabi's experiment in Sudan threatened Egyptian national security because it attacked the foundations of the Egyptian regime's legitimacy and offered an alternative social and political order. The Sudanese regime's promotion of Islamic internationalism was the aggressive side of this political-religious ideology that validated and reified the demands of Egyptian Islamists. This ideology challenged the legal foundations for the exclusion of Islamists from political power as well as the core values of the Egyptian state—the *official* noninterference of religion in politics codified by the constitutional prohibition of religious political parties. Furthermore, Turabi's message appealed to Islamists because he challenged the structure of religious authority in Egyptian society. Turabi's call for greater use of *ijtihad* (independent reasoning) undermined the state-aligned Azhari shaykhs' status as the sole interpreters of Islam.

For Saudi Arabia, the concern about Sudan's ideational power grew out of the effects of the Gulf War on Saudi Arabia's tumultuous domestic environment in the early 1990s. The Gulf War was the catalyst for domestic unrest in Saudi Arabia. It created a crisis of legitimacy for the Saudi regime.[52] The government had mismanaged the economy. In addition, its inability to build a defense system led it to make some uncomfortable choices that had serious domestic political implications. In essence, the Saudi regime was forced to rely on foreign troops to defend the kingdom.

While the causes of the Islamist opposition predated the war, both moderate and radical Islamist opposition exploited King Fahd's decision to invite foreign troops to defend Saudi Arabia as a way to voice their discontent with the government and mobilize supporters. The strongest criticism came from young religious scholars who questioned if it was legitimate for Saudis to rely on non-Muslims to fight fellow Muslims.[53]

The Sahwa, or awakening sheikhs, formed the most important part of the opposition. These Islamist sheikhs represented a blend of Muslim Brotherhood/ Qutbist-style political activism combined with Salafi puritanical practices. Fostered by the state in the 1980s to bolster the regime's religious legitimacy and guard against revolutionary Islamic impulses (i.e., neo-Ikhwan), these sheikhs led the Islamic resurgence in Saudi Arabia. They were significant since they came from within the religious establishment and were extremely popular. Influenced by their Muslim Brotherhood instructors who had fled secular regimes in the 1960s, this new generation opposed the quietism of the Saudi *ulama*, epitomized by the Grand Mufti's fatwas related to Saudi foreign policy. They also advocated the full implementation and strict adherence to shari'a.

Two of the most prominent members of the Sahwa were Dr. Safar al-Hawali, dean of the Islamic College of Umm al-Qura University, and Salman al'Auda, a faculty member at Imam Muhammad Ibn Saud University. At a general level, al-Hawali argued that the West, not Iraq, was the real enemy, and expressed these views in a letter to Sheikh Abdel Aziz ibn al-Baz, the head of the higher council of the *ulama*. Salman al-'Auda, whose Friday sermons and lectures were widely circulated during the Gulf War, called for greater Islamization of society, and like Hawali he warned against the dangers of Western cultural imperialism. Hawali, 'Auda, and other Sahwa sheikhs also opposed the Saudi regime on the grounds that the political causes of Palestine, Chechnya, Iraq, Kashmir, and Bosnia also affected the *umma*.

These sheikhs not only ruptured the expected quietism of the Saudi religious establishment, they also shattered the taboo against publicly criticizing the regime. The famous Letter of Demand (1991) and Memorandum of Advice (1992) were sent to the King through Abdel Aziz ibn Baz and contained over a hundred signatures representing many opposition groups including 'Auda, Hawali, Mohammed Ma'asari, Saad al-Faqih, and Osama bin Laden.

These public petitions, expressing the rising criticisms about Saudi domestic and foreign policy, encouraged others to push for political reform. During this period of *infitah* (openness), some pressed for greater freedom and liberalism. But some of the activities in pursuit of these goals, such as the November 6, 1990 event in which forty-five women openly violated the law banning women from driving, drove the Islamist opposition to intensify their criticism that the presence of foreign troops would corrupt Saudi society.[54]

Osama bin Laden represented one of the most radical forms of Saudi Islamist opposition. After fighting against the Soviets in Afghanistan and founding al-Qaeda toward the end of the decade, bin Laden returned to Saudi Arabia a hero of the jihad in Afghanistan. Saudi Arabia's decision to rely on the United States for security after Iraq's invasion of Kuwait put bin Laden at odds with the monarchy. In a meeting with Prince Turki al-Faisal, the head of Saudi intelligence, Osama is said to have offered to "prepare one hundred thousand fighters with good combat capability within three months." Bin Laden then promised, "You don't need Americans. You don't need any other non-Muslim troops. We will be enough . . . .We will fight them with faith."[55] This offer was ignored and bin Laden's opposition grew stronger, more public, and more personal against King Fahd. Similar to much of the Saudi Islamist opposition, bin Laden viewed Abdel Aziz ibn Baz's fatwa that permitted the deployment of non-Muslim troops on Saudi soil simply as a desperate attempt to provide religious legitimacy to a political decision of the regime and, in turn, increased the attacks on the religious establishment and the House of Saud. In fact, in his first major public address to the Muslim world, bin Laden attacked ibn Baz for religiously sanctioning both the stationing of Western troops on Saudi soil and support of the Arab-Israeli peace process.[56]

By 1994, Saudi Arabia had no choice but to revoke bin Laden's citizenship. But by this time, he had been living in Sudan for almost four years and continued to live there until 1996.[57] Bin Laden's first contacts with Sudan took place while he began to challenge the Saudi regime's policies. Bin Laden was offered attractive business opportunities to settle in Sudan and he employed other Arab Afghans and Islamic militants who were unwelcome in their countries of origin.[58] As fresh recruits and stateless returnees flocked to Khartoum, bin Laden set up training camps for Islamic militants. He invested in the country and was awarded contracts to build an airport in Port Sudan and several major roads, becoming Sudan's only business tycoon.[59]

But the threat from al-Qaeda and Osama bin Laden carried greater symbolic weight than military punch. The kingdom was largely spared from violent attacks throughout the 1990s, and there was no campaign of violence
comparable to Algeria or Egypt. As for the ideology behind al-Qaeda's drive,
it was based on extreme pan-Islamism, not social-revolutionary ideology.[60]
Thus, the real threat was Osama bin Laden's ability to spread ideas that undermined the ruling regime's legitimacy, and this threat was based in Sudan.

Sudan's "betrayal" of supporting Iraq turned to ideological hostility. Turabi
openly assailed the Saudi regime for its un-Islamic positions and dependence
on the West. Turabi and other Sudanese leaders echoed Saddam Hussein's language about a holy war against the West and the stationing of troops, delegiti-
mizing the Saudi regime for allowing foreign troops on sacred soil. This was
seen as a direct challenge to Saudi Arabia's religious and political authority over
Arab Islamic matters. Saudi leaders assailed Sudan for supporting Iraq and were
concerned that Turabi could exploit the growing popular opposition to the war.
In response to Sudan's policy, Saudi Arabia cut its economic assistance, stopped
supplying oil, and began to back Sudan's southern rebels.[61]

Turabi's message had great potential to mobilize opposition groups and in
some cases appealed to important constituencies within the Islamist opposition. At the most general level, Turabi projected an Islamist message, putting
these ideas at odds with a Saudi regime supported by Islamic religious quietism, not Islamic political activism. Many moderate and conservative Islamists
shared Turabi's views on the Gulf crisis as well as his efforts to support Islamic
movements (especially when Muslims were under siege) opposing Western
imperialism and the Arab regimes they supported. In addition to appealing
to Sunni Islamist groups, Turabi's emphasis on the pan-Islamic character of
the Islamic revival, characterized by his outreach to Shi'a groups and Iran,
may have appealed to the Shi'a opposition. Turabi's ideas about democracy
appealed to nonviolent Shi'a opposition groups that pushed for greater political reform and civil rights. Turabi's ideas had the greatest influence among
Sahwi intellectuals.[62] Most importantly, Sahwi intellectuals were attracted to
the boldness of Turabi's (and Ghannoushi's) Islamism that sought to establish
a conservative Islamic democracy.[63]

How Sudan's alliances projected the ideational threat

Sudan's alliance choices with state and nonstate actors were a great concern for both Egypt and Saudi Arabia because they affected the ideational

balance of power. Sudan formed close relationships with Iraq and, most notably, Iran; hosted a number of nonstate actors, such as al-Gama'a al-Islamiyya and al-Jihad, that wished to topple the Egyptian regime; and, as previously discussed, supported Osama bin Laden. Even in cases that enhanced Sudan's military capability to pressure Egypt, these alliances were more important for their symbolic value.

During the run-up to the Gulf Crisis (1990–1991), Hassan al-Turabi made numerous attempts to position himself as an Arab mediator and dissuade Arabs from joining the U.S.-led UN coalition to drive Iraq out of Kuwait. Sudan, along with Yemen, Jordan, and the PLO, were the only Arab parties that did not join the coalition. Hassan al-Turabi exploited the Arab coalition's position on this conflict to question their commitment to Arab Islamic causes.

Both Egypt and Saudi Arabia strongly opposed Sudan's support of Iraq. The previous pages described how this was a source of domestic vulnerability for Saudi Arabia. Egypt grew concerned about the growing relationship between Iraq and Sudan, enshrined in a protocol of cooperation. The most disconcerting part of this understanding was the security cooperation, since this arrangement meant that Egypt's foe, Iraq, could gain a foothold in Khartoum.[64] Egypt accused Sudan of receiving Scuds from Iraq prior to the invasion of the U.S.-led coalition, which Cairo claimed were meant to target the Aswan Dam.[65] Thus, as a warning to Sudan after demonstrators in Khartoum called for an attack on the Aswan Dam, President Mubarak conducted military exercises near the Sudanese border. Mubarak also threatened that Egypt would attack Sudan if he found evidence that Iraq had transferred weapons to Sudan.[66]

Yet, the Iraqi-Sudanese relationship did not seem to alter the military balance between Egypt and Sudan in an appreciable way, or at the very least it did not prompt Egypt to move beyond the level of issuing threats and military maneuvers. In an interview with al-Akhbar, Interior Minister Abdel Halim Musa claimed that Iraq did not possess the capability to threaten Egypt and Sudan should "think a thousand times before turning its territory into a site of aggression against Egypt."[67]

Instead, the Sudan-Iraq alliance posed a threat to Egypt in two ways, some of which apply to Saudi Arabia as well. First, the alliance challenged Egypt's leadership status and brought attention to the international order Egypt and Saudi Arabia supported. Despite their differences on what the order should look like and Saddam's brutal repression of Islamists in the past,[68] Sudan and Iraq shared the goals of overturning the regional order, supported by Egypt, which had a stake in maintaining the status quo. Ultimately, Egyptian officials viewed Sudan's response to the Iraqi aggression against Kuwait as a violation of the proper Arab Islamic response, and, more notably, as a challenge to Egypt's authority to speak for Arab Islamic collective interests. Egyptian officials clearly saw that Sudan's vision of the international order posed a challenge.

Second, Sudan's alliance choice posed a threat to Egypt by enhancing Sudan's nonmaterial capabilities. Sudan's support of Iraq enhanced its popular standing among those who opposed the idea of their governments collaborating with Western military forces against an Arab Muslim-majority state. Sudan's alliance with a secular leader demonstrated its commitment to a transnational ideal of defending Muslims under siege.[69] Although there was not much sympathy for Saddam Hussein and most Arabs interpreted his use of religious symbols as opportunistic, Saddam's rhetoric created a shift in the discourse about the war.[70] Islamists and secular nationalists protested against the Gulf War and, more specifically, Egypt's role in the war. The Gulf Crisis created political opportunities for a charismatic leader, such as Turabi, armed with a powerful ideology, to mobilize discontent.

The Sudanese-Iranian alliance was a major concern for Egypt. The "axis," as the Egyptians called it, constituted one of the greatest sources of hostility in Egyptian-Sudanese relations. From the perspective of military capabilities, this alliance posed the most significant threat to Egypt. Sudan and Iran developed an ideological and strategic partnership through high-level diplomatic exchanges as well as cultural, military, and economic agreements shortly after Bashir came to power.[71] There was considerable military cooperation and coordination between Iran and Sudan including military assistance, intelligence sharing, training in conventional and asymmetric warfare, advising, and, quite possibly, combat activities. In December 1991 Iran's president, Ali Akbar Hashemi-Rafsanjani, and leaders of Iran's Islamic Revolutionary Guard visited Khartoum and agreed to supply free oil and sell arms to Sudan, and the two states signed a military pact.[72] Sources also relate that the Iranian Navy used Port Sudan, and the Iranian Air Force was granted special landing privileges within Sudan.[73] An Egyptian pro-regime paper even claimed there were over 10,000 Iranian soldiers in Sudan (although these numbers were likely inflated because the source quoted was the Sudanese opposition).[74]

Indeed, Egyptian authorities were keenly aware of Iran's activities to improve Sudan's asymmetric capabilities.[75] In the early 1990s, there were between 1,000 to 2,000 Iranian revolutionary guards in Sudan training Islamic fundamentalist militants from Sudan, Algeria, Tunisia, Egypt, and the Persian Gulf region.[76] Iran also sent several hundred Revolutionary Guards to help Sudan wage *jihad* against the rebels.

From Egypt's perspective, this alliance represented a level of threat located somewhere between an immediate and an indirect threat.[77] The immediate concern was that Sudan could more easily imperil some of Egypt's vital strategic interests, such as Egypt's water supply in the Nile Basin, access to the Horn of Africa and Africa, and the Red Sea—the strategic extension of the Gulf.[78] Moreover, Iran, utilizing this alliance, could contribute its resources to support terrorism and export the Islamic revolution throughout the Middle East and, in particular, Egypt.[79]

But the ideological aspect of this alliance posed a greater threat than the military element. Iran set the terms of the alliance as the stronger power. As such, it was highly unlikely that Iranian support, even in the context of military agreements, would extend much beyond training, advisers, and stationing of troops even if reports were correct. In fact, Iran did not react to the border skirmishes between Egypt and Sudan over Halaib.

From the beginning, Bashir had cast the burgeoning relationship in Islamic (religious-political) terms. Iran's adoption of independent policies set "an exalted and civilized example of an Islamic state," Bashir said, and Sudan was "determined to make use of the worthwhile experiences of Iran in our government structure and in political, economic and other fields."[80] In this context, Bashir reaffirmed Sudan's pan-Islamic message and proposed a new normative structure for international politics: "all Muslim nations to cooperate and adhere to Islamic principles."[81]

Egypt saw this alliance through the filter of a transnational ideological threat—political Islam and Islamic extremism—inspired and promoted by Iran. As a parliamentary report indicated at the time, Egypt believed that Iran, through Sudan, could bring "the revolution to Egypt" just as Egypt was "the target of Khomeini's revolution."[82] Denouncing the Sudanese regime (and Iran), the comments of a pro-regime newspaper are telling of the Mubarak regime's attitude: "this regime has turned the country into a branch for Tehran's rulers and for the institution they are running to export their backward thought and terrorist schemes to Egypt."[83]

Some Egyptians may have also been aware of the more subtle religious aspects of this ideological alliance between two "Islamic republics." Turabi's emphasis on *ijtihad* must have won favor in the eyes of Iranian Shi'a clerics, and possibly some liberal Islamists and conservative reformists, while upsetting traditional and quietist, state-aligned *ulama* in the Arab Sunni world. For reform and renewal to occur in Islam, Turabi's theological doctrine stressed the need to reintroduce the institution of *ijtihad*, a practice that Shi'a clerics continued to exercise. In fact, in initial discussions with the Iranian hierarchy in Iran, Bashir, coached by Turabi, emphasized the importance of reviving the practice of *ijtihad* as a way to connect with their Iranian hosts.[84]

Saudi Arabia also saw the Sudan-Iran alliance as a symbolic threat in which its political-communicative value far outweighed its military might. From the perspective of regional power politics, Saudi Arabia was understandably concerned Sudan would be a gateway for Iranian influence into East Africa, and in particular as an access route to the Red Sea, a sphere of influence and strategically sensitive. The Iran-Sudan relationship was also perceived as an alliance of states sponsoring Islamic radicalism and terror that used these asymmetric tactics to destabilize regimes. Saudi Arabia was certainly alarmed by the military cooperation between the two countries. The Saudi-owned *al-Hayat* reported that there were between 4,000 to 12,000 Iranian troops in Sudan and discussed the arms deals with Iran brokered by China.[85]

But it is unclear how this military cooperation could have posed a military threat, especially at a time when the U.S. military and other foreign armies were stationed on Saudi soil. Instead, the Saudi leadership perceived these moves as evidence of Iranian ideological penetration in Africa's largest country. The relationship communicated that the Sudanese model, a Sunni Islamic republic, could bridge Sunni-Shi'a and Arab-Persian divides. This capability, and the open policy toward Islamists throughout the region, raised the possibility that perhaps the charismatic al-Turabi might be even more successful in the Arab Sunni world where he was already popular. This new relationship, which allied Sudan with a major regional player ruled by the first Islamist regime to come to power through popular revolution, added to Sudan's prestige.

The symbolic value of Sudan's support
of Egypt's Islamist opposition
One of Egypt's top concerns that related to its domestic and foreign policy was Sudan's support of Islamic movements inside Egypt, particularly the violent

Islamic insurgency that plagued Egypt during the 1990s. As part of its Islamic internationalist policy, Sudan pledged support for those Islamists who wished to change the political and social order of society along Islamic lines. Consequently, from 1990 to 1996 Sudan became a haven for Islamic radicals including the a'idun, or returnees, who fought against the Soviets in Afghanistan and were not allowed to reenter their countries of origin.[86] Sudan welcomed these militant Islamists by not requiring a visa from any Arab, and in some cases they provided diplomatic passports.[87] Egypt's State Security Investigation Service (SSI) was very concerned about the training camps for these Arab Afghans under the control of the Islamist NIF.[88]

Two overlapping interests motivated Sudan's support of Egypt's violent and nonviolent opposition groups. First, Sudan wanted to demonstrate its ideological commitment to Islamic movements. Second, Sudan hoped to destabilize, or at least to weaken, Egypt. From a capabilities perspective, Sudan's support of asymmetric warfare did not constitute a direct threat to the Mubarak regime's survival, although it imposed material costs on Egypt. Rather, this foreign policy tool aimed to create the conditions under which Islamic movements might challenge the Egyptian regime.

Cairo was primarily concerned about Sudan's support of al-Gama'a al-Islamiyya (Islamic Group) and al-Jihad, Egypt's fiercest Islamic militant groups, which violently confronted the Egyptian state during the late 1980s and 1990s. According to a senior Egyptian security official, Egypt was concerned that Turabi could act as a model for the Islamic Group.[89] Sudan provided the Islamic Group and al-Jihad with logistical support and set up training camps.[90] Egyptian Security Services emphasized the strategic-ideological aspects of Sudan's strategy by identifying the NIF's involvement in training these militants.[91]

Egypt also accused Sudan of supporting the Muslim Brotherhood, the most serious political opposition to the Mubarak regime. Some security officials believed that the Brotherhood saw Turabi as a model of inspiration.[92] Egyptian officials often tried to link the Brotherhood, Turabi, and foreign sponsors of terrorism. After the assassination attempt against Mubarak, Egyptian Minister of Interior Hassan al-Alfi arrested thirty senior Brotherhood officials, accusing them of having links to Turabi and foreign terrorists.[93] Dismissing the differences between the Brotherhood and Turabi as "details," al-Alfi claimed that there were various forms of coordination between the NIF and the Brotherhood. The Mubarak regime was also aware of the Egyptian

Brotherhood members' attendance at the PAIC; the regime often denied some members from attending.[94]

While Sudan's policies were a serious security challenge for Egypt, they enhanced Sudan's ideational power. Egypt perceived Sudan's support of these nonstate groups as an ideological threat to its domestic political stability for a few reasons. First, irrespective of the level of actual support Sudan actually provided the Egyptian militants and its impact, the insurgency caused a steep drop in tourism and led to a significant decline in state revenue. Therefore, Egypt viewed any aid that could help the insurgents prolong this condition as a threat to its domestic political stability.

Second, Sudan's support undermined Mubarak's delicate strategy to increase and maintain Egypt's legitimacy by accommodating, co-opting, and selectively repressing the violent and nonviolent Islamist opposition. During the 1980s, the Mubarak regime allowed the Brotherhood to operate more freely, since this enhanced Mubarak's credibility and public image; the Brotherhood ran candidates as independents in the 1987 elections.[95] The growth of the Brotherhood's popularity and societal influence coincided with a rise in Islamic militancy against the state in the late 1980s and throughout the 1990s. In order to bring the insurgency led by the Islamic Group and al-Jihad under control, the Mubarak regime executed massive crackdowns and collective punishments from 1992 to 1997 on segments of the population. This, however, further eroded civil liberties in Egypt and weakened the Mubarak regime's administrative legitimacy. Despite his own authoritarian rule, Turabi was able to exploit this situation. He chastised the Mubarak regime for disregarding human rights and brutally attacking the Islamic movement, which, Turabi claimed, represented the true aspirations of the Egyptian people in search of deliverance from tyrannical rule.

Sudan and the PAIC:
International Institutions as a Symbolic Threat

One of Sheikh Hassan al-Turabi's major successes at the ideational level was the establishment of the Popular Arab Islamic Conference (PAIC). Hassan al-Turabi established the PAIC in the wake of the Gulf Crisis as a response to the Arab League's and Organization of Islamic Conferences' perceived betrayal of Islam. Turabi claimed these organizations acted out of self-interest and greed during the Gulf Crisis.[96] The PAIC challenged the religious and political authority of the OIC, which sought to maintain the existing political and social order. For example, PAIC's first conference took place in Khartoum, April 25–28, 1991, at the same time as the OIC's meeting in Cairo.[97] The size and scope of the meeting, which included over 200 representatives from forty-five countries, projected Sudan as the center of Islamic internationalism. Over the course of the decade, senior leaders from the Muslim Brotherhood; Islamist radicals from Tunisia, Algeria, and Afghanistan; and officials from Iran were regular attendees. Kepel observes, "The goal, of course, was to blend all these ingredients into an international Islamism with a much more radical program—colored by populism and Third World ideology—than the one offered by the Wahhabites. It saw itself as a durable alternative to such puppets of Saudi control and influence as the OIC and the Muslim World League, and it called other meetings in 1993 and 1995."[98]

Consciously representing itself as a type of "Islamic Cominterm," which merged ideology and practice, the Sudanese regime (through Turabi) aimed to coordinate "all anti-Imperialist, Muslim movements" and bring them toward revolution. Logistically, the PAIC was important for improving cooperation and ultimately uniting Islamic revolutionaries with similar goals but different ideologies. For example, Hassan al-Turabi worked together with Osama bin Laden, a large financial supporter of the PAIC, to heal rifts among Egyptian militant groups; this experience brought bin Laden closer to many senior Egyptian militant Islamists.[99] In addition, these PAIC meetings helped facilitate the creation of social networks and the planning of violent operations.[100]

Representing both a concern about the conference and a pretext to attack its enemies, the PAIC enhanced the Islamist regime's symbolic and ideational power. The Sudanese government heralded the first meeting of the PAIC as the "most significant event since the collapse of the Caliphate."[101] To boost his image and the role of Sudan as an Islamic mediator,[102] General Secretary Turabi used this Islamic institution "for mediating disputes in countries from Afghanistan to Algeria. Through this forum he was able to assert himself as an adjudicator in domestic and international policy quarrels within the *umma*, the global Muslim family."[103] Turabi clearly tried to present himself as a mediator, portraying his actions as similar to the way that the Prophet Mohammed brought hostile tribes together under the Medina Charter. This metaphorical act was meant to enhance his legitimacy and authenticity and raise his status as an Islamic leader.

Egypt accused Turabi of using the sessions to coordinate terrorist activities.[104] The Mubarak regime also claimed that the Muslim Brotherhood had links to terrorist groups that attended the conference as well.[105] The most significant public or official reaction denouncing Turabi and the PAIC came from the Egyptian Security Services. They were especially concerned about Turabi's involvement in bringing together Islamic militant factions including the Muslim Brotherhood.[106] Interior Minister Alfi accused Turabi of trying to help unite Egypt's two main radical groups. This accusation revealed the Egyptian Security Services' tremendous fear that Turabi's efforts would prove successful.[107]

Most importantly, Egypt regarded Hassan al-Turabi's establishment of the Popular Arab Islamic Conference as a symbolic and practical vehicle to launch Sudan's expansionist ideology and bring Islamic movements toward revolution. Symbolizing his *Islamic internationalism*, Turabi used this Islamic international institution as a coordinating device for Islamic movements to contest Egypt's authority as a spokesman for Arab-Islamic collective interests. The activities of the PAIC, which created opportunities for Islamists to cooperate and coordinate violent and nonviolent action, combined with the powerful ideological symbolism of an "authentic" international Islamic institution and strengthened Sudan's Islamic regime as an ideological threat.

These activities naturally constituted an ideational threat to Saudi Arabia as well. After all, the PAIC was established to challenge the Saudi-backed OIC; the international order the PAIC promoted was also a challenge to Saudi Arabia's status and legitimacy. Moreover, the challenger was not within Saudi Arabia's "peer group" so to speak. The founder of the PAIC was from a poor, black African state that Saudi Arabia had kept afloat financially. More importantly, the list of PAIC members included representatives from the most popular Islamic groups and movements in the region, which added credibility to his message and claims. Turabi capitalized on Sudan's poor, "third world" status to promote the authenticity of his Islamic vision and contrast it with the material corruption of Saudi Arabia.

Containing Ideational Power Projection through Ideational Balancing

Cairo and Riyadh sought to contain Sudan's ideational power projection by balancing against it through a variety of tactics and countermeasures. Egypt's general approach to Sudan during the first half of the 1990s was containment. This strategy consisted of alignments and limited armed engagements with

Sudan in the external realm, and nuanced strategies in the domestic realm. Egypt employed ideational balancing tactics and traditional balancing behavior to contain, isolate, and pressure Sudan. On the informational front, Egypt attempted to undermine the credibility of the source of the symbol—the Islamist regime led by Hassan al-Turabi and Omar al-Bashir.

The Mubarak regime, through the Egyptian media, utilized three approaches to reduce Turabi's influence and mitigate his ability to mobilize Egyptian domestic opposition using Islamic symbols. The media focused on creating unflattering images of Turabi. First, Egypt exposed Turabi's shortcomings as the leader of a failed state. To reduce Turabi's appeal, Egypt's message tried to communicate that these failures were a result of Turabi's ideological extremism. According to a senior Egyptian diplomat closely involved with African affairs at the time, the Egyptian media tried to portray Sudan as an economically failing state consumed by bloodshed.[108] This strategy hoped to expand the criteria upon which Turabi's legitimacy should be judged to include economic prosperity.[109] This exposure would show that the leader of the "Islamic model" had not ameliorated suffering and eliminated bloodshed.

The Egyptian media also portrayed Turabi as a fanatic, associating him with Ayatollah Khomeini in an attempt to marginalize Turabi and his message. One Egyptian columnist went so far as to compare Turabi's fanaticism to Khomeini's but also claimed that Turabi lacked Khomeini's charisma.[110] Egyptian officials also framed Turabi as hostile to Egyptian national interests by bringing attention to his links with Islamic radicals. Specifically, Egyptian officials linked Turabi to Egyptian militants who had killed Egyptian citizens, sown seeds of societal division, and caused severe economic damage. Mubarak assailed Sudan's rulers by claiming, "[They changed] our neighbor country into a place exporting terrorism to Egypt and other Arab countries and to a country harboring murderers and criminals."[111] Ultimately, Egypt attempted to neutralize the threat Sudan posed by undermining the credibility of the source of the Islamic symbols. Without the requisite authority of a credible interpreter of Islamic symbols, the Sudanese regime would be less of a threat.

Egypt also contested Turabi's claim as the authoritative interpreter of Islam, its symbols, and their meaning. Specifically, Cairo countered Khartoum's claims by asserting that "Egyptian Islam," as represented by Al-Azhar, was a moderate and authentic Islam. In countering Sudan, Egypt's close strategic cooperation with Tunisia and Algeria served two important purposes on both practical and cultural levels. Practically, their counterterrorism cooperation included intelligence sharing on Sudan's support of violent and nonviolent Islamic movements. On a cultural level, these regimes consciously constructed their antiterrorist and anti-extremist cooperation as a fight between tolerant, moderate, enlightened, and rational Islam and extremist, radical, and fundamentalist Islam. Egypt, Tunisia, and Algeria promoted their regimes as representing the commonly held belief that true, authentic Islam was moderate in nature. Thus, the role of these Arab incumbent regimes was to protect Islam from extremists, and this role would in turn provide the regimes with religious legitimacy.

Meanwhile, Saudi Arabia sought to manage the external ideological threat through ideational balancing, including counterframing and resource mobilization. Saudi Arabia both mobilized and denied resources to Sudan as a means to undermine the credibility of the source of the ideational threat. The effects of Saudi Arabia's denial of aid and its support for Sudan's southern rebels supported Khartoum's claims that the Sudanese model was a failure. The fact that Saudi Arabia's strategic interests favored Sudanese unity, but aided the southern rebels, suggests how Saudi Arabia ranked the threat. As a whole, the purpose of this policy was to associate instability and disorder with Turabi to bolster the claim that Turabi was in no position to promote his model.

Despite largely denying the existence of some challenging issues in the press as Turabi rose to prominence and popularity in the early 1990s, the Saudi press's attacks against Turabi went beyond his stance on Iraq. The Saudi-owned international Arab daily, al-Sharq al-Awsat, featured scathing critiques of Turabi along with Saddam Hussein and portrayed them as opportunists. To question Turabi's genuine commitment to Islamic causes, the Saudi media pointed out the fact that Turabi was now aligned with a secular Ba'athist leader who had crushed Islamic movements in Iraq.[112] In addition, these battles in the press were intended to attack supporters of Turabi inside the kingdom and also to reveal some of the greatest concerns of the regime.

The public dispute between the Sahwa sheikh and Turabi sympathizer Salman al-'Auda and Ghazi al-Qusaibi, a state official, public intellectual, and ally of the royal family, reveals how the Saudi regime defended itself against what it feared. The dispute was part of an escalation of the ongoing debate between conservatives and modernists that started in the late 1980s.[113] Conservative Sahwa responded harshly to Qusaibi's assertion of his right to speak about religion.[114] Joined by others, al-'Auda attacked al-Qusaibi for his secularism in a sermon titled "Islamic Tape: An Assessment."[115] Al-Qusaibi responded in a series of newspaper articles, later collected in a book known as *Hata la Takun Fitnah* (Until There Is No More Discord), where al-Qusaibi accused the religious right of attempting to destabilize Saudi Arabia and calls them "Khomeinis" and "Saddamists."[116] While the energy of this debate was internal, the regime was still concerned about external influences, particularly from Turabi who had the support of influential Saudi clerics.[117]

From Brinkmanship to Reconciliation: The Decline of Islamic Internationalism (1995–2000)

On June 26, 1995, a group of Islamic militants tried to assassinate President Hosni Mubarak as he arrived at the Addis Ababa airport to attend the Organization for African Unity Summit. Mubarak promptly left Ethiopia and returned to Egypt. Al-Gama'a al-Islamiyya claimed responsibility for the assassination attempt, its third assassination in recent years, and the terrorist group promised to keep trying "until every Islamist is freed from Egyptian jails and Islamic law is applied in Egypt."[118]

Mubarak immediately blamed Turabi and the Sudanese regime for their involvement in the plot and for their continued support of Egyptian militants. The next eighteen months were the most volatile period in Sudanese-Egyptian relations, consisting of military maneuvers, threats, and limited but deadly border clashes. Armed clashes broke out in Hala'ib, and Egyptian forces killed two and wounded seven policemen in a raid on three police stations. [119] Yet, by the end of the decade, full diplomatic relations had been restored and normalization was underway. Relations with Saudi Arabia improved as well. What was so threatening about this crisis and how can we explain the subsequent decline in Egypt's threat perception as well as Saudi Arabia's?

The challenge of religious symbolism

The assassination attempt against Mubarak and the intense period that followed demonstrate Turabi's potentially threatening use of evocative Islamic symbols. In the middle of this diplomatic crisis, Sheikh Turabi tried to put Mubarak on the defensive by linking a vital national security interest, the Nile, with a commonly held belief that the Egyptian regime's legitimacy was contested through the use of religious metaphor. First, Turabi played the "water card" to expose Egypt's vulnerability. "We don't want tensions to come to a head . . . but water supplies are from this land. And they [Egypt] don't have any ground water supply, and if Sudan faces agitation, Sudan will repudiate its water treaty agreements, and this will be a dangerous affair."[120] Following this, Turabi linked this national security interest, the Nile, directly to religious legitimacy of the Egyptian regime by alluding to its secular nature: "[Egypt has] a deficiency in religion," and "the Nile flows north to purify Egypt."[121] Turabi went even further. Referencing Sadat's assassins who proclaimed "Death to Pharoah," Turabi implicitly sanctioned the assassination and the practice of *takfir* by the Islamic militants who tried to kill Mubarak, saying, "The group of mujahidin left Egyptian territory to chase after the Egyptian Pharaoh."[122]

Regardless of the type of player we label Turabi (political opportunist or religious ideologue), the payoffs for utilizing Islamic terminology during times of crisis, uncertainty, and strain on the political system were enhanced.[123] Turabi aimed to give the assassination attempt additional salience by placing it within the context of Islamic history and, in doing so, transform this symbol into a focal point for coordinating collective action against the Egyptian regime. Turabi hoped that these powerful cultural-religious images of the Egyptian regime's vulnerability and impiety would somehow resonate in a dissatisfied and dispossessed population. In addition, the assassination attempt itself, supported by its weak neighbor, Sudan, posed a direct threat to the regime and was surely an embarrassment to Egypt's security and intelligence services.

The assassination attempt marked a climax as well as a red line for Turabi's Islamic internationalism. The assassination attempt may have been too much for Turabi's potential sympathizers in Egypt, where a rally around the flag effect (Mubarak) took hold. Even within Turabi's own regime, the assassination attempt led to dissent.[124] Indeed, mounting isolation and international pressure convinced many leaders in the RCC, notably Bashir, that rapprochement with Cairo was a necessity for political survival. Ironically, the assassination, which signaled the malicious intent of the Sudanese regime, was also a catalyst for a growing power struggle between Bashir and Turabi.

Egypt's perception of Sudan changed in response to what it did not observe. In other words, it was the diminution or absence of the ideational projection of Islamic internationalism that led to a decline in threat perception. At the diplomatic level, Sudanese officials mostly eschewed harsh ideological rhetoric and personal attacks against Mubarak.

Sudan's alliance policy and foreign relations also changed. Sudanese-Iraqi relations had already died as a significant issue by this time and, more significantly, Iranian-Sudanese relations cooled. This may have had more to do with Iranian decision-making. For Iran, the costs and risks of the relationship outweighed the benefits. Once Iran's association with Sudan as a pariah state jeopardized the expected utility of Iran's strategy to engage with the West, the relationship became a liability for Tehran. The threat from the Sudan-Iran axis also declined because of personal disagreements. An example of this is the Iranian discontent with Turabi for his attempts to portray himself as Khomeini's successor. Sudanese support was no more remarkable compared to other states' sympathy for the Iraqi people's plight under UN sanctions, which was widespread throughout the Arab world.

Nonetheless, the activities of the PAIC, the Islamic institution that best symbolized Islamic internationalism, subsided. Although Sudan did not hand over wanted Egyptian militants, which was still a major source of contention between the two countries, Sudan seemed to refrain from supporting Islamic Group and al-Jihad as it had in the past. The departure of Osama bin Laden from Sudan along with a number of top Islamic Group and al-Jihad leaders, who would later form their core elite after they joined al-Qaeda, was a significant statement.

Sudan's decision to encourage or ask Osama bin Laden to leave the country represented a retreat from its expansionist ideology and signaled a desire to improve relations with Egypt (Saudi Arabia and other countries as well). Bin Laden had been a business partner, an investor, a financer of Sudan, and an important financial contributor to the PAIC. Thus, Turabi's decision to ask bin Laden to leave Sudan was a costly signal of change, since it not only had financial repercussions but also contradicted the Islamist regime's claims that it was the center of Islamic internationalism. In pursuit of closer relations with Egypt, Sudan emphasized the countries' shared Arab identity and mutual interest in the Nile.[125] In an interview with the Egyptian weekly *al-Usbu'a* in 1997, Turabi emphasized Sudan's and Egypt's shared ethnic and religious identity to dissuade Egypt from negotiating with the Sudan People's Liberation Army (SPLA)'s John Garang, whose interests, according to Sudan, were inimical to Arabs and Muslims.[126] These developments were a significant change from the earlier emphasis on Sudan's Islamic character and the regime's intent to export the revolution.

In response to Sudan's retreat from activities supporting its Islamic internationalism, Egypt agreed to reopen trade and travel routes (air flights and sensitive border crossings), and it eventually restored diplomatic relations. It was much easier in this atmosphere for Egyptian officials to emphasize their shared interests with Sudan as seen in the renewed public statements by Egyptian officials reiterating they supported a unified Sudan.[127] By 1998, Egypt and Sudan constructed a general plan to normalize relations. By the end of 1999, Egypt openly backed Bashir in his power struggle with Turabi. Bashir framed this struggle as a second "coup" to reclaim his power.[128] As part of this struggle, Bashir dissolved parliament, effectively ending Turabi's position as speaker, and declared a state of emergency. Bashir sent Turabi to jail in 2000, and thereafter full, normalized relations between Egypt and Sudan were restored.

Saudi Arabia's decline in threat perception followed a very similar pattern. The increased international pressure on Sudan, particularly from the United States following the assassination attempt against Hosni Mubarak in June 1995, had a similar effect on the Sudanese-Saudi relationship as it did on the Sudanese-Egyptian relationship. A few weeks after the assassination attempt, Bashir traveled to the Gulf to explain Sudan's position and to repair relations with the Gulf countries. It is quite likely Bashir embarked on these travels as a way to distance himself from Turabi and cultivate external alliances that would push Turabi out of power.

But it was also clear something had changed. From July 1995 onward, we find fewer examples of hostile Sudanese statements toward Saudi Arabia and, in fact, more conciliatory ones. The PAIC's diminished activities and bin Laden's departure from Sudan in 1996 also indicated that Sudan had taken a different path. Sudan ceased to project its ideology.

President Bashir's hajj to Saudi Arabia, accompanied by a number of high-level officials from the ministries of defense and foreign affairs, stands out as an attempt to move the reconciliation process forward. Upon his departure Bashir related that Sudan was "keen to remove the problems that faced bilateral relations after the Persian Gulf War."[129] More importantly, on the day of Bashir's departure, he replaced the presidential adviser for *originalization* and strategic planning.[130] This (religious) symbolic act communicated and acknowledged the legitimacy and authority of Saudi Arabia's religious leadership.

A more robust message of conciliation followed. Sudan's message acknowledged Saudi Arabia's important regional role connected to its Islamic identity:

"The Sudan acknowledges the leading role by Saudi Arabia for disseminating Islam in Africa, Asia and Europe."[131] To reciprocate, Saudi Arabia publicly reassured Sudan that they opposed the division of Sudan: "Saudi Arabia cannot in any case accept the division of Sudan."[132] Saudi Arabia followed Egypt's lead on reconciliation and watched carefully for the rift between Turabi and Bashir to widen. The Gulf states and Egypt supported forces that further isolated Turabi internally until his imprisonment in 1999.

Conclusion

This chapter has examined Egypt's and Saudi Arabia's relations with Sudan before and after Islamists took power there. Evidence from these cases supports my argument that the projection of transnational ideological threats influenced threat perception and foreign policy. Egypt and Saudi Arabia perceived the Sudanese Islamist regime's use of religious symbols in the form of messages and foreign policies as a threat to regime security and stability. The sociopolitical logic of this ideational threat was that these subversive ideas could affect commonly held beliefs about regime legitimacy, exploit state-society tensions, and facilitate collective political action among opposition groups. These were the major fears.

Egypt and Saudi Arabia responded to this nonmilitary threat through ideational balancing to contain Sudan's ideational power projection. They did, however, employ different tactics because the situations were slightly different. Egypt responded to these threats through ideational balancing to mitigate the ideological-political threat from Sudan. The counterframing aspect of the response consisted of *denial*—ignoring the threat; *neutralization*—undermining the credibility of the source; and *defense*—bolstering Egypt's image. When the Bashir-Turabi regime modified external manifestations of its ideology, such as support for Islamic radicalism, its alliance with Iran, and its aggressive rhetoric, Egypt's perception of Sudan changed and Egypt pursued a more accommodating foreign policy.

Saudi Arabia responded with counterframing and resource allocation. The former policies included *neutralization*—undermining Turabi's credibility in the press as Egypt did (undermining the credibility of the source); allocating resourcing to Sudan's opposition; and denial of resources to Sudan in terms of the discontinuation of aid, which was actually a response to Sudan's support of Iraq during the war.

As in the case of Egypt, some of Saudi Arabia's domestic polices were also responses to local internal challenges. It is often difficult to separate them from policies responding more directly to domestic threats that emerged independently of the external ideational threat. But the external ideational threat may have amplified the internal threat.

These dynamics are captured by the ideational security dilemma. The escalation between Egypt and Sudan that resulted in low-level armed clashes, and promised more, shows how nonmaterial threats can lead to military confrontation. More importantly, the structure of this ideational competition can be destabilizing in and of itself. Egypt and Saudi Arabia feared Sudan's ability to destabilize through ideational power projection. More generally, viewing the dyads in these terms serves as an important analytical framework to understand how ideational factors matter in interstate relations.

Let us now turn to some of the alternative explanations while highlighting additional observations that come out of this chapter. The argument that a shift in the balance of power affects threat perception does not explain why Egypt feared Sudan's Islamist regime. In fact, Egypt's relative military capability actually increased during the Turabi-Bashir regime. While Egypt received debt relief because of its role in the Gulf War and continued to receive aid as a result of the Camp David agreement, Sudan was still fighting a civil war.

Another possible explanation why Egypt feared Sudan's Islamist regime is that it was perceived as an irrational actor that could threaten the flow of the Nile. This perception is based on the belief that religious fundamentalists or extremists are risk-averse. Egypt certainly described the regime this way, and editorials consistently urged Sudan to return to a "rational" foreign policy. Egypt's primary concern was that Sudan would alter the flow of the Nile and thus put Egypt's most important national resource at risk. Indeed, one of Egypt's most famous journalists and historians, Mohammed Hassasnein Heikel, writes in a *Foreign Affairs* article in 1978, "Since Egypt's very existence depends on the waters of the Nile, the first consideration of any Egyptian government is to guarantee that these waters are not threatened."[133] However, in the same article Heikel acknowledges that technological limitations contribute to the unlikelihood of this event. Similarly, many Egyptian and foreign experts agree that the diversion of the Nile is not a realistic possibility.[134]

Geography is important insofar as shared borders encouraged outcomes that were consequences of the ideational threat, not causes of the conflict. These events were: the armed clashes between Sudan and Egyptian forces in the disputed border region; the "securitization" of water as a way to mobilize support against Sudan and the Islamist regime in power; and the movement of Islamic militants between Egypt and Sudan. However, geography did not affect factors in the traditional security realm, such as the offense-defense balance, because shifts in military power did not affect threat perception.

Geography is highly correlated with a contagion effect. Thus it is reasonable to assert that the demonstration effect resulting from the establishment of the first Sunni-Arab government on Egypt's border was a cause for alarm. Not only is there a psychological element here, it is likely that the perception of close networks linking Islamists in both countries, porous borders, and the ability to move resources between the two countries all contributed to the Egyptian regime's threat perception of Sudan's Islamist regime.

The shared ethnic and religious identities of the two countries came into play in a few respects. First, there were fewer identity barriers for the transnational ideology to traverse, and within this Sunni context the Egyptian regime saw Sudanese Islamists' and Egyptian Islamists' shared ideological origins as a potential source of cooperation and threat. Moreover, the shared ideational factors might motivate Egypt's Islamists to seize power either through inspiration or jealousy. After all, Egypt was the birthplace of two of political Islam's greatest ideologues, Hassan al-Banna (the founder of the Brotherhood) and Sayyid Qutb. In addition, the Egyptian Brotherhood's southern and poor offshoot, the NIF, had established the first Arab-Sunni Islamic state on Egypt's border. On a more general level, the NIF was the only Sunni Islamist movement to seize power, and it was also the only movement ready to fill the vacuum left by Ayatollah Khomeini's death earlier that year.[135]

It is likely that after watching the Islamist military officers, supported by Turabi's party, seize power, Egyptian leaders reflected on their own domestic context. Less than ten years prior to the coup, radical Islamist groups had penetrated the Egyptian military and assassinated President Sadat. This precedent doubtlessly reminded the regime of the risk posed by even a few radical Islamists in the military. But Islamist penetration of the military in Sudan exposed a deeper concern. Egyptian officials understood this military takeover as qualitatively different from the numerous coups and attempted coups Sudan had experienced in the past; this event was part of a broader transnational threat posed by a monolithic Islamic movement. "The coup of July 1989 was not a traditional military one because the Islamic movement was inside the Sudanese army."[136] In another sense, this coup could have also caused fear of an internal demonstration effect of Islamists seizing power through a combination of military infiltration and electoral success.

Second, the shared identities limited some of Egypt's options for how to combat the ideational threat. Egypt could not counterframe the conflict as a sectarian or an ethnic one. Instead, Egypt promoted itself as the guardian of "moderate" Islam. But here too Egypt was on shaky ground. This Arab republic maintained a political system that banned religious parties and repressed Islamists. Moreover, the state was in the midst of fighting an Islamic insurgency during the 1990s. This challenge forced the regime to rely on state-sponsored religious institutions such as al-Azhar, whose credibility was already in decline, for political support.

These ideational factors lead us to an important puzzle highlighting the argument that ideology must be projected. The question is: Why did Egypt's threat perception not change when Numeiri imposed Islamic law in 1983 and declared an Islamic republic? Even if it is true that Numeiri's Islamization was a survival tactic to gain the support of Islamists, this declaration seemed to signal a shift in domestic priorities. As part of his Islamization program, Numeiri restricted the power of the courts and employed "Islamic punishments" (*hudud*), banned European-style dancing and alcohol, and introduced changes in taxation and banking (Zakat Tax 1984).[137] Numeiri also instituted changes in the army,[138] and he tried to pass a law that would give the president (him) the title of Imam.[139] Meanwhile, Egypt was still adjusting to the potential effects of the Iranian revolution and the assassination of President Sadat by Islamic militants.

There are two possible reasons this apparent change in Sudan's political ideology did not affect Egyptian threat perception. First, in the words of a former Egyptian ambassador for African affairs, "Egypt was simply busy with internal matters."[140] This answer, however, implies that Egypt would have cared had they been more aware of the long-term implications. Instead, Egypt's attention was focused on the implications of renewed fighting in the south, not the motivation of the policy that caused it. A more convincing explanation is that while Numeiri's ideology did not contain an expansionist and aggressive intent toward Egypt, numerous aspects of the Turabi-Bashir regime's ideology did. The latter regime defined itself as a "dissatisfied" state that aimed to transform the international order. Numeiri, on the other hand, was allied with the United States and did not have such intentions.

While it is clear that ideational projection emerges as a necessary condition for a change in threat perception, how did Egypt's domestic conditions affect its perception of threat? It is plausible that the stabilization of the Egyptian domestic environment and the containment of violent and nonviolent opposition during the mid- to late 1990s contributed to a decrease in the perception of the ideological threat. The Mubarak regime's interaction with al-Azhar may have been one contributing factor. The state-led Islamization of society, which included granting more autonomy to al-Azhar to rule on personal status issues, was a response to growing (observable) religiosity and weakened regime legitimacy and also a necessary tradeoff to brutally repress the militants who were popular in many segments of society (especially in upper Egypt). The best outcome of this co-optation strategy was turning society's growing piety into direct support for the regime or, more realistically, encouraging religious quietism instead of the Islamic political activism practiced by the Brotherhood. However, one caveat to this explanation is that the state's co-optation meant that the state-aligned clerical establishment would still remain the interpreter of religion.

By 1996, the Egyptian Security Services had subdued the Egyptian Islamic militants and there were quiet discussions of a ceasefire.[141] Despite the Luxor massacre in 1997, in which renegade elements of the Islamic Group slaughtered fifty-nine tourists, the insurgency was already at its end. On the nonviolent front, the regime had crushed the opposition by imprisoning numerous high-ranking Brotherhood officials and restricting the political space within which the Brotherhood could operate. The economic situation was slowly improving, which provided additional breathing room for the regime. Egypt's declining domestic vulnerability meant that the Sudanese regime, and in particular Turabi, had fewer political opportunities to exploit.

As I have asserted, Egypt feared Sudan's Islamist regime's capability for using Islamic symbols to challenge the Mubarak regime's legitimacy. A contributing factor to this concern was the Egyptian regime's tension with society over the role of religion (Islam) and the state. This perennial tension essentially limited Egyptian responses and policy options, especially in the discursive realm. Egypt could not choose a strategy that invalidated normative structure of the game, such as insulting Islam, as an extreme example, because it would not be convincing and would cost the regime greatly. The co-optation strategy, which Egypt frequently employed to combat religious challenges to its legitimacy, also ran the risk of delegitimating the co-optee or exposing the regime's legitimacy deficit.

The strategies Egypt employed to counter this threat point to the rational mechanism of the fear. Egypt's concern was that the Turabi regime had the potential to facilitate collective political action and use Islamic symbols to coordinate action among opposition groups. Egypt targeted the source or communicator of the symbol in an attempt to undermine the credibility of the message. Egypt chose a strategy aimed at undermining Turabi's legitimacy by exposing Sudan's failures and highlighting Turabi's ideological extremism. Sudan's involvement in the assassination attempt against Mubarak raised the level of tension and confirmed Egypt's depiction of Turabi as a fanatic who had gone too far. Together with the waning threat of the Islamic insurgency and the decline in hostile rhetoric coming from Sudan, Egypt's threat perception decreased.

In the Saudi case, a number of interconnected issues seem to have affected Saudi-Sudanese relations during the 1990s: Sudan's support of Iraq during the Gulf War, Osama bin Laden, Iran-Sudan relations, and Hassan al-Turabi's challenge and potential appeal to opposition groups in Saudi Arabia. Sudan's support for Iraq (communicated though official neutrality) was not perceived as a military threat; it was seen as a betrayal of Saudi largesse. But this support, along with the establishment of the PAIC in opposition to the OIC and the hosting of bin Laden, enhanced Turabi's credibility as a source, spokesman, and interpreter of Islamic symbols.

The relationship between Osama bin Laden and Sudan did not transform Sudan into a military threat for Saudi Arabia. Rather, the presence of the legendary bin Laden enhanced Sudan's prestige and its image as a true haven for the venerated Afghan Arabs. In addition, bin Laden's presence helped validate Turabi's vision of turning Sudan into the headquarters of an international Muslim community that would carry the Islamic revolution to other countries. Sudan's alliance with neither Iran nor Iraq shifted the balance of power. Instead, these relationships enhanced Sudan's ideational power as demonstrating a principled stand on foreign policy issues in contrast to its own regime.

The Saudi regime responded directly to the threat Turabi posed by trying to undermine his credibility in the press. As part of an internal struggle unrelated to Turabi, the Saudi regime exiled several religious leaders of the Sahwa, some of whom agreed with Turabi. This could be considered an attempt at denial by trying to remove their voices from the local scene; however, they could still communicate from exile. Ultimately, the regime's activities to co-opt some conservative religious forces and bring them in line with the state also had benefits to mitigate Turabi's influence.

This case is also significant because it involved two Sunni Muslim countries; one vaunted as the model of an Islamic state and the other declaring itself as the center of the Islamic revival. Both states battled over the meaning of Islam and their ability to control its symbols.

The contrast between the two states could not be greater. Saudi Arabia is one of the wealthiest countries on the planet, while Sudan is one of the poorest. Although both are Muslim-majority Sunni countries, the majority of the population in Saudi Arabia adheres to Wahhabism, which is highly antagonist toward the Sufi practices found among a majority of Sudanese Muslims. Although these differences cannot explain relations between Sudan and Saudi Arabia over the last thirty years, they may be able to inform our understanding.

In sum, this case or cases of dyads demonstrates how a militarily and economically weak state can pose a threat to a much stronger state through transnational ideological appeals.

5   Indirect Power Projection and Ideational Balancing after Khomeini

THE DEATH OF AYATOLLAH KHOMEINI, THE SUPREME leader of the Islamic Republic of Iran, brought an estimated three million mourners to the streets of Tehran. The crowds were so huge and frenzied that there was doubt if authorities would be able physically to bury the Ayatollah.[1] The body eventually had to be transported by an army helicopter because it could not make it through the crowds of mourners.

At the international level, this leader had embarrassed and infuriated one of the two superpowers by seizing the United States' embassy and holding U.S. citizens hostage for 444 days. Gone was the charismatic leader who had revolutionized state-society relations and the balance of power through religious symbols by leading the region's only true social revolution. Nonetheless, Ayatollah Khomeini's death did not mean the end of the Islamic Republic or its profound impact on Middle Eastern politics. What did emerge, rather than a direct ideational power projection, was an indirect ideational power projection.

This chapter examines Saudi Arabia's and Egypt's threat perception and policies of this type of ideational threat during the 1990s and 2000s. The period also overlaps with important structural changes such as the Gulf War (1990–1991), the peace process, the Iraq War (2003), and Iran's development of its nuclear program. During this period, other regional events such as the Arab-Israeli conflict also affected this dynamic.

This chapter shows that ideational power can threaten indirectly through symbolic policies that have communicative political value. Moreover, ideational balancing by Saudi Arabia and Egypt took on more of a coordinated effort as seen in how Riyadh and Cairo framed the Iranian threat in sectarian terms. This securitization of sectarianism attempted to coordinate policies at the domestic and international levels and had slightly different meanings for each state. While it would seem that Iran's pursuit of its nuclear program should trigger traditional forms of balancing (which it did), this chapter points out how fears of this development enhanced the ideational threat and reaction at home.

Lastly, the developments within these two dyads show how the ideational security dilemma comes into play. Iran's efforts to project its ideational power to Arab publics aimed to undermine regime security; Arab leaders' ideational balancing as a response sought to combat this challenge to domestic political stability. In doing so, Arab responses that framed Iran's efforts as a sectarian project ran the risk of destabilizing domestic balances that could translate into escalation at the level of foreign policy.

Iran-Egypt Relations during the 1990s

Ayatollah Khomeini had become the symbol and source not only for Iranian revolutionary energy at home and abroad; his image was feared and reviled by many Arab Sunni leaders. Thus, the passing of the supreme leader on June 3, 1989, which brought millions of mourners into the streets of Tehran, repeating chants of "We are orphaned," did not have the same effect in the streets of Cairo. Over a thousand miles away, Egyptian officials met Khomeini's death with relief and a feeling of cautious optimism. They initially viewed Khomeini's successor, Ali Akbar Rafsanjani, as a pragmatist who favored economic development and state interest over ideology in contrast to his ideological predecessor. Iran's "good behavior" during the Gulf War (1990–1991), meaning its passive support for the U.S./UN-led led coalition, strengthened this perception. There were even reports of direct contacts made between Egypt and Iran.[2]

But this cautious optimism soon reverted to growing suspicion of Iran. Disagreements over the conditions of rapprochement led to the resumption of a propaganda war between Egypt and Iran.[3] Iranian leaders called Mubarak's regime illegitimate, anti-Islamic, and serving Western imperial interests, while Egypt charged Iran with exporting Islamic radicalism and terrorism.[4]

Iran's activities challenged Egypt within its three traditional spheres of influence: the Gulf, the Arab-Israeli conflict, and Africa. In the Gulf arena, as mentioned above, Iran's "good behavior" of not intervening in the Gulf War won it favor from many of its traditional rivals. But Iran's pursuit of its strategic interests in its backyard (the Gulf) caused great alarm. Iran strongly opposed an "Arab deterrent force" composed of Syrian and Egyptian troops stationed in the Gulf to defend against future aggressors as proposed in the Damascus Declaration in 1992. The same year, Iran seized Abu Musa and the Greater and Lesser Tunbs in 1992. Egypt also saw these moves as far exceeding that of its defensive needs.[5] According to one pro-regime newspaper, this latest Iranian venture was seen as "part of a slow takeover of Arab lands under the veil of Islam."[6]

Iran's position directly challenged Egyptian interests. Egypt's most important foreign policy area for regional influence was the Arab-Israeli conflict or, more specifically, Israeli-Palestinian relations. This area was particularly crucial as Egypt sought to reintegrate itself into the Arab fold after the Gulf War and as the only Arab state with diplomatic relations with Israel. Throughout this period, Egypt played the most important Arab role in the peace process. Egypt also engaged in the Arms Control Regional Security (ACRS) talks and supported the Oslo Accords. Egypt's support and encouragement also took the form of hosting various regional conferences, such as the Sharm El-Sheikh agreement in 1999, for the Israelis and Palestinians to implement past agreements.[7]

Iran strongly opposed the Madrid Conference (1991), a multilateral venue that started the peace process, as well as the Oslo Accords. In fact, Iran led the rejectionist front through its statements and support of nonstate actors such as Hezbollah, Hamas, and the Palestinian Islamic Jihad. Iran's support for these populist symbols challenged Egypt's interests and accentuated the gap between the Egyptian regime's foreign policy interests and its society's preferences.

Since Iran's leadership of the rejectionist front featured support for populist, anti-Israeli actors such as Hezbollah and Hamas, Egypt had to tread carefully. Egypt portrayed Iran's leaders as not living in the "real world" and being an opponent of peace.[8] In an interview in 1993 with *al-Jumhuriyya*, a progovernment newspaper, Mubarak defended Egypt's position in support of the peace process as in line with the views of the rest of the world in contrast to Iran, which opposed peace.[9] Egypt blamed Iran for the lack of success in the peace process.

Iran's alliance with Sudan during the first half of the 1990s challenged Egypt in another sphere of influence—Africa. This alliance (1990–1996), discussed in the previous chapter, gave Iran access to Egypt's strategic depth and sought to compete with Egypt for political and economic influence. Africa had long been important because of the Nile River, and not just because Egyptians considered the river valley and parts of Sudan as a part of Egypt. During Nasser's time, newly independent countries were an extremely important source of support for Egyptian political leadership. Nasser considered Africa an important "sphere of activity."[10] Most importantly, the Nile River is Egypt's lifeblood.

While Egyptian officials were concerned about Iran's reach into Africa and its access to the Indian Ocean, the alliance of two allied Islamic states supporting popular causes that could resonate within Egyptian society became a source of threat. And this was also proof, once again, of Iran's ideological goal to topple the Egyptian regime and spread Islamic extremism throughout the Middle East.[11]

> With regards to Egypt, it was the target of Khomeini's revolution since its establishment. Iran was planning to bring the revolution to Egypt and then Egypt would handle the export of the revolution to the remaining countries of the world, similar to what happened in the days of the four rightly guided caliphs at the beginning of the Islamic call.[12]

> Through Sudan, Iran could bring "the revolution to Egypt."[13]

These geopolitical challenges to Egypt's spheres of influence should not be discounted. However, these threats were seen as a part of a broader, more serious, nonmilitary ideational threat aimed at undermining regime, not state, security. Ibrahim Nafee, the editor of Egypt's official newspaper al-*Ahram*, lays out this view: "Iran's plans to export its revolutionary model are more acute than worries about its fast-paced re-armament."[14] Nafee explains how and why this ideological threat from Iran is so serious for Egyptian national security:

> Tehran spends $30 million a month in Lebanon . . . because it attaches great importance to building a Shiite belt of supporters in the heart of the Arab world stretching from Iran to southern Iraq to the Mediterranean, a move that totally threatens national security in the region . . . . This is an attack being waged from inside our countries, which is not as easy to stop as, say, an Iranian invasion of the gulf.[15]

The key point here is the idea that Iran presented an internal threat that is harder to combat than an external military one. But how and why is this internal threat waged from inside? The answer is that a volatile domestic environment exacerbated by a growth of Islamic fundamentalism and extremism enhanced the regime's threat perception. During the 1990s, Egypt fought a brutal Islamic insurgency that killed over 1,400 civilians and caused enormous economic damage. While the insurgency had many domestic causes, it was linked to a broader wave of Islamic insurgencies and rebellions across North Africa and the Middle East. Radical Islamists fought the "near enemy" to topple their regimes, and in some cases moderates were caught in the middle. Many Arab leaders in the region blamed Iran for supporting the "march of Islam" materially and politically. Egypt, for example, accused Iran of aiding the Islamic Jihad and Islamic Group through their cooperation with and training in Sudan.

Egypt also accused Iran supporting its small Shi'a community. The security services arrested members of the very small Shi'a community for their active support of Hezbollah.[16] In fact, these crackdowns were enough to cause Hezbollah's religious leader, Sheikh Muhammad Husain Fadlallah, to protest the Egyptian government's repression of Shi'a in Egypt as a political statement.[17] Some of the government claims about Iranian support are probably true, while others may be suspicious. Even if, for example, the claims about Shi'a cells in Egypt are untrue, it tells us something very important about what the regime was concerned about by what it was trying to do—frame Iran as a supporter of forces that were against Egyptian national interest.

Saudi Arabia–Iran Relations during the 1990s

For Saudi Arabia, Iran presented a similar symbolic threat. As millions of supporters mourned the death of Ayatollah Khomeini in Iran, Khomeini's last will and testimony read on Tehran radio blasted the Kingdom of Saudi Arabia. Khomeini labeled King Fahd as "a traitor to God" [18] and as one who "spends a large part of the people's wealth every year on . . . publicizing the anti-Koranic, totally baseless and superstitious faith of Wahhabism."[19]

Surprisingly, Khomeini's last invective did not set the tone for the thaw or détente, as many have called it, in Saudi-Iranian relations during the 1990s. King Fahd regarded Khomeini's successor, Ali Akbar Hashemi-Rafsanjani, with cautious optimism and the press initially described him as a pragmatist.[20] From the Saudi perspective, Iran's behavior during the Gulf War signaled a willingness to cooperate on some issues, and Rafsanjani did not produce the same level of hostile rhetoric.[21] Saudi Arabia removed Hajj quotas for Iran, and official diplomatic relations were reestablished in 1991. Moreover, following reformist candidate Mohammed Khatami's election as president of Iran in 1997, Iran and Saudi Arabia exchanged high-level visits and came to a number of economic (particularly oil) and cultural agreements.[22]

Despite the relaxation in tensions, a latent threat still existed. Iran's foreign policies were much less confrontational as it reoriented its foreign policy to reintegrate itself into the international order.[23] Cooperation could exist alongside competition within a set of rules of the game. For example, the two sides continued jockeying for power and influence in Afghanistan, the former Soviet Republics, the Gulf, and the Levant.

However, Saudi Arabia perceived Iran's steps to reassert and reintegrate itself in a pragmatic manner as an indirect ideational threat. Iran's reinvention of its "Islamically oriented" foreign policy through its support for Islamic movements, Islamic causes, international institutions, and the conduct of its foreign relations with other states were symbolic acts to compete for leadership of the Islamic world. This indirect ideational power projection and leadership competition focused on three main issues areas: the Rushdie affair, leadership in the OIC, and Palestine.

The Rushdie Affair

Following the widespread protests in the Muslim world in response to the publication of Salman Rushdie's controversial book *The Satanic Verses*, Ayatollah Khomeini issued a fatwa in February 1989 condemning the Iranian-born novelist to death for blasphemy. While this generated renewed fears in the West, informal Islamic groups identified with Khomeini's fatwa by expressing their readiness to carry it out, challenging the quietist, state-aligned local religious authorities.[24] Khomeini's intentional political use of this Islamic institution aimed "to mobilize his Islamic clientele by stressing his claim to being not only the leader of the Iranian Islamic Revolution, but also of the whole Islamic umma."[25] Iran also utilized the Rushdie affair to downplay sectarian antagonisms, a potential limitation of its ideational power and obstacle of reintegration, and to project itself as the real custodian of Islam and Islamic values, struggling against "American Islam."[26]

The Saudi regime responded to this challenge in two ways. Internally, the media ignored it; and externally, the regime stated the Rushdie affair should not be "politicized."[27] More importantly, this defensive and tepid reaction revealed a number of things about the Saudi regime's vulnerabilities and threat perception. The Saudi regime's ability to address this threat on religious grounds was limited by the fact that it could not "outbid" Iran in the Islamic sphere because of Saudi Arabia's alignment with the West. Yet, at the same time, the regime had to quiet the reactions of Saudi *ulama*, the religious guarantor of the House of Saud's right to rule, which had also declared Rushdie an apostate.[28] By not addressing the issue on religious grounds, the Saudi state's defensive reaction revealed its weakness as a credible religious authority, enabling Iran to reengage the Sunni Islamic world by suggesting the possibility of overcoming Sunni-Shi'a cleavages.

The Organization of Islamic Conferences (OIC)

The Rushdie affair served as a gateway for Iran, the self-appointed spokesman for outrage in the Muslim world, to contest a vital instrument of Saudi ideational power and regime credibility, the Organization of Islamic Conferences (OIC).[29] The OIC served an important purpose in protecting and promoting Saudi Arabia's image. After Jerusalem's holy sites fell under Israeli control, Saudi Arabia helped establish this UN-affiliated international institution to bolster its Islamic credentials against growing charges of the monarchy's moral and financial corruption. Moreover, King Faisal created this institution to help Saudi Arabia balance its engagement with the modern (Western) world using very conservative elements at home.[30] The Kingdom of Saudi Arabia's strong position in the OIC allowed it to control the agenda, shape consensus, and manage issues that could potentially become an embarrassment. For example, during the 1980s, Saudi Arabia sidelined Iran's protests and charges, essentially marginalizing the Islamic Republic. After the Hajj massacre in 1987, Iran boycotted the annual summit and stayed out of the picture.

During the 1990s, Iran used the OIC to challenge Riyadh's leadership across a number of issues including the need to support "Muslim causes" in Bosnia, Kashmir, Afghanistan, Lebanon (Hezbollah), Palestine, and Algeria.[31] For example, the same year that relations were reestablished between Iran and Saudi Arabia (1991), President Rafsanjani assailed the Saudis at the Islamic Summit in Dakkar by calling for the continuation of jihad as a way to put Saudi Arabia on the defensive for its support of the peace process. Iran's military and diplomatic support for Islamic oppositions during the Algerian Civil War restored its credibility in the eyes of some Sunni Islamist groups.[32] During the Balkan conflict, Iran utilized the OIC summit to pledge resources to this Islamic cause that Saudi Arabia could not support due to the king-dom's relationship with the United States. At one meeting, Iran pledged to send 10,000 troops and supplies, which forced Saudi Arabia to respond to the Bosnia crisis even if it meant diplomatic statements of support or aid.[33] More generally, however, Saudi Arabia's responses were constrained by its strategic interests of supporting the unpopular, status-quo-oriented, Western-aligned authoritarian regimes combating the Islamic movements and its overall rela-tionship with the United States. The change in dynamics of this international institution has had significant consequences. According to an adviser to the Qatar foreign ministry, "today Saudi Arabia cannot use the OIC against Iran because Iran is very Islamic."[34]

Palestine

Challenges to Saudi Arabia's leadership role were not limited to international institutions such as the OIC. Asserting its Islamic leadership, Iran presented itself as an opponent of the peace process on religious grounds. In doing so, Iran indirectly attacked Saudi Arabia's quiet support of the peace process, beginning with the Madrid Conference (1991) as a betrayal of the Islamic val-ues for which Iran stood.[35] Ayatollah Khomeini, the highest religious author-ity at the time, called it a great injustice, and Hojjat ul-Islam Mohteshami, a former minister of interior, predicted, "The participants in the conference will be detested by the people."[36] But Mohteshami went even further to claim it was a religious imperative to rebel against the conference participants:

> To take part in America's so-called Middle East peace conference means to declare war on Islam and Muslims, and the participants are classed as moharebs [those who wage war against God and deserve death], for they have committed an unforgivable crime; and in accordance with Islam [Islamic law], the blood of a mohareb enemy must be shed. And no doubt the revolu-tionary Muslims, at the earliest appropriate opportunity, will carry out their religious duty against them, under any circumstances.[37]

Iran increased its efforts during the 1990s (which would intensify in the fol-lowing decade) to proclaim its leadership of the Palestinian cause. President Rafsanjani relates, "Palestine is the most important problem in the world and our history. It is only Iran, out of 180 countries in the world, which says that it does not accept the negotiations . . . . That is a basic source of pride for us."[38] This initiative also involved making Palestine a religious issue and thus an

Islamic symbol of resistance. This framing was emphasized in Iran's support for religiously oriented groups who opposed the peace process, such as Hezbollah, Hamas, and the Palestinian Islamic Jihad.

Iran's support of Hamas offers both a good example of how Iran challenged Saudi Arabia with this issue and what its limitations are. Founded in 1987 at the beginning of the Intifada, Hamas slowly transformed the Israeli-Palestinian conflict from an ethno-religious conflict to more of a religious conflict through its symbols, tactics, and rhetoric. It became the main source of organized Palestinian opposition to the PLO-supported peace process. Although Hamas received a majority of funding informally from the Gulf, and especially from Saudi Arabia, Iran openly aided and backed Hamas as more than an expression of support and sympathy. The effect was that Iran's support for the rejectionist or revisionist forces served to reconcile relations with Sunni Islamic movements.[39]

Saudi Arabia continually faced a dilemma over how to respond to Iran's increasing support for these populist, "authentic" movements and nonstate actors. On the one hand, if the regime played its matching Islamic card against Iran on the Israeli-Arab conflict, it risked being outbid by its own Islamic opposition groups because it could not take a position that might threaten its relationship with the United States.[40] On the other hand, if the Saudi regime used its religious authority to support the peace process, it risked a loss of credibility.

Ultimately, Saudi Arabia played a mixed hand in response to Iran's challenges on the Arab-Israeli issue. In other words, Saudi Arabia treated the Palestine issue as an Arab issue but used its religious credibility to demonstrate its authority to speak for Arab Muslims. The Saudi regime's attempt to undermine the credibility of the source, Iran, raised the issue of ethnicity: "Iran considered that one of its legitimate rights, as though it was an Arab country with a direct or indirect link to this thorny issue which belongs to the Arabs alone."[41] On the religious side, support for the peace process came with the senior Saudi Mufti ibn Baz's fatwa stating that peace between Jews and Muslims was compatible with shari'a, citing the Prophet's example.[42] Ibn Baz even issued a fatwa permitting Muslims to visit al-Aqsa, which was interpreted as a way to have peace with Israel on a temporary basis (*hudna*).[43] Lastly, the Saudi regime used Islam to cement the two issues and enhance its authority when it reconciled with Arafat while he performed the "umra to Mecca."[44] The context of this reconciliation communicated that the Saudi regime could bring the secular, nationalist leader of *the* pan-Arab cause to Islam's holiest sites, which were under Saudi control.

These events took place during considerable domestic upheaval and turmoil in Saudi Arabia. The Saudi government's decision during the Gulf Crisis to call on an international force led by the United States became the catalyst for domestic challenges across many sectors of society and from within the religious establishment. Mobilized opposition included: clerics within and outside the official religious establishment; exiled Saudi nationals; Shi'a political activists; liberals; and Sunni Islamists (from moderates to militants, including neo-Ikhwan and al-Qaeda types who advocated violence against the state).

The Sahwa (al-Sahwa al-Islamiyya, "Islamic awakening") movement led the most important challenge to the regime.[45] Composed of Islamist *ulama* from both inside and outside the official religious establishment, they demanded political reform and the greater Islamization of the state in what some have called the "Sahwa Intifada."[46] In providing the most formidable opposition to the Saudi regime, the Sawha took a number of unprecedented steps in the political sphere that mobilized support and countermobilized the state. These *ulama* denounced the Saudi regime and its policies in a very public way through the formation of organizations, petitions, letters, and fatwas. Beginning with the first petition sent to King Fahd in May 1991, Islamists' demands for the stricter Islamization of the Saudi state intensified.[47] The formation of the Committee for the Defense of Legitimate Rights (CDLR) in 1993, the first group to openly challenge the monarchy and the foundation of the state, was a major development. Because some of the clerics came from within the religious establishment and included well-known and respected clerics and intellectuals, these grievances carried weight within Saudi society, the regime, and the religious institutions of the state.

These challenges were not limited to domestic matters. After all, it was a foreign policy decision that served as the catalyst for these protests. Leading Sahwi scholars of the "council of preachers" (*majlis al-du'at*), an independent religious authority formed to compete with the state-sponsored religious institutions, issued their own fatwas in opposition to the official religious establishment and government policy.[48] One of these included an open letter to Sheikh Ibn Baz against the peace process and for the continuation of Jihad.[49] Another fatwa condemned the Saudi government for its lack of support for the Bosnian cause.[50] These, of course, were causes the Iranian regime heralded as their own.

The Saudi state shut down the thrust of the Sawha insurrection through exiling, imprisoning, and silencing its leaders by the mid-1990s. It also weakened the Sahwa opposition by supporting countermovements that eroded bases of support.[51] But the end of the insurrection did not mean the opposition challenges went away. Osama bin Laden, who served to bring jihadi support for the Sahwa after the creation of CDLR in 1993, carried on the struggle in a more radical and violent direction. Other challenges from radical Shi'a groups, such as the one responsible for the Khobar Towers bombing, did not have the same societal support. Perennial tensions between regional identities seemed ripe for exploitation.[52] Meanwhile, there were nagging concerns about succession after King Fahd's debilitating stroke in 1995.

These forces illustrate the potential for domestic instability and give even more weight to why the Saudi regime should have concerned itself about challenges to its leadership. One related and puzzling question is why Iran did not exploit this opportunity to more directly challenge Saudi Arabia. It leads one to speculate that had there been more direct ideational projection, it may have increased Saudi threat perception during this period.

Iran may have been involved in supporting and exploiting tension within Saudi Arabia but not at the larger societal level and not in the aggressive way it did in the 1980s. There is reason to believe there was Iranian involvement in the attacks on Khobar. Propaganda also continued during this period, as discussed previously. The ideational power potential was latent; Khomeini's bold project inspired some Saudi intellectuals in their desire to create a "conservative Islamic democracy."[53] But Iran did not project this power even though, despite sectarian obstacles, the early 1990s may have been ripe for exploitation.

Iran's Ideational Opening: Egypt and Saudi Arabia after the Iraq War

The election of the reformist cleric, Iranian President Mahmoud Khatami, in 1997 brought some measure of cautious optimism to both Saudi Arabia and Egypt. Khatami's talk about the "dialogue of civilizations" featured encouraging signs that could decrease tension and bring opportunity for rapprochement not just with the West but also within the region. *Al-Ahram,* Egypt's official newspaper, announced a significant change in Iranianp.[54] To some extent, there were attempts at this rapprochement particularly in the late

1990s and 2000s. One example of the new mood was the meeting in Cairo between Iranian and Egyptian officials. In addition to security, trade, and religious issues, the discussion also included talks about the resumption of diplomatic relations.[55] Saudi Arabia and Iran meanwhile made similar types of moves. For example, the former president, Ali Akbar Hashemi Rafsanjani, visited Saudi Arabia for two weeks in April 1998, marking the first visit of a senior official since the revolution. As he claimed, the trip had melted a "mountain of ice."[56]

Nonetheless, this new atmosphere did not lead to a major breakthrough. Egyptian officials remained suspicious of Iran and security officials publicly tried to play down expectations.[57] The sentiment that prevailed was that Iran "speaks with two tongues."[58] Latent suspicion remained, many of Iran's provocative activities continued, and international events exposed fears and uncertainty of Iran exploiting international opportunities. The relations between Iran and these two countries would soon change with the Iraq War (2003) and, most significantly, with the election of President Mahmoud Ahmedinejad in Iran.

The Iraq War (2003) set the stage for an intensification of threat perception and hostilities that dramatically increased in the 2000s, particularly after Mahmoud Ahmedinejad came to power in Iran. The overthrow of Saddam Hussein disrupted a relatively stable regional order and regional security complex in the Gulf.[59] It created a power vacuum both in the Gulf and elsewhere in the Middle East that Iran could now fill. Reflecting this sentiment, Egyptian President Hosni Mubarak remarked that while Saddam was in power, "Iran did not dare meddle with Iraq, or to move freely in the Gulf, or to work with Hamas or stir up trouble in the region."[60] This statement may be a bit of an exaggeration but it contains some truth from a strategic perspective and also indications about Mubarak's threat perception. For Saudi Arabia, Iraq's demographic realities, a Shi'a-majority population with religious and political links to Iran meant that a more representative government might one day ally with Iran against Saudi Arabia.[61]

This concern about Iran's ability to exploit the new sectarian balance of power was not limited to Iraq, nor was the concern limited to Saudi Arabia or Egypt for that matter. In 2004, months before Iraq's first democratic election, King Abdullah of Jordan warned of a "Shi'a crescent" emerging across the Middle East being driven by Iran.[62] This statement sparked controversy and can be marked as a major turning point in sectarian relations. Saudi officials certainly agreed with this framework and were committed to preventing a Shi'a crescent to emerge, enacting domestic and foreign policies to combat this threat.[63] Along similar lines, President Hosni Mubarak commented to the news channel al-Arabiyya that "definitely Iran has influence on Shias" and "most of the Shias are loyal to Iran, and not to the countries they are living in."[64] And to emphasize the point that regional power shifts were being viewed in ethnic or sectarian terms, President Mubarak, in an interview with *al-Musawwar* in March 2006, said that the Arab role is to preserve the Arab character of Iraq.[65]

Sectarianism became both an expression of a particular ideational threat and a tactic of ideational balancing—a way to frame the existing threat and mobilize domestic and international constituencies around the symbol of the Shi'a threat. Ideational balancing activities coordinated an ideational response with allies to mitigate Iranian influence. But this securitization of sectarianism overlapped with Iran's indirect projection of ideational power after President Mahmoud Ahmedinejad came to power in 2005. From this period, Iran began to pursue a much more regionally activist foreign policy in areas of strategic importance whose effects were even at the level of domestic politics. "Ascendant Iran" took a more active role in sensitive areas of Middle East politics, such as Israel/Palestine and Lebanon, and pursued a nuclear program in defiance of Western pressure. Complementing these policies were President Mahmoud Ahemdinejad's extremely provocative statements about Israel. His denials of the Holocaust and promises to "wipe Israel off the map" certainly found receptive ears in many Arab domestic publics. These statements also challenged Egypt and Saudi, states that had peace treaties with the Zionist entity and its closest ally the United States. Iran's foreign policies in support of Syria, Hezbollah, and Hamas became part of a larger regional rivalry with Saudi Arabia and other U.S.-allied, status-quo-oriented Arab Sunni states, such as Egypt. While the provocative statements may have primed domestic sentiments in many cases, it was the combination of Iran's activities during times of the regional crises that communicated powerful symbolic messages, exacerbating state-society relations by bringing Egyptian and Saudi foreign policy under intense scrutiny.

Iran's role in aiding militant Palestinian groups during and after the Second Intifada, such as the Karine-A affair, was not considered a setback but a boost for Iran in the Arab world. The focus, however, was on Hamas. After Hamas's parliamentary success in 2006, Iran pledged $250 million to Hamas after funding dried up due to an international boycott.[66] Hamas's violent coup in 2007 added to its financial problems as Israel and Egypt, tacitly supported by Saudi Arabia, imposed a blockade of Gaza in response. This focus soon revolved around the blockade of Gaza, which became the leading Palestinian humanitarian and political cause in many Arab societies. The rift between the regime's policy and its society's preferences was ripe for exploitation. President Ahmedinejad personally attacked the king of Saudi Arabia for his inability to end the siege of Gaza: "King Abdullah, the puppet king of Saudi Arabia, is not expected to ignore the demands of his American and Zionist masters and frown at what is going on in Gaza."[67]

But the issue and the Hamas-Israel conflict in Gaza was much more sensitive for Egypt given the Muslim Brotherhood's ideological connection to Hamas and Egypt's concerns about border security. Egypt's participation in the blockade of Gaza following Hamas's coup in 2007 became a domestic political liability. The perceived collusion between Israel and Egypt against Hamas was an easy target for the Muslim Brotherhood and other critics of the Mubarak regime. As articulated by a Brotherhood official and spokesman, Dr. Essam al-Eryan, "We are, of course, calling for lifting the siege, and giving the Palestinians a normal life. . . . But the Israelis and Americans are pushing Egypt to secure the Israelis. And this is not our duty . . . the Palestinians are no threat to Egypt."[68]

This statement shows the vulnerability of the Mubarak regime on this issue. Already on the defensive against criticisms that it was aiding Israel's occupation of the Palestinians, the Mubarak regime was extremely sensitive to any escalation in the Israeli-Palestinian conflict, particularly in Gaza, because clashes could directly implicate Egypt and risk an armed confrontation with Palestinians. Therefore, the Gaza War (December 2008–January 2009) that resulted in over a thousand Palestinian deaths, many of them civilians, created tremendous strain on the Mubarak regime's legitimacy. Known in the Arabic press as the Gaza Massacre or *mujra ghaza*, images broadcast on sallellite stations such as al-Jazeera showed the public gruesome images of Israel's destruction of Gaza and the deaths of Palestinian civilians.

But the Egyptian public had already been primed before the violence erupted. Days before the Egyptian-brokered ceasefire between Hamas and Israel was due to expire, Brotherhood members stepped up pressure on the government's policy toward Gaza by accusing the ruling party of helping continue the Israeli occupation of Palestine. National Democratic Party (NDP) parliamentarians shot back by accusing the Brotherhood of allowing Iran to gain a foothold in the region and promoting policies that would hurt Egyptian national security. A fistfight in parliament even broke out. When the images of Palestinian suffering reached the media, the Brotherhood's position was vindicated in the public's mind.

And only a year after the Gaza War, one of the regime's worst fears was realized—armed clashes with Palestinians. Since the Israeli disengagement from Gaza in 2005, Egyptian leaders had been extremely anxious about enforcing security on their side of the border because it might risk armed confrontation with Palestinians. While minor clashes had occurred since the disengagement, including Hamas's breaching of the border in 2008, the incidents of January 2010 were different. Egyptian soldiers fired shots at Palestinians demonstrating against Egypt's enforcement of the blockade of Gaza. After one Egyptian soldier was killed, the official state media attacked Hamas, and implicitly Iran and the Egyptian Muslim Brotherhood, for undermining Egypt's security interests.[69]

Saudi Arabia was also affected by these clashes in Gaza, but the ideational battles were more openly with Iran. The most intense period came during and after the Gaza Christmas War of 2008–2009. President Ahmedinejad proclaimed his support for Hamas and the Palestinians while explicitly and implicitly attacking the Saudi regime. In a letter to King Abdullah, President Ahmedinejad writes: "It is expected of you as the Saudi Arabian King and the Custodian of the Two Holy Places, i.e. Makkah and Medina, to break your silence on the catastrophic events and the massacre taking place in Gaza and take a clear stance on the murder of your children, who are dear to the Islamic Ummah."[70] Iranian religious authorities added fuel to this religious fire by pledging to send 70,000 volunteers to Gaza, a statement that was later toned down.[71]

The Saudi regime was in a difficult position. Riyadh's foreign policy enabled its critics to claim it took the side of the Arab Islamic world's bitter enemy—Israel. Saudi-supported media outlets, such as al-Arabiyya, tried to subdue the coverage and did not allow the use of the word *shaheed*, or martyr, to describe Palestinian casualties. But Hezbollah's spiritual leader, Sheikh Hassan Nasrallah, assailed the channel and its backers by calling it *al-Ibriya* (the Hebrew one).[72] Saudi officials lashed out at Hamas and Iran in response. The pro-Saudi *al-Sharq al-Awsat* compared Hamas's reckless instigation to Hezbollah's move that started the 2006 Lebanese war.[73]

The conflict paid dividends for Iran. Not only did Saudi Arabia end up on the losing side because it appeared to support Israel, but immediately following the fighting the Hamas leader Khaled Meshaal went to Tehran to thank Iran for its support.[74] This event was tracked all over the international media, including the Arab press. The image of the embrace after Hamas's journey to Tehran was carried on many Arabic news outlets.

For Saudi Arabia, however, the most important battleground with regards to ideational power was Lebanon. This three-week conflict in the summer of 2006 between Israel and Hezbollah would leave over a thousand Lebanese dead and have tremendous immediate and medium-term costs as well as political consequences. The public relations and media battle was just as, if not more, important than the military conflict. This was the first time such strong criticism against Hezbollah was leveled publicly by Arab states, especially Saudi Arabia, Egypt, and Jordan, in contrast with or even defiance of public opinion.[75] Many Arabic media outlets, such as al-Jazeera, framed the struggle as a pan-Arab issue and Hezbollah presented it this way too. But Hezbollah also framed the struggle as a religious one that was also against the Arab governments who were against Arab and Islamic causes. "A defeat for us is a defeat for the whole Muslim nation," proclaimed Sheikh Nasrallah.[76]

The official Saudi response publicly condemned Hezbollah and implicated Iran:

> The kingdom would like to clearly announce that a difference should be drawn between legitimate resistance and rash adventures carried out by elements inside the state and those behind them without consultation with the legitimate authority in their state and without consultation or coordination with Arab countries, thus creating a gravely dangerous situation exposing all Arab countries and its achievements to destruction with those countries having no say. The kingdom views that it is time that these elements alone bear the full responsibility of these irresponsible acts and should alone shoulder the burden of ending the crisis they have created.[77]

A few days later in an emergency session of the Arab League, Saudi Foreign Minister Prince Saud al-Faisal criticized Hezbollah's attacks on Israel as "unexpected, inappropriate and irresponsible acts."[78] The logic behind this official public-messaging campaign was to connect Hezbollah's irresponsible move as helping Iran extend its influence in the region, thus implying that support for Hezbollah was support for Iran.[79]

Other Saudi responses were even harsher. A prominent Saudi cleric and member of Saudi Arabia's higher religious council, Sheikh Abdullah bin Jibreen, issued a fatwa making it a sin to pray for or support Hezbollah because it is Shi'a.[80] The influential Safar al-Hawali, one of the most important Islamist opposition clerics in the 1990s, echoed these religious-political sentiments in his fatwa forbidding support for Hezbollah.

These statements became the center stage for the war of images and words fought in various media outlets. Al-Jazeera, representing a more pan-Arab, pro-Hezbollah perspective, faced off against al-Arabiyya, representing a Saudi perspective. As the war dragged on, images of the destruction dominated the airwaves and the Saudi position became more untenable. Comments of this nature disappeared.

Iran gained an important symbolic victory in the short term as Hezbollah's most important patron state. Besides Syria, Iran was the only Middle East state to back Hezbollah's resistance to Israel. Sheikh Nasrallah's and Iran's status in the region increased.[81] The battle did not end with the cessation of fighting. A proxy war over the rehabilitation of Lebanon became part of the ongoing political battles in Lebanon over Hezbollah's status and the durability of the March 14th coalition established in the wake of 2005 parliamentary elections and the Hariri assassination.

For Egypt, the sectarian angle was much more of a political challenge than a religious one. Fears of Shi'ism may have resonated with some conservative Islamic trends and even sentiments within the opposition Muslim Brotherhood, but the government's main focus was to communicate that certain political activities challenged government policies. Matters portrayed as "Shi'a" were meant to communicate they were illegitimate. During the Hezbollah-Israel war in the summer of 2006, Egypt faced domestic pressure to take diplomatic action by breaking relations with Israel or, in some cases, to do more. The Brotherhood proclaimed they were prepared to send 10,000 volunteers to help Hezbollah.[82] Sheikh Hassan Nasrallah in particular became widely popular among the Egyptian public and the view of Iran increased as well.[83] President Hosni Mubarak, in opposition to this public pressure, came out strongly against Hezbollah and particularly against Iran's role in instigating this conflict.[84]

Following the Lebanon War (2006), statements framing Iran's growing influence in the region as part of the Shi'a threat increased. One manifestation of this fear, and a countermobilization strategy, was elites' concern about conversions to Shi'ism. Both as an indicator of threat and a strategy to combat it, Egyptian and Jordanian presses warned of Shi'a proselytizing in staunchly Sunni countries in late 2006 and early 2007.[85] This strategy and perception was given religious credibility when al-Azhar criticized the number of pro-Shi'a books in Egypt and warned of the threat of conversion to Shi'ism.[86] Finally, the editor of the pro-regime periodical *Ruz al-Yusuf* even warned the (secular) elite that they needed to wake to the Shi'a threat.[87]

But the Mubarak regime's fear of the Shi'a threat was not that Shi'ism would spread throughout the Middle East and into Egypt or that there would be mass conversions to Shi'ism. Rather, the Mubarak regime feared the *political conversion* to what could be considered Shi'a causes; Hezbollah, Hamas, and anti-Western policies.[88] Understood by incumbent regimes in a zero-sum context, the increasing support for Iranian foreign policies presented one of the biggest domestic challenges because these policies, rhetoric, and symbols could mobilize opposition forces.

Iran's Nuclear Ambitions and Ideational Power

Thus far we have not discussed the role of Iran's nuclear program in triggering Saudi and Egyptian threat perception and policy. There is no question that Cairo and Riyadh were extremely concerned about Iranian proliferation efforts.

It is impossible to know with certainty exactly how much this fear of hard power factors into the decision-making calculuses of individuals leaders, especially as the shifts in ideational and military power occur at the same time. Nonetheless, it is possible to see how some responses suggest that hard power is not the most immediate fear and that this shift in hard power may enhance the ideational threat.

In the Egyptian case, a strong argument can be made that Iran's pursuit of a nuclear program has triggered "hard" balancing. During the 2000s, Egypt increased its political, military, and intelligence cooperation with Saudi Arabia and Jordan. The Gulf Cooperation Council +2 (Jordan and Egypt) met on a more frequent basis about issues related to Gulf security. In 2006, Egypt announced that it would restart its civilian nuclear program, and widespread speculation arose as to what was really motivating this move and if Egypt was simply pursuing "nuclear hedging."

But there is more to this story at the domestic and foreign policy levels. In terms of foreign policy, the strengthening of relations was also a response to Iran's growing geopolitical influence and thus cannot be easily separated from other factors. Yet, GCC leaders and Egypt did not view Iran's nuclear threat with the same concern. The climax of this division was the GCC's letter in 2005 accusing Amr Musa, the secretary general of the Arab League, of siding with Egypt.[89] Finally, these Arab leaders all face a formidable Islamist challenge within their respective borders, suggesting additional motivations for their increased cooperation.

There are other reasons to call into question the idea that Egypt was reacting to the military threat posed by Iran's nuclear program, and these stem from domestic politics. First, the timing could be attributed to a number of factors including Egypt's loss of relative prestige and status. Gamal Mubarak specifically mentioned long-term economic benefits and also spoke of the need to bring Egypt into the twenty-first century.[90] Second, Gamal Mubarak, who announced this initiative at the ruling party's annual conference, faced challenges from the opposition and the military as he was being courted to succeed his father. It was assumed that identification with a project of nature would give him credibility as a national and international leader.

The Saudi case also raises a few questions. For years, analysts have speculated about Saudi Arabia's motivations to acquire nuclear weapons. Saudi Arabia clearly considers Iranian acquisition of nuclear weapons capability a serious national security threat. In recent years, Saudi Arabia has threatened privately to acquire a nuclear weapon of its own should Iran get one.[91] Saudi fears of Iranian nuclear proliferation are that this weapon could be used to coerce Saudi leaders over its political alliances in the Gulf or Shi'a minorities in Saudi Arabia. The amount this would shift the balance of power between Iran and Saudi Arabia is less important than the questions it will raise about U.S. resolve to defend Saudi Arabia against a nuclear-armed state. Iran's acquisition of this weapon would provide it with escalation dominance in any future crisis between Saudi Arabia and a possible means to deter the United States from involvement in regional conflicts.

Yet, an Iranian nuclear weapon could have a more immediate impact on its ideational power. According to a Saudi official, "there is prestige for Iran especially if the US pushes."[92] Iran has framed this issue as a symbol of Western fear of a sovereign Muslim country pursuing its right to acquire nuclear technology and develop nuclear power in accordance with an international agreement. Iran's resistance to Western pressures over the nuclear issue stands in contrast to a regime that has appeared to yield to U.S. foreign policy interests.

Furthermore, the development of this technology exposes the technological gap between these two rivals and certainly makes a symbolic statement about Iran being a modern, advanced country worthy of leading the Muslim world.

While it is difficult to isolate Saudi responses by the type of threat, military or ideational, and the source of the threat (i.e., the nuclear balance, Iraq, etc.), it is possible to identify some of the clear cases and illustrate examples of ideational balancing. Saudi responses to Iran since the Iraq War have included both hard and soft policies. Saudi Arabia's vast arms purchases, including some of the most advanced jets, can be considered internal balancing, and strengthening relations with GCC+2+1 can be considered a form of external balancing. The decision to more publicly support a nuclear-weapons-free zone in the Gulf contra the Egyptian position is a sign of how serious the nuclear issue is.

But these arms purchases can also be considered a way to acquire prestige and it is unclear if Saudi Arabia has the capability to actually use this military hardware effectively. Moreover, Saudi Arabia has also provided arms and material to Sunni groups in Iraq in their power struggle against Iranian-backed military and political organizations. Military support for its allies against Iranian proxies have also included supporting interests in Lebanon, the Gulf countries, Afghanistan, and Yemen (in the latter it was also directly involved in armed conflict).[93] These are hardly ways to fully balance against a nuclear threat.

Some prominent scholars suggest that Saudi Arabia has played the sectarian card for domestic reasons.[94] While this may be true, I suggest that framing the conflict in sectarian terms is an aspect of the Saudi regime's ideational balancing. As such, Saudi leaders have aimed to undermine Iran's ideational power, mobilize domestic support, coordinate regional policies, and try to bolster the collective legitimacies of Arab Sunni regimes. By reframing the conflict as sectarian, Saudi Arabia sought to undermine the credibility of the source. Not only is Iran, of course, non-Arab, it is Shi'a—and for many, particularly those in Wahhabi Saudi Arabia, Shi'a are equated with non-Muslims. Therefore, the message was to be wary of supporting a political cause supported by the Iranians because their Shi'ism could not possibly make them an "authentic" Islamic leader that represents Arab and Muslim interests.

Conclusion

This chapter has examined how ideational threats can be projected indirectly through symbolic foreign policies. Information is projected and communicated about the sender (Iran) and the targeted regimes in Egypt and Saudi Arabia. Egypt and Saudi Arabia responded through ideational balancing to mitigate these nonmilitary threats.

After the death of Ayatollah Khomeini, the ideological threat Iran posed took a much subtler and less direct course as it reoriented its foreign policy to reassert and reintegrate itself in the international order.[95] This did not mean the threat went away, however. By supporting revisionist, anti-imperialist causes, which were framed as Islamic causes, Iran's foreign policies took on symbolic significance and challenged Egypt's and Saudi Arabia's status and legitimacy. Even though the early 1990s showed some outward signs of a relaxation in tensions, Riyadh and Cairo still considered Iran's ideational power a national security threat. This is because Iran projected this threat indirectly.

The structural change caused by the overthrow of Saddam Hussein became a catalyst for Iran to take advantage of political opportunities created by the intersection of unstable domestic and regional environments. Regional crises exacerbated societal discontent and served as focal symbols for mobilization. The war in Afghanistan, the Global War on Terror, the Intifada, and the U.S. invasion of Iraq provided no shortage of resonant symbols. The discontent that mobilized around these symbols was not just directed against the United States or Israel, it was also an expression of protest against Egyptian foreign policy.

These tensions between public opinion and foreign policy were certainly nothing new. President Sadat's peace initiatives toward Israel and Egypt's participation in the Gulf War (1990–1991) are just two examples of foreign policies that sparked protest and dissent. Attempts by foreign actors to stoke these fires were seen in Khomeini's rhetoric and Saddam Hussein's rhetorical attacks on Egypt. What was new, however, was the way in which Iran's activities exploited this gap indirectly and pressured the Egyptian regime. Iran's actions projected its message without directly attacking Egypt's leadership.

Iran's activities drew attention to one of the most resonant issues for Arab publics, the Palestinian-Israeli conflict and Arab regimes' inability or unwillingness to take a stance that would satisfy public opinion. After coming to power in 2005, President Mahmoud Ahmedinejad's provocative statements challenging Israel's legitimacy and the Holocaust found a receptive audience. Many Arabs welcomed a leader willing to speak out on issues that their own leadership would not. Furthermore, Ahmedinejad's rhetoric was complemented by Iran's actions—its material and diplomatic support for Hamas, Palestinian Islamic Jihad, and Hezbollah.

Saudi Arabia's and Egypt's primary ideational balancing tactic revolved around counterframing the ideational threat as "sectarianism." This move to "securitize sectarianism" became both a way to frame the threat perception and a focal symbol to coordinate an ideational response with allies to mitigate Iranian influence. Saudi officials shared King Abdullah of Jordan's 2004 warning of an Iranian-driven Shi'a crescent emerging across the Middle East. Both Saudi and Egyptian domestic policies had tinges of sectarianism influenced by the regional politics environment. Because of the much larger Shi'a population in Saudi Arabia and the proximity to other Shi'a populations in the Gulf, this issue received much more attention in Saudi Arabia.

Egypt and Saudi Arabia's ideational balancing tactics that played the sectarian card are examples of how the ideational security dilemma is potentially destabilizing. This ideational competition at the systemic level between Iran and its adversaries occurred alongside the game of domestic politics. Playing the sectarian card in Egypt and Saudi Arabia appeased and even pleased groups more conservative than the government. Saudi Arabia has a significant Shi'a population (10–15%) and an even more significant Sunni population that is virulently anti-Shi'a. The policy in Saudi Arabia ran the risk of forcing the government into a corner where it might suffer some type of audience cost by backing down from a confrontation. In the Egyptian case, the talk of Shi'ism, even though it also represented an aversion to anti-status-quo politics, mobilized Salafi forces that supported the Mubarak regime. But this mobilization has also run the risk of raising expectations in state-society relations and forcing stronger rhetoric to make unrealistic demands on Egyptian power.

6 Conclusion: Balancing the Brotherhood

FEW MIDDLE EAST EXPERTS PREDICTED THE EVENTS OF 2011 even though many were aware of the factors and conditions that gave way to the unrest.[1] The alacrity, unpredictability, and extent of change in the Middle East has made it difficult to answer important questions about the timing of these events, the conditions and factors that facilitated the protests, and why some rebellions succeeded and others failed. As one wave of events succeeded another, attention was given to new questions. What is known, however, is that these monumental protests set in motion a series of historic changes that will affect not only domestic politics but also international relations for years to come. In the wake of the uprisings, Islamists, the feared and repressed opposition of Arab authoritarian regimes, came to power in many North African states. But only two-and-a-half years later, Islamists had won and lost power in Egypt, a focal point of the Arab uprisings.

One of the most interesting and relevant stories is how other states responded to Islamists coming to power. While some states welcomed or warmed to the Muslim Brotherhood–led Egypt, such as Qatar and Turkey, other states, primarily Saudi Arabia and the UAE, balanced against the Brotherhood. This concluding chapter examines how the Gulf states of Saudi Arabia and the UAE pursued ideational balancing strategies in response to the rise of an Islamist regime in Egypt. It will also discuss the role of Turkey, an interesting case of a regional power, governed by a liberal Islamist party, that did not aggressively project its ideational power. The second part of the chapter will provide a summary of the findings in this book.

The Domestic and International Context

In retrospect, it is almost inconceivable that the self-immolation of a fruit seller in southern Tunisia in December 2010, done in protest of corruption, cronyism, and police abuses, would have such a massive impact on Tunisia and the region for years to come. There had been martyrs in the past, and these grievances had been around for a long time: "Yet something was different this time."[2] From Mohamed Bouazizi's town of Sidi Bouzid, protests spread to other cities, leading to the departure of President Zine el-Abidine ben Ali from Tunisia on January 14, 2011. Mobilized by their own symbols of corruption and humiliation, such as Khalid Said, the Egyptian Revolution broke out on the national holiday Police Day on January 25, 2011. Growing protests lasted for eighteen days, culminating in the resignation of President Hosni Mubarak, who had ruled Egypt with an iron fist for three decades. Meanwhile, Libyans took to the streets to overthrow one of the most brutal and erratic dictators in the Arab world, Muammar Qaddafi. By September 2011, Libyan rebels, aided by American and NATO forces, had overthrown his regime. Fierce clashes leading to civil war and insurgency broke out in Syria and Yemen. In other states, such as Bahrain, large-scale protests were brutally repressed. The international aspects of the uprisings were largely dominated by the spread of ideas through collective identities and experiences.

The uprisings, which many have called revolutions, overthrew the old order in some states and placed regimes under enormous pressure to reform. In the latter set of cases, states such as Jordan or Morocco enacted narrow reforms or provided material benefits to preempt domestic unrest and prevent any real pushes for political reform.[3] Even in cases in which the regime did not change, such as Morocco, an Islamist became prime minister for the first time in its history as a result of elections. Other states, such as Saudi Arabia, led the counterrevolutionary charge by offering payoffs to their own citizens as well as their allies in an effort to ensure regime stability.

Other responses varied. Iran's Ayatollah Ali Khamenei claimed the uprisings were an "Islamic awakening" in an effort to show the impact of its revolution three decades earlier.[4] Al-Qaeda claimed these uprisings were not a defeat but an opportunity: "Our mujahideen brothers in Tunisia, Egypt, Libya and the rest of the Muslim world will get a chance to breathe again after three decades of suffocation," wrote Anwar al-Awlaki in al-Qaeda's English-language magazine *Inspire*.[5] Israel's prime minister Benjamin Netanyahu initially urged Western capitals to support the embattled Mubarak and feared that Egypt "will go in the direction of Iran."[6]

Attention naturally focused on Egypt, the most influential Arab state. Saudi Arabia and the UAE initially responded to the overthrow of their ally with serious concern. King Abdullah of Saudi Arabia criticized the protesters and voiced support for President Mubarak.[7] Riyadh publicly opposed the United States' position and was terrified by the contagion of revolutionary fervor as well as the fear that their long-standing ally, the United States, had abandoned their longtime friends, such as Hosni Mubarak, and could do the same to them. Thus, the revolt that broke out in Bahrain in 2011 was a red-line event. Saudi Arabia and the UAE sent approximately 2,000 military personnel and police to help the Bahraini regime suppress the revolt.[8] This attempt to prevent the spread of contagion on their border was also a way to send a message to their domestic constituency, the United States, and safeguard regional security interests vis-à-vis Iran.

As such, this fear of revolutionary contagion and the spread of ideas about political reform prompted these conservative monarchies to bolster their counterrevolutionary efforts both at home and abroad. They dedicated massive financial resources to satisfying their own populations. Saudi Arabia announced $36 billion in new projects and jobs.[9] They sent aid to their allies to prevent revolutionary contagion as well as creeping Iranian influence.[10] Gulf states were concerned that the revolutionary contagion would spread to other monarchies and thus invited Morocco and Jordan to join the Gulf Cooperation Council.[11]

Saudi Arabia had a very close eye on Egypt. So when Islamists did come to power under Mohammed Morsi in Egypt, these Gulf states embarked on ideational balancing to mitigate a future potential ideational threat. Why did Saudi Arabia fear the rise of a regime that was ostensibly committed to promoting Islamic values and opposed secular nationalism? In fact, the relationship between the Muslim Brotherhood and Saudi Arabia, and the UAE as well, went back to the 1950s and 1960s, when Saudi Arabia took in exiled Brotherhood members from Syria and Egypt.

The concern about the Brotherhood seizing power stems largely from three main factors. First, these states feared an Islamist-dominated Egypt would be soft on Iran and at worst ally with it. Hosni Mubarak had a very negative view of Iran shared by many of his top security advisers. Immediately after his overthrow during the period of the Supreme Council of Armed Forces (SCAF) rule, the new foreign minister, Nabil al-Araby, broke new diplomatic ground by allowing Iranian ships through the Suez Canal. This move was unprecedented because no Iranian ship had passed through this important waterway since the days of Anwar al-Sadat. And while this may have been a way to communicate a more independent foreign policy, and not necessarily an alliance with Iran, the move alarmed not just Israel and the United States but also Egypt's Gulf allies.

When Mohammed Morsi came to power, Saudi Arabia was concerned that Egyptian-Iranian relations would warm. So when the president of Iran visited Egypt in 2011, there was tremendous concern. However, the visit turned out to be a diplomatic fiasco. During President Ahmadinejad's historic visit to Cairo, protesters hurled shoes at him and he was publicly berated by one of Egypt's top clerics.[12]

An even greater concern was that an Islamist-dominated regime in Egypt might export its ideology and revolutionary character. Many critics see the Brotherhood as an international organization, whose members swear loyalty to the supreme guide in Egypt. In July 2012, Dubai's police chief Dhahi Khalfan warned of an international plot to overthrow Gulf countries. "There's an international plot against Gulf states in particular and Arab countries in general," claimed Khalfan.[13] These fears and tensions led to a number of arrests. Around January 2013, several members of the Egyptian Muslim Brotherhood living in the UAE were arrested, accused of holding "secret meetings" and recruiting Egyptian expatriates, and raising large amounts of money and spying. Khalfan continued, "The Egyptian Muslim Brotherhood has conducted many courses and lectures for the members of the secret organization regarding the election and the ways of changing regimes in Arab countries."[14] Ninety-four were put on trial, which caused major tensions with Egypt. Lastly, Khalfan has stated that the Brotherhood poses a greater security risk than Iran. Saudi Arabia also employed a similar crackdown against potential Brotherhood supporters.

This leads to my central and final point. The reason these Gulf monarchies have had a hostile relationship with the Brotherhood is that they fear the spread of an activist political trend, which includes ideas about politics, religion, and a nationalism that could resonate within society if projected.

This trend seeks to challenge the political status quo through symbols that could mobilize opposition against the rulers. The Muslim Brotherhood offers an alternative religious interpretation that sees political activism, which pushes for reform, as a religious imperative. Moreover, Saudi Arabia blames the Brotherhood for infecting their Wahhabism with a Qutbist type of activism that produced the likes of Osama bin Laden—citizens who were educated by exiled Muslim Brotherhood members.

The most important aspect of these state responses were the public (dis) information campaigns through new media technologies, such as satellite television, Facebook, and Twitter, to shape public attitudes toward the Muslim Brotherhood and its activities. Saudi Arabia and the UAE waged a powerful public anti-Brotherhood campaign with some of the most public examples, noted earlier, coming from the Dubai police chief.[15] Statements by officials were also part of this strategy.

The House of Saud's attitudes toward the Morsi regime were clearly expressed when the military took over power from Morsi in July 2013.[16] King Abdullah of Saudi Arabia supported the military's gambit in the strongest terms: "Let the entire world know that the people and government of the Kingdom of Saudi Arabia stood and still stand today with our brothers in Egypt against terrorism, extremism and sedition, and against whomever is trying to interfere in Egypt's internal affairs."[17] Saudi Arabia, the UAE, and Kuwait pledged $12 billion for the new government—roughly four times the combined aid of the United States and European Union. While this may have also been in response to the U.S. threats to cut aid, Saudi information campaigns to promote and justify the Sisi takeover and criminalize the Muslim Brotherhood became clear.

Turkey, the Arab Uprisings, and the Nonprojection of Ideational Power

At the beginning of the Arab uprisings in 2011, Turkey's prime minister Recep Tayyip Erdogan was considered the most respected Middle East leader by a wide margin.[18] He came to power in 2003 as the leader of the AKP (Adalet ve Kalkınma Partisi), also known as the Justice and Development Party. Many in the Arab world, particularly Islamists, have upheld this liberal Islamist party as a model. For its admirers, the "Turkish model" is an example of how an Islamist party can successfully govern by providing jobs for its citizens and also by satisfying the democratic aspirations of its citizens. At the same time same, this NATO member-state, whose predecessors ruled over the Middle East and parts of Europe for almost six hundred years, reengaged the region as an emerging leader.

Throughout the 2000s, Turkey, or more accurately Prime Minister Erdogan, became increasingly popular because of its foreign policy stance. Turkey's catchall "zero problems" foreign policy presented its diplomatic forays in an attractive frame. But most notably, it was Prime Minister Erdogan's strong stances against Turkey's former strategic ally, Israel, which won him praise among Arab publics.[19] In 2006, major events that won Turkey a great amount of popularity included Erdogan's public attack on Israeli President Shimon Peres in Davos, Switzerland, and Turkey's involvement in the Gaza flotilla affair in 2009.

Turkey's ideational power or, as some claimed at the time, its "soft power" grew over the decade. While Turkey's ideational power was not considered to have the same impact on domestic politics as Iran's power, attitudes began to change more publicly toward the end of the decade. Some of the policies that won the Erdogan administration favor among Arab publics, such as its activities in the Arab-Israeli conflict, challenged the leadership positions and policies of the Arab leaders. The Palestinian issue is one example. In 2009, some Egyptian newspapers and officials began to criticize the Turkish role in challenging Egyptian policy over the blockade of Gaza. According to a U.S. State Department official based in Cairo, "Egyptians have been biting their lips for some time."[20] In fact these sentiments may have been expressed more widely had officials not been constrained by their hope that Turkey would become a "Sunni balancer" against an Iranian threat and that Foreign Minister Davutoglu's "zero problems" with neighbors policy would not apply to Iran. After all, the Turkish model, as a political alternative, demonstrated that elected Islamists could run a country well and have an influential role in international affairs.

After the popular uprisings of 2011 that overthrew the ruling regimes in Tunisia, Libya, and Egypt, many prominent moderate Islamists praised the Turkish model as their inspiration. Rashid al-Ghannoushi, the charismatic Islamist leader who returned to his country to found and lead the largest political party, al-Nahda (Ennahda, or Renaissance party), credited Turkey led by the AKP as a model for Tunisia in pioneering the democratic experience.[21] Vigorous debates in the Egyptian press pondered the feasibility of that option for Egypt.

But the enthusiasm about Turkey and its model decreased after Prime Minister Erdogan's "tour" of the new Middle East in December 2011. After first receiving a hero's welcome in the region, Prime Minister Erdogan tour exposed the limits of Turkey's appeal. During Erdogan's visit to Cairo, he advised Egyptians (particularly Islamists) not to be afraid of secularism.[22] These and other remarks were interpreted as patronizing and (mis)interpreted as a call for secularism,[23] angering the Muslim Brotherhood.[24]

Despite these tensions, Prime Minister Erdogan supported the Muslim Brotherhood and condemned the overthrow of Mohammed Morsi in the strongest terms. Prime Minister Erdogan claimed Morsi was the legitimate president of Egypt.[25] He even went so far as to blame Israel and the Jews for Morsi's overthrow.[26]

In sum, the post–Arab Spring situation demonstrates that Saudi Arabia and the UAE balancing the Brotherhood policies are a form of ideational balancing to prevent the regime from projecting its politically destabilizing ideology. These policies include domestic crackdown and counterframing activities as well as tensions with the Morsi regime (and its backer, Qatar). The strong backing of General Sisi's seizure of power and his crackdown on the Brotherhood might even be considered evidence of a roll-back strategy against any future attempts to project the ideational power of Islamists from the region's most influential state. Meanwhile, the Turkish example underscores not only how important promotion is as a condition for triggering threat perception but also how ideological affinity may not preclude future competition and rivalry.

The Future

In the years ahead, greater opportunities may exist for ideational projection to threaten domestic political stability as a foreign policy tool. New media technologies will continue to connect Arab publics within and across borders. The importance of religion will not fade in the near future either. Weak domestic structures could mean a return to the 1950s and 1960s in which power was defined by how well another state's leader could manipulate a foreign policy. But it is also likely we could see the counterrevolutionary trends produce a new type of authoritarianism.

Whatever direction the region takes, the ideational security dilemma will continue to be a feature of Middle Eastern politics and a potential source of regime instability. Even if there are major shifts in the military balance of power, from Iranian nuclear weapons for example, ideational power and ideational balancing will remain important determinants of regime security and regional stability.

Summary of Findings

This book has explored some of the ways that ideas affect international politics, focusing on how and why states' projection of nonmilitary power affects threat perception. It offered a different way to think about threat perception by focusing on a type of power and a set of state policies that are often overlooked. While evidence presented in the chapters showed that ideational factors in the form of ideational power trigger threat perception in the absence as well as the presence of military power, the purpose was not to generate a universal theory outlining the conditions under which ideational factors trump material factors. Instead, the goal was to advance this debate by examining how and why ideas can threaten.

The cases examined Egyptian and Saudi Arabian threat perceptions and policies before and after Islamists came to power in an effort to understand how and why ideas can threaten. The findings from these cases suggest that states, or more specifically regimes, may consider ideational power a national security threat because this nonmilitary force could undermine domestic political stability. The sociopolitical logic that underpins this fear is that projection of ideational power through a subversive transnational ideology could affect a society's beliefs about the targeted regime's legitimacy and that the culturally resonant symbols used to project this transnational political ideology may serve as focal points to facilitate social mobilization. Symbols are important as the most powerful delivery vehicle of this ideational threat, and they also illustrate the ways in which ideas can constitute a national security threat.

The book has presented a second argument connected to the first. Targeted states have engaged in *ideational balancing* to mitigate an adversary's ideational power. As shown throughout the text, these policies aimed to mitigate an ideational threat's political-symbolic power through resource mobilization and counterframing. Consisting of domestic and foreign policies, this state behavior bolsters commonly held beliefs about its own legitimacy and seeks to undermine the credibility of the source of the ideational threat. Examining the ways in which states respond provides additional insight about how and why ideas threaten.

These arguments and findings come together to form the basis for a new analytical framework for understanding international politics: the ideational security dilemma. As I mentioned at the outset of the book, this framework allows us to understand a specific type of strategic interaction in the ideational realm that brings together domestic and foreign policies. At the heart of what drives this phenomenon is not state security or military power but ideational threats to regime security. In some cases, "outbidding" can lead to military confrontation; but for the most part, ideational power, when projected, is enough to make regimes perceive their survival is at risk. This leads states to resort to ideational balancing. Introducing the concepts of ideational balancing and the ideational security dilemma are this book's major contributions to the field.

Realism and ideational factors

The cases in this book confirm that ideational factors, such as ideational power, can be robust determinants of threat perception just as much as material factors. Ideational power can threaten another state's regime security and survival. In the selected cases, the rise of Islamist regimes, or "Islamic states," triggered threat perception and ushered in a period of hostility with former allies. But capabilities-based explanations derived from a balance of power approach could not explain these changes. Iran's relations with Egypt and Saudi Arabia improved as Tehran's relative military power increased. Immediately following the revolution, Iran's military power declined but Egypt's and Saudi Arabia's threat perception of Tehran increased. Meanwhile, Sudan never possessed serious military capabilities to threaten Egypt and Saudi Arabia yet it was considered a national security threat.

An identity-based explanation also reveals a difficulty in explaining the changes in threat perception. In all the cases examined, a difference or similarity in state identity was not a robust determinant of threat perception. For example, Saudi Arabia and Egypt, two Arab Sunni-majority states, were allies in the 1970s and enemies for the last three decades with Persian Shi'a-majority Iran. Ethnic and religious (sectarian) similarities did not prevent Saudi Arabia and Egypt from clashing with their former ally, Sudan, during the first half of the 1990s.

A related hypothesis—that the establishment of an "Islamic state," as a state identity and regime type, was the change that triggered a shift in threat perception—did not provide an adequate explanation either. If the national security concern revolved around a change in domestic regime type, domestic ideology, or state identity, then we should expect these types of changes to trigger threat perception. However, Egypt and Saudi Arabia did not initially consider these nascent Islamic republics a threat. Riyadh sought accommodation with Tehran initially, and in the case of Sudan, both Riyadh and Cairo were cautiously optimistic about the new leadership in Khartoum.

Two related examples that can be found within important cases underscore the previous point. The first is that Sudan's Islamization from the late 1970s to 1980s, including Numeiri's imposition of shari'a in 1983, was encouraged by Saudi Arabia and tolerated by Egypt. In other words, this top-down domestic Islamization did not affect Riyadh's and Cairo's threat perception in a negative way. The second example is that Egyptian and Saudi rapprochement toward Sudan took place in the mid-1990s even though Sudan's domestic political system had not changed. What Sudan did change, by not projecting its subversive ideology, was its foreign policies.

This leads us to an important point. Egypt's and Saudi Arabia's threat perceptions changed when Iran and Sudan *projected* their domestic political ideologies as ideational power. These cases showed that the projection of the transnational ideology, or ideational power, was a key condition for an ideology to become a threat. Islamist regimes became threats when they projected their ideologies directly through statements that included aggressive rhetoric or indirectly through alliances, financial and military aid, and international institutions. The way these Islamic states projected their ideational power also mattered because it affected the type of ideational balancing tactics that were employed.

The targeted regime's domestic political environment conditioned the level of perceived ideational threat. Periods of societal crisis, during which state-society relations were strained, provided political opportunities for an external ideational challenger. During these periods of enhanced dissent toward a local political authority, alternative visions of political order closely connected to identity could become more attractive. Moreover, regimes feared that projected culturally resonant symbols could coordinate political action among different opposition groups.

In sum, these conditions explain why Egypt and Saudi Arabia did not immediately consider the rise of these Islamist regimes as threats, why there is variation in a targeted state's policy response, and why other Islamist regimes were not considered ideational threats.

How Identities Matter

The previous discussion does not mean identity is unimportant. Ideologies may appeal to identities and their cultural reference points as the basis or justification for collective behavior toward a political goal. Ideational power relies on aspects of shared identity to make a case for what a polity based on this identity should look like and why the local political authority should be contested. But just as transnational identities link populations across political boundaries, they can also divide them. My findings suggest that identity plays a crucial role as both a resource and limitation of ideational power. In interstate relations, identity can be called upon as a source of cooperation or a way to frame conflict. Iran and Saudi Arabia claimed to cooperate on Islamic grounds in their establishment of the Organization of Islamic Conferences in 1969, but after the Islamic Republic of Iran was established their religious differences became a source of conflict. This book has shown how Saudi Arabia and Egypt highlighted these religious differences as a way to undermine Iran's influence among Arab Sunni-majority populations.

The identity around which an issue is framed and who frames the issue matters because transnational identities in the region circumscribe the way issues are discussed and which ideas resonate. Iran is at a distinct disadvantage in this area because it does not share ethnic and sectarian identity with the majority of the population in Arab states. Therefore, when an issue, such as the Israeli-Palestinian conflict, is discussed as an Arab interest, Iranian leaders have to shift the conversation if it seeks to use the issue to score political points. Iran tried to do this in the early 1980s with limited success; it was much more successful in the 2000s due to the overall change of the types of ideas that had become resonant—namely, political Islam. Hezbollah and Hamas play a crucial role in this regard. These nonstate allies of Iran may not share the same ethnic identity, but the religious-political foundations of these groups and the way they frame the conflict (religious and nationalist) within the Arab world creates opportunities for Iran to insert its voice and make its interventions that much more credible.

Iran has done well when it has been able to keep the message universal and pan-Islamic and not narrowly sectarian. In the periods examined, the ideational power Iran possessed was conditioned by the extent to which its adversaries, Saudi Arabia and Egypt, were able to undermine its leadership credibility on ethnic and religious grounds. This is why Saudi and Egyptian hard balancing against Iran during the 1980s had immense political value as an example of ideational balancing. The Iran-Iraq War became a convenient way to reframe the political threat from Iran as an ethnic interstate conflict between Persians and Arabs with sectarian overtones.

Twenty years later, counterframing along mostly sectarian lines became a way to coordinate the positions of Arab states seeking to contain Iranian regional influence and neutralize domestic dissent after the fall of Saddam Hussein. Some local conflicts became part of broader intraregional struggles, such as the new "Arab Cold War," and identified as part of a sectarian agenda driven by Iran. The transformation of the Houthi rebellion in northern Yemen is a prime example. In 2004, Hussein Badr al-Din al-Houthi launched a rebellion against the government motivated by a demand for greater resources for his community from the central government. The focus of the conflict became the fact that the insurgents were Zaidis, a Shi'a offshoot that is closer to Sunnism than Shi'ism. Yemeni officials during this period accused Iran of supporting this insurgency. The sectarian tensions within the region as a result of the Iraq War clearly had an effect on changing how this conflict was viewed locally. Many Yemenis at the time commented that the terms of reference for religious identity were not as politicized and generally avoided Sunni versus Shi'a distinctions.[27] By 2009, the Houthi rebellion came to be seen largely as a larger struggle between Iran and Saudi Arabia along sectarian lines. Saudi Arabia's military intervention was partly justified by accusations of Iranian support for the rebels. At that time, officials in Egypt and Saudi Arabia were convinced that Iran's involvement went beyond diplomatic support.

How does a greater overlap of shared identities (ethnic and sectarian) affect how states respond to an ideational threat? Sudan promoted its policies and ideology as representing an "authentic" vision of Islam that was consistent with Arab interests. Since Sudan considered itself Arab and Sunni, Egypt and Saudi Arabia could not easily use these identity categories to mitigate Sudan's ideational power. Instead, Cairo's and Riyadh's ideational balancing consisted of selectively denying the existence of the ideational challenge at times (in the case of Saudi Arabia). When they chose to engage, they argued that extremist ideological models, such as the one found in Sudan, would only bring ruin. Saudi Arabia used its resources to reinforce its ideational-balancing tactic of undermining the credibility of the messenger by withholding needed aid and supplying the southern rebels. Egypt also participated by enhancing the status of Sudanese rebels through working with them and by mobilizing its diplomatic resources to isolate Sudan internationally. However, one strategy to delegitimize the source of symbols and ideas, Hassan al-Turabi, may have backfired. Cairo's and Riyadh's denunciation of Sudan's support of Saddam Hussein against a Western-led, Arab coalition in the run-up to the Gulf War (1990–1991) may have actually raised Turabi's profile among the Arab public.

Theoretical Contributions

This book makes important theoretical and empirical contributions to the study of Middle East politics, international relations of the Middle East, and international relations theory. The book's primary contribution is its focus on the ideational and identity component of regime conceptions of threat. The most important research findings underscore the significance of ideational threats in accounting for changes in interstate relations. In particular, it develops and applies two new concepts: ideational balancing and the ideational security dilemma.

These findings build on an emerging literature on regime security that overlaps in many ways with a growing body of scholarship within the realist tradition—neoclassical realism. These complementary approaches include unit-level and perceptual variables to explain state behavior. My findings that these Arab regimes reacted to a transnational ideological threat, and not necessarily a military threat, does not mean this work is outside the realist tradition.[28] Demonstrating the role of ideational factors as a threat to regime security is a key contribution to this literature. For neoclassical realism, the focus on regime security and domestic politics as an intervening variable engages their core research agenda. I have shown that realism's focus on external balancing, bandwagoning, and arms racing as indicators and responses to threats may not capture what really threatens a state. What this work contributes, as outlined by ideational balancing, is that it shows how responses to threat perception are not found just in alliance formation. Instead, states enact domestic policies and other types of foreign policies to mitigate the power of the ideational threat.

The application of the terms "ideational power" and "threat" forms the foundation of this contribution. The international relations literature has largely revolved around the idea that hard, or material, power matters. The abundant literature on how hard power is defined does not compare to the dearth of theoretical literature on nonmilitary forms of power. This disparity is quite striking if we think about how much soft or smart power has been used in foreign policy discourse about the United States, China, Iran, and many other countries. While its conceptual elusiveness might be frustrating for some, the openness of the term provides opportunities for refining and building on an underdeveloped yet extremely important part of international politics. The unique contribution of this project is that it looks at ideational power as a potentially threatening force to a regime. We tend to think of ideas as a benign force in international politics. But for a state that may be weakened by its society's changing beliefs and attitudes, the spread of ideas could pose a threat to domestic political stability.

While my argument's emphasis on nonmilitary power clearly contributes to aspects of constructivists' broader research agenda on the role of ideas, it also engages this literature from other angles. First, it demonstrates that identity affects state behavior as a resource and limitation, but it is not the most important determinant. Second, shared identities can be a source of conflict or cooperation.

Finally, the topic naturally contributes to our understanding of the role of religion in international security. Both Samuel Huntington's famous work and the surge in religiously inspired political violence and terrorism in the last two decades have encouraged this new interest among academics. This project provides additional insight about political actors' use of religious symbols to threaten another state. I have tried to show how religion is relevant for international peace and security.

Outside the international relations realm, this work contributes to the literature on authoritarian regimes in comparative politics. Prior to the Arab uprisings, the durability and survival of authoritarian regimes have been explained by a number of factors including: the coercive apparatus, path dependency, culture, and institutions such as multiparty elections. This book has illuminated a different source of threat for an authoritarian regime—a transnational ideological threat—and focused on authoritarian strategies of using a state's ideological apparatus to control information and social behavior.

Notes

Chapter 1

1. Author interview with midlevel military officer, Cairo, Egypt, November 2005.

2. Robin Wright and Peter Baker, "Iraq, Jordan See Threat to Election from Iran," *Washington Post*, December 8, 2004.

3. Marc Lynch, *The Arab Uprising: The Unfinished Revolutions of the Middle East* (New York: Public Affairs, 2012), 8.

4. I discuss the terms "Islamic state," "Islamist regime," and "Islamic republic" later in the chapter.

5. Morton Valbjorn and Andre Bank, "Rediscovering the Arab Dimension of Middle East Regional Politics," *Review of International Studies* 38, no. 1 (January 2012): 10; Lynch, *Arab Uprising*, 29.

6. Michael Barnett, *Dialogues in Arab Politics: Negotiations in Regional Order* (New York: Columbia University Press, 1998), 158.

7. By transnational ideology, I refer to a set of ideas about how political life should be organized across national and territorial boundaries.

8. Kenneth Boulding, *Conflict and Defense* (New York: Harper & Row, 1963). This point is developed further in the following chapter. See also Kieran Webb, "The Continued Importance of Geographic Distance and Boulding's Loss of Strength Gradient," *Comparative Strategy* 26 (2010): 295–310.

9. Mark L. Haas, *The Ideological Origins of Great Power Politics, 1789–1989* (Ithaca: Cornell University Press, 2005). Haas argues that ideological distance is a driving factor.

10. Curtis R. Ryan, *Inter-Arab Alliances* (Gainesville: University Press of Florida, 2009).

11. Barnett, *Dialogues in Arab Politics*, 43. See also Zdzislaw Mach, *Symbols, Conflict, and Identity* (Albany: State University of New York Press, 1993), 36.

12. As such, threat perception is generally treated as an intervening variable. See Raymond Cohen, *Threat Perception in International Crisis* (Madison: University of Wisconsin Press, 1979).

13. David J. Singer, "Threat-Perception and the Armament-Tension Dilemma," *Journal of Conflict Resolution* 2 (1958): 94. For a classic work on this subject, see also Klaus Knorr, "Threat Perception," in *Historical Dimensions of National Security Problems*, ed. Knorr (Lawrence: University Press of Kansas, 1976). Knorr discusses the importance of predisposed beliefs.

14. Kenneth Waltz, *Theory of International Politics* (New York: Addison-Wesley, 1979).

15. John J. Mearsheimer, "The False Promise of International Institutions," *International Security* 19, no. 3 (Winter 1994/95): 10–11. Also see Waltz, *Theory of International Politics*, 88–89 and 116–128. In contrast, some "soft" realists contend that conflict (and threat perception) may result from a state's inability to determine intention, misperception, or belief system. See Deborah Welch Larson, *Anatomy of Mistrust* (Ithaca: Cornell University Press, 1997), 3. Other soft realists argue that capabilities do not determine the image formed. See Robert Jervis's works, *The Logic of Images in International Relations* (Princeton: Princeton University Press, 1970) and *Perception and Misperception in International Politics* (Princeton: Princeton University Press, 1976).

16. For the argument that a shared sense of identity can limit a perception of threat, see Ted Hopf, *The Social Construction of International Politics* (Ithaca: Cornell University Press, 2002); and Alexander Wendt, *Social Theory of International Politics* (Cambridge: Cambridge University Press, 1999). For the argument that shared identity may lead to conflict, see Michael Barnett, "Identity and Alliances in the Middle East," in *The Culture of National Security: Norms and Identity in World Politics*, ed. Peter Katzenstein (New York: Columbia University Press, 1996). See also Markus Kornprobst, "Ireland's Selection of the Status Quo Norm," *International Organization* 61, no. 1 (2007): 73–74.

17. Ontological security challenges the notion that foreign policy is driven by physical survival and instead posits that states are identity/security seekers. It challenges both realist and mainstream constructivist assumptions that physical survival is a national interest. See Brent J. Steele, *Ontological Security in International Relations* (New York: Routledge, 2009); Jennifer Mitzen, "Ontological Security in World Politics: State Identity and the Security Dilemma," *European Journal of International Relations* 12, no. 3 (September 2006): 341–370.

18. See Barry Buzan, Ole Waever, and Jaap de Wilde, *Security: A New Framework for Analysis* (Boulder, CO: Lynne Rienner, 1998). This approach tries to bring together constructivism and classic realism.

19. Stephen M. Walt, *The Origins of Alliances* (Ithaca: Cornell University Press, 1987).

20. Steven R. David, "Explaining Third World Alignment," *World Politics* 43, no. 2 (January 1991): 233–256; and specifically chap. 3 of Steven R. David, *Choosing Sides* (Baltimore: Johns Hopkins University Press, 1991).

21. Malik Mufti, *Sovereign Creations and the Political Order in Syria and Iraq* (Ithaca: Cornell University Press, 1996)

22. See Michael Barnett, *Dialogues in Arab Politics: Negotiations in Regional Order* (New York: Columbia University Press, 1998). Less focused on explicit outcomes of threat perceptions, Marc Lynch asserts that domestic politics and interaction with international public space changed Jordan's identity and interests. Marc Lynch, *State Interests and Public Spheres: The International Politics of Jordan's Identity* (New York: Columbia University Press, 1999).

23. Barnett, *Dialogues in Arab Politics*, 5.

24. Mark Haas argues that ideological distance, as an independent variable, helps explain alliance behavior under certain conditions. Haas, *Ideological Origins of Alliances*, 2.

25. See F. Gregory Gause III, "Balancing What? Threat Perception and Alliance Choice in the Gulf," *Security Studies* 13, no. 2 (Winter 2003/4): 273–305. In this article, Gause tries to get at the idea of how states identify threats, which he feels Walt does not address. See also F. Gregory Gause III, "Systemic Approaches to Middle East International Relations," *International Studies Review* 1, no. 1 (Spring 1999): 23–24.

26. Ryan, *Inter-Arab Alliances*, 8.

27. Ibid., 12. See also a number of important works related to the regime security approach including: *David, "Explaining Third World Alignment"*; Gause, "Balancing What? Threat Perception and Alliance Choice in the Gulf"; Hein Goemans, *War and Punishment: The Causes of War Termination and the First World War* (Princeton: Princeton University Press, 2000); and Etel Solingen, *Nuclear Logics: Contrasting Paths in East Asia and the Middle East* (Princeton: Princeton University Press, 2007).

28. Gause, "Balancing What?"

29. Ryan, *Inter-Arab Alliances*, 208.

30. Barnett, *Dialogues in Arab Politics*, 9.

31. Lynch, *State Interests and Public Spheres*.

32. See Bahgat Korany, Paul Noble, and Rex Brynen, "The Analysis of National Security in the Arab Context: Restating the State of the Art," in *The Many Faces of National Security in the Arab World*, ed. Korany, Noble, and Brynen (New York: St. Martin's Press, 1993), 10. The authors expand the concept of national security to include the threats to basic values and interest of Arab states and societies. Conflict within society and between state and society are included in this framework.

33. On regional security systems see Barry Buzan and Ole Waever, *Regions and Powers: The Structure of International Security* (Cambridge: Cambridge University Press, 2003). For a discussion about the Middle East and its relationship to the global, systemic level, see Leonard Binder, "The Middle East as a Subordinate International System," *World Politics* 10, no. 3 (April 1958): 408–429.

34. Nigel Gould-Davies, "Rethinking the Role of Ideology in International Politics during the Cold War," *Journal of Cold War Studies* 1, no. 1 (1999): 102.

35. Ibid.

36. There has been a growth of literature on religion and international affairs. See Monica Duffy Toft, Daniel Philpott, and Timothy Samuel Shah, eds., *God's Century:*

Resurgent Religion and Global Politics (New York: W. W. Norton, 2011); Ron E. Hassner, *War on Sacred Grounds* (Ithaca: Cornell University Press, 2009); Jack Snyder, ed., *Religion and International Relations Theory* (New York: Columbia University Press, 2011); Jonathan Fox and Shmuel Sandler, *Bringing Religion into International Relations* (New York: Palgrave Macmillan, 2004); Brenda Shaffer, *The Limits of Culture: Islam and Foreign Policy* (Cambridge, MA: MIT Press, 2006); and Elizabeth S. Hurd, "Political Islam and Foreign Policy in Europe and the United States," *Foreign Policy Analysis* 3 (2007): 345–367. For an excellent review article on religion and politics, see Eva Bellin, "Faith in Politics: New Trends in the Study of Religion and Politics," *World Politics* 60, no. 2 (2008): 315–347. See also David C. Rapoport, "Four Waves of Terrorism," in *Attacking Terrorism: Elements of Grand Strategy*, ed. Audrey Kurth Cronin and James M. Ludes (Washington, DC: Georgetown University Press, 2004), 46–73.

37. Benedict Anderson, *Imagined Communities* (New York: Verso, 1983); Snyder, *Religion and International Relations*.

38. There are many works on this subject. See Fawaz Gerges, *The Far Enemy: Why Jihad Went Global* (Cambridge, MA: Cambridge University Press, 2010); Gilles Kepel, *Jihad: The Trail of Political Islam* (Cambridge, MA: Harvard University Press, 2002); and Thomas Hegghammer, *Jihad in Saudi Arabia: Violence and Pan-Islamism since 1979* (Cambridge: Cambridge University Press, 2010).

39. Samuel P. Huntington, "The Clash of Civilizations?" *Foreign Affairs* (Summer 1993): 22–49.

40. Vali Nasr highlights the regional implications for changes in the sectarian balance of power between Sunnis and Shi'a in Iraq for the regional balance of power. Vali Nasr, "The Regional Implications for a Shi'a Revival in Iraq," *Washington Quarterly* 27, no. 3 (Summer 2004): 1.

41. See Frederic Wehrey, Theodore W. Karasik, Alireza Nader, Jeremy J. Ghez, Lydia Hansell, and Robert A. Guffey, *Saudi-Iranian Relations since the Fall of Saddam: Rivalry, Cooperation, and Implications for U.S. Policy* (Santa Monica, CA: RAND Corporation, 2009).

42. Huntington, "Clash of Civilizations?" 22. Rather than include an exhaustive list of academics, intellectuals, and political leaders who contest his argument, I refer to his response (which does not address many of the criticisms), Samuel P. Huntington, "If Not Civilizations, What? Samuel Huntington Responds to His Critics," *Foreign Affairs* (November/December 1993): 186–194.

43. Jason Seawright and John Gerring, "Case Selection Techniques in Case Study Research," *Political Research Quarterly* 61, no. 2 (June 2008): 296.

44. Alexander George and Andrew Bennett, *Case Studies and Theory Development in the Social Sciences* (Cambridge, MA: MIT Press, 2005), 166–167.

45. For more on the comparative case study method, see Harry G. Eckstein, "Case Study and Theory in Political Science," in *Handbook of Political Science*, vol. 7, *Strategies of Inquiry*, eds. Nelson Polsby and Fred Greenstein (Reading, MA: Addison-Wesley, 1975), 79–137; Alexander L. George, "Case Studies and Theory Development: The Method of Structured Focused Comparison," in *Diplomacy: New Approaches*

in History, Theory and Policy, ed. Paul Gordon Lauren (New York: Free Press, 1979), 43–68; Arend Lijphart, "Comparative Politics and the Comparative Method," *American Political Science Review* 65, no. 3 (September 1971): 682–693; Stephen Van Evera, *Guide to Methods for Students of Political Science* (Ithaca: Cornell University Press, 1997); Alexander George and Andrew Bennett, *Case Studies and Theory Development in the Social Sciences* (Cambridge, MA: MIT Press, 2005); and Gary King, Robert O. Keohane, and Sidney Verba, *Designing Social Inquiry* (Princeton: Princeton University Press, 1994).

46. There is little consensus among practitioners and scholars, and the literature covering this subject is enormous. For other distinctions and a different categorization, see Peter Mandaville, *Global Political Islam* (New York: Routledge, 2007).

47. Paul Noble, "The Arab System: Pressures, Constraints, and Opportunities," in *The Foreign Policies of Arab States*, eds. Bahgat Korany and A. Hillal Dessouki (Boulder, CO: Westview, 1991).

48. Van Evera, *Guide to Methods*, 77.

Chapter 2

1. John Herz, *Political Realism and Political Idealism* (Chicago: University of Chicago Press, 1951), 157.

2. Charles Glaser, "The Security Dilemma Revisited," *World Politics* 50, no. 1 (October 1997): 172.

3. Shiping Tang, "The Security Dilemma: A Conceptual Analysis," *Security Studies* 18, no. 3 (2009): 288.

4. See chap. 2 in Curtis Ryan, *Inter-Arab Alliances: Regime Security and Jordanian Foreign Policy* (Gainesville: University Press of Florida, 2009).

5. Morton Valbjorn and Andre Bank, "Rediscovering the Arab Dimension of Middle East Regional Politics," *Review of International Studies* 38, no. 1 (January 2012): 3–24.

6. Barnett, *Dialogues in Arab Politics*, 7

7. Mohammed Ayoob, "Unraveling the Concept: National Security in the Third World," in *The Many Faces of National Security in the Arab World*, eds. Bahgat Korany, Paul Noble, and Rex Brynen (New York: St. Martin's Press, 1993), 32. Gregory Gause and Rex Brynen both argue that state strength increased from the 1970s but remained vulnerable to penetration of different types of influences, including ideological ones.

8. Bassel F. Salloukh and Rex Brynen, "Pondering Permeability," in *Persistent Permeability? Regionalism, Localism, and Globalization in the Middle East*, eds. Bassel F. Salloukh and Rex Brynen (London: Ashgate, 2004), 5.

9. Noble, Brynen, and Korany, "Conclusion," 279.

10. David, *Omnibalancing*; Gause, "Balancing What?"

11. Ryan, *Inter-Arab Alliances*, 2009.

12. Barry Buzan, Ole Waever, and Jaap de Wilde, *Security: A New Framework for Analysis* (Boulder, CO: Lynne Rienner, 1998).

13. Ayoob, *Third World Security Problematic*, 263.

14. Ryan, *Inter-Arab Alliances*, 23.

15. Barnett, *Dialogues in Arab Politics*, 10.

16. Ibid., 156.

17. Bruce Bueno de Mosquita, "An Expected Utility Theory of International Conflict," *American Political Science Review* 74, no. 4 (December 1980): 917–931.

18. A broad discussion about the concept of power is beyond the scope of this paper. For four alternative conceptualizations of power from a constructivist perspective, see Michael Barnett and Raymond Duval, "Power in International Politics," *International Organization* 59, no. 1 (January 2005): 39–75. Important constructivist works on the Middle East by Barnett and Lynch fall into this category as well.

19. See John French and Bertram Raven, "The Bases of Social Power," in D. Cartwright, ed., *Studies in Social Power* (Ann Arbor: Institute for Social Research, University of Michigan, 1959), 150–167.

20. See Rodney Bruce Hall, "Moral Authority as a Power Resource," *International Organization* 51, no. 4 (August 1997): 591–622.

21. For an overview of soft balancing, see articles by Robert Pape, "Soft Balancing against the United States," 7–45; T. V. Paul, "Soft Balancing in the Age of U.S. Primacy," 46–71; Stephen G. Brooks and William Wohlforth, "Hard Times for Soft Balancing," 72–108; and Kier A. Lieber and Alexander Gerard, "Waiting for Balancing: Why the World Is Not Pushing Back," 109–139, *International Security* 30, no. 1 (Summer 2005). For the use of normative power, see Chaka Ferguson, "The Strategic Use of Soft Balancing: The Normative Dimensions of the Chinese–Russian 'Strategic Partnership,'" *Journal of Strategic Studies* 35, no. 2 (2012): 197–222.

22. Joseph S. Nye Jr., *Bound to Lead: The Changing Nature of American Power* (New York: Basic Books, 1991); and Joseph S. Nye Jr., *Soft Power: The Means to Success in World Politics* (New York: Public Affairs, 2004).

23. Nye, *Soft Power*, 6.

24. Ibid.

25. Incidentally, structural differences gave the Soviets an advantage in the larger geopolitical struggle. Because the Soviet system was less susceptible to penetration, Western powers could only transmit ideas by radios and images to the Soviet bloc, whereas the Soviets could direct parties to promote their interests. See Nigel Gould-Davies, "Rethinking the Role of Ideology in International Politics during the Cold War," *Journal of Cold War Studies* 1, no. 1 (1999): 104.

26. This term is associated with Malcolm Kerr's famous work, *The Arab Cold War*, which describes the conflict between Egypt and its republican allies against the conservative monarchies aligned with the West. Malcolm Kerr, *The Arab Cold War* (New York: Oxford University Press, 1967).

27. See Barry Buzan, Ole Waever, and Jaap de Wilde, *Security: A New Framework for Analysis* (Boulder, CO: Lynne Rienner, 1998), 144.

28. For more on the idea of national security as a subjective and objective term, see Arnold Wolfers, "'National Security' as an Ambiguous Symbol," *Political Science Quarterly* 68, no. 4 (December 1952): 481–502. See also the discussion of security having these qualities in Buzan, Waever, and De Wilde, *Security*, 30.

29. Davies, "Rethinking the Role of Ideology," 101.

30. Ayoob, "Unraveling the Concept," 33.

31. Shibley Telhami, "Power, Legitimacy, and Peace-Making in Arab Coalitions," in *Ethnic Conflict and International Politics in the Middle East*, ed. Leonard Binder (Gainesville: University Press of Florida, 1999), 51.

32. Telhami, "Power, Legitimacy, and Peace-Making in Arab Coalitions," 52. For the classic work on sources of authority, see Max Weber, *Economy and Society* (New York: Bedminister, 1968).

33. Telhami, "Power, Legitimacy, and Peace-Making in Arab Coalitions," 52.

34. Stephen M. Walt, *The Origins of Alliances* (Ithaca: Cornell University Press, 1987), 146. The term "legitimacy" is widely used but is often left undefined.

35. Kenneth Boulding, *Conflict and Defense* (New York: Harper & Row, 1963).

36. F. Gregory Gause III, *International Relations of the Persian Gulf* (Cambridge: Cambridge University Press, 2010), 278.

37. Marc Lynch, *State Interests and Public Spheres: The International Politics of Jordan's Identity* (New York: Columbia University Press, 1999), 43.

38. Thomas Schelling, *Strategy of Conflict* (Cambridge, MA: Harvard University Press, 1960), 144.

39. Nye, *Soft Power*, 101.

40. See Charles Hirschkind, *The Ethical Soundscape: Cassette Sermons and Islamic Counter Publics* (New York: Columbia University Press, 2006), 6.

41. Emmanuel Sivan, *Radical Islam: Medieval Theology and Modern Politics* (New Haven: Yale University Press, 1990), 13.

42. Hugh Miles, *The Inside Story of the Arab News Channel That Is Challenging the West* (New York: Grove Press, 2005); Noami Sakr, *Arab Television Today* (London: I. B. Tauris, 2007).

43. For a good discussion of the politics behind these media outlets, see Mamoun Fandy, *Uncivil War of Words: Media and Politics in the Arab World* (Westport, CT: Praeger Security International, 2007).

44. Marc Lynch, *Voices of the New Arab Public: Iraq, al-Jazeera, and Middle East Politics Today* (New York: Columbia University Press, 2007).

45. See Alia Malek, "al-Alam's game," *Columbia Journalism Review*, http://www.cjr.org/feature/alalams_game.php, accessed September 2, 2009; see also "Iran TV targets Iraq," April 3, 2003, http://news.bbc.co.uk/2/hi/middle_east/2913593.stm, accessed September 2, 2009.

46. Doug MacAdam and Dieter Rucht, "The Cross-National Diffusion of Movement and Ideas," *Annals of the American Academy of Political and Social Science* 528 (July 1993): 56–71. See also Sidney Tarrow, *The New Transnational Activism* (Cambridge: Cambridge University Press, 2005).

47. See Janine A. Clark, "Islamist Women in Yemen," in Quintan Wiktorowicz, ed., *Islamic Activism: A Social Movement Theory Approach* (Bloomington: Indiana University Press, 2004), 166. On radicalization aspects, see Marc Sageman, *Leaderless Jihad: Terror Networks in the Twenty-First Century* (Philadelphia: University of Pennsylvania Press, 2008); John Horgan, *The Psychology of Terrorism* (New York: Routledge, 2005). Many argue that the most important function of networks is recruitment.

48. Wiktorowicz, "Introduction," in *Islamic Activism*, 24.

49. Recent research that has applied Social Movement Theory to explain Islamic activism has also focused on transnational linkages between Islamic movements. See Diane Singerman, "The Networked World of Islamist Social Movements," in Wiktorowicz, *Islamic Activism*.

50. Neo-Sufism, which was more orthodox in practice and spirit, became the popular religion and was largely responsible for the spread of Islamic revival movements, particularly in central Asia and India. See chap. 12 of Fazlur Rahman, *Islam* (Chicago: University of Chicago Press, 1966), 193–211. For more on how this Islamic revival movement became an anticolonial movement in Central Asia and India, see Kemal Karpat, *The Politicization of Islam* (New York: Oxford University Press, 2001).

51. This Islamic movement revolted against British-Egyptian rule and established a theocratic state (Mahdist state) for about fourteen years until it was defeated by the British; see Rahman, *Islam*, 211. See also H. R. Dekmejian and Margaret Wyszormirski, "Charismatic Leadership in Islam: The Mahdi of Sudan," *Comparative Studies in Society and History* 14, no. 2 (March 1972): 193–214.

52. Laurence Louer, *Transnational Shia Politics* (New York: Columbia University Press, 2009).

53. Literally, this term means a source of imitation. A *marja'a* (or *marja'a taqlid*) is a cleric who serves as a religious reference or source for Shi'a Muslims.

54. Quintan Wiktoworicz, *The Management of Islamic Activism: Salafis, the Muslim Brotherhood, and State Power in Jordan* (Albany: State University of New York Press, 2004).

55. O'Neill describes three varieties that capture what symbols are and how they may affect a strategic environment: message symbols, focal symbols, and value symbols. Message symbols are nonlinguistic acts that are expressed in a language immediately understood by the audience. A focal symbol "induces observers to commonly expect a certain outcome in a game they will be playing with each other, through considering a certain part/whole relationship and each others' views of the same." A focal symbol may have no sender and can be an event. A value symbol may have a multiplicity of meanings and is something that represents ideas about which people value and hold strong beliefs. My use of symbols includes all three types. Barry O'Neill, *Honors, Symbols and War* (Ann Arbor: University of Michigan Press, 2001), 3.

56. Definitions of symbols vary across social science disciplines. In political science, selected works include: Murray Edelman, *The Symbolic Uses of Politics* (Bloomington: University of Illinois Press, 1985); Robert Jervis, *Perception and Misperception in International Politics* (Princeton: Princeton University Press, 1976);

O'Neill, *Honors, Symbols and War*; and Michael Barnett, *Dialogues in Arab Politics* (New York: Columbia University Press, 1998). Some definitions describe symbols as part of a culture's repertoire that helps maintain and enhance social solidarity. Definitions may also emphasize their emotive qualities based on primordial attachments to explain violent conflict, while other approaches view symbols as political constructs. See Stuart Kaufman, "Symbolic Politics or Rational Choice," *International Security* 34, no. 4 (Spring 2006): 45–86. Some definitions describe symbols as part of a culture's repertoire that helps maintain and enhance social solidarity. Definitions may also emphasize their emotive qualities based on primordial attachments to explain violent conflict, while other approaches view symbols as political constructs.

57. Barnett, *Dialogues in Arab Politics*, 43. See also Zdzilaw Mach, *Symbols, Conflict and Identity* (Albany: State University of New York Press, 1993), 36.

58. Dale Eickelman and James Piscatori, *Muslim Politics* (Princeton: Princeton University Press, 1996), 57–65.

59. Irving Goffman, *Frame Analysis* (New York: Harper & Row, 1974). For a similar approach in the political psychology literature, see Foong Khong Yuen, *Analogies at War: Korea, Munich, Dien Bien Phu, and the Vietnam Decisions of 1965* (Princeton: Princeton University Press, 1992).

60. David Snow and Robert Benford, "Ideology, Frame Resonance, and Participant," *International Social Movement Research* 1, no. 1 (1988): 198.

61. Ibid., 7.

62. "Common knowledge" is a game-theoretic concept that means "I know that you know that I know" and so on. This system of second-order beliefs is essential for understanding coordination games. For a mutually beneficial outcome to occur, it is not sufficient that actor A knows what actor B's expected behavior is. Instead, actor A must know that actor B knows that actor A knows that actor B knows. For a clear discussion of this concept, see Michael Chwe, *Rational Ritual* (Princeton: Princeton University Press, 2001).

63. Chwe, *Rational Ritual*, 28; Victor Turner, *The Ritual Process: Structure and Anti-Structure* (Chicago: Aldine, 1969).

64. The Arab League, or League of Arab States, was founded in Cairo in 1945. The headquarters moved from Cairo to Tunis during 1979–1989 when Egypt was suspended from the Arab League for signing a peace treaty with Israel. Summits were held in various locations throughout the Arab world.

65. E. W. Rothenbuhler, *Ritual Communication: From Everyday Conversation to Mediated Ceremony* (Thousand Oaks, CA: Sage, 1998), 51. He argues that institutional actors might attach their invented ritual to an authentic one.

66. In other words, a *coordination problem* exists when individuals want the same thing but a lack of information of the others' expected behavior prevents the optimal outcome. As such, a dissatisfied individual will not participate in a demonstration unless he knows others will because the risk of being the lone protester is too high. This strategic setting is often represented by a Stag Hunt. For a clear discussion of this, see O'Neill, *Honors, Symbols and War*, 48–49. Thomas Schelling

discusses focal points in *Strategy of Conflict* (Cambridge, MA: Harvard University Press, 1960), 57.

67. Ann Swidler, "Culture in Action: Symbols and Strategies," *American Sociological Review* 51, no. 2 (April 1986): 277.

68. Ibid.

69. Schelling, *Strategy of Conflict*, 57.

70. O'Neill, *Honors, Symbols and War*, 6.

71. Schelling, *Strategy of Conflict*, 144.

72. Barnett, *Dialogues in Arab Politics*, 43.

73. Saudi scholar Madawi al-Rasheed asserts that while Saudi authoritarianism relies on physical coercion and oil revenues, it is much more dependent on "sacred narratives"; see Madawi al-Rasheed, *Contesting the Saudi State: Islamic Voices from a New Generation* (New York: Cambridge University Press, 2007), 213.

74. Ibid.

75. See Lisa Weeden, "Acting 'As If': Symbolic Politics and Social Control in Syria," *Comparative Studies in Society and History* 40, no. 3 (2003): 503–523.

76. Chwe, *Rational Ritual*, 19.

77. Ibid., 83.

78. Kuran argues that preference falsification is what maintains an authoritarian regime. For more on preference falsification, see Timur Kuran, *Private Truths, Public Lies: The Social Consequences of Preference Falsification* (Cambridge, MA: Harvard University Press, 1997).

79. Thomas Schelling is known to have coined the term "tipping point." See Timur Kuran, "Sparks and Prairie Fires: A Theory of Unanticipated Political Revolution," *Public Choice* 61, no. 1 (1989): 41–74; and Susanne Lohmann, "The Dynamics of Informational Cascades," *World Politics* 47, no. 1 (1994): 42–101.

80. See Michaelle Browers, *Political Ideology in the Arab World: Accommodation and Transformation* (Cambridge: Cambridge University Press, 2009).

81. Chwe, *Rational Ritual*, 12.

82. Robert D. Benford and David A. Snow, "Framing Processes and Social Movements: An Overview and Assessment," *Annual Review of Sociology* 26 (2000): 626.

83. Yaroslav Trofimov cites that there was almost no discussion of Juhayman's siege of Mecca in the Saudi press. See his *The Siege of Mecca: The Forgotten Uprising in Islam's Holiest Shrine and the Birth of Al-Qaeda* (New York: Doubleday, 2009).

84. "The Rise of Official Islam in Jordan," in Michael Robbins and Lawrence Rubin, *Politics, Religion & Ideology* 14, no. 1 (2013), 59–74.

Chapter 3

1. Author interview with Dr. Abdel Monem Said, Cairo, Egypt, December 17, 2005.

2. This is only one aspect, and not the more important regional and domestic story. See Malcolm Kerr, *The Arab Cold War: Gamal Abdel Nasser and His Rivals, 1958–1970* (Oxford: Oxford University Press, 1975).

3. "Nasser Shuts Embassy in Iran in Retaliation," *New York Times*, July 27, 1960, 5.

4. James Jankowski, *Nasser's Egypt, Arab Nationalism, and the United Arab Republic* (Boulder, CO: Lynne Rienner, 2001), 141. During the beginning of the reign of King Saud (1953–1964), Saudi Arabia's policies were actually geared toward cooperating with Egypt in an anti-Hashemite alliance, but this ended by early 1958. For more on these shifting alliances see chapter 4 in this volume.

5. Other states including Jordan and Great Britain also contributed diplomatic, military, or economic aid.

6. Nasser did try to increase pan-Arab sympathies in the Ahvaz region of Iran, populated by Persian-speaking Arabs, but this did not threaten political stability.

7. Anwar Sadat, *In Search of Identity* (New York: Harper & Row, 1977), 212–213.

8. William Quandt, *Saudi Arabia in the 1980s: Foreign Policy, Security, and Oil* (Washington, DC: Brookings Institution, 1981), 38.

9. Trita Parsi, *Treacherous Alliance: The Secret Dealings of Israel, Iran, and the United States* (New Haven: Yale University Press, 2008), 37.

10. Drew Middleton, "Who's Next in Atom Club?" *New York Times*, May 26, 1974, 162.

11. Rouhollah K. Ramazani, *Revolutionary Iran: Challenge and Response in the Middle East* (Baltimore: Johns Hopkins University Press, 1988), 70.

12. Dana Adams Schmidt, "Britain Cuts Some Old Ties: Trucial States," *New York Times*, December 5, 1971, E4. In 1970, Iran finally said it would accept a plebiscite on Bahrain's sovereignty.

13. From 1970 to 1978, Iran's defense expenditures were nearly 1.5 times Saudi Arabia's. Iran's arms imports ranged from 1.7 to 16 times Saudi Arabia's arms importation during that period of time. See Anthony H. Cordesman, *The Gulf and the Search for Strategic Stability* (Boulder, CO: Westview Press, 1984), 160. Cordesman reports this data from the U.S. Arms Control and Disarmament Agency.

14. For more on the Saudi reaction, see Quandt, *Saudi Arabia in the 1980s*, 39.

15. Saeed M. Badeeb, *Saudi-Iranian Relations 1932–1982* (London: Centre for Arab and Iranian Studies 1993), 60–61.

16. See Graham Fuller, *Center of the Universe: The Geopolitics of Iran* (Boulder, CO: Westview Press, 1991), 110.

17. Gwenn Okruhlik, "Saudi Arabia–Iranian Relations: External Rapprochement and Internal Consolidation," *Middle East Policy* 10, no. 2 (Spring 2003): 115.

18. "Iran on Fringe of Arab World, Akhbar al-Yawm Warns of Repetition of Iran Developments," *Foreign Broadcast Information Service*, Near East Section 1/11/79, D3–4, NewsBank, Stamford, CT, 1979–1980.

19. Yazid ibn Mu'awiyya (645–683) was the second Caliph of the Umayyad dynasty and is condemned by Shi'a for his impiety and, more importantly, for his role in the Battle of Karbala that resulted in the Martyrdom of Hussein in the year 680.

20. Sunni radicals also referred to Sadat this way. After shooting Sadat, Khalid Islambouli, Sadat's assassin, yelled, "I have killed the pharaoh!" See Gilles Kepel, *Muslim Extremism in Egypt: The Prophet and Pharaoh* (Berkeley: University of California Press, 1993), 192.

21. Ehud Sprinzak, "The Process of Delegitimization: Towards A Linkage Theory of Political Terrorism," *Terrorism and Political Violence* 3, no. 1 (Spring 1991): 50–68.

22. Kepel, *Prophet and the Pharaoh.*

23. See Rudi Matthee, "Egyptian Opposition on the Iranian Revolution," in *Shi'ism and Social Protest*, ed. Juan R. Cole and Nikki Keddie (New Haven: Yale University Press, 1986), 247–274.

24. For more on Al-Jihad's views see Sivan, "Sunni Radicalism in the Middle East and Beyond," *International Journal of Middle East Studies* 21 (1989): 26.

25. Although Egypt technically lost the war, the surprise attack and the crossing of the Suez Canal is remembered as a great achievement.

26. Nader Entessar claims that the tension increased after 1982. See Entessar, "The Lion and the Sphinx: Iranian-Egyptian Relations in Perspective," in Hooshang Amirahmadi and Nader Entessar, eds., *Iran and the Arab World* (New York: St. Martin's Press, 1993), 171.

27. "The Shah's Flight into Egypt," *Newsweek*, April 7, 1980.

28. See Raphael Israeli, "The Role of Islam in President Sadat's Thought," *Jerusalem Journal of International Relations* 4, no. 4 (1980): 1–12.

29. The Sadat and Mubarak regimes also combined these efforts with other policies. After Sadat's assassination in October 1981, Hosni Mubarak throughout the 1980s and 1990s used "selective repression" to confront the ideological threat by isolating radicals and, at the same time, bolstering the regime's religious legitimacy by providing resources for state-run religious institutions and political space (at times) to the Muslim Brotherhood. This term "selective repression" is borrowed from Robert Bianchi, *Unruly Corporatism: Associational Life in 20th Century Egypt* (New York: Oxford University Press, 1994). For more on this domestic bargain struck and similar ideas see Julie Taylor, "Prophet Sharing: Strategic Interaction between Islamic Clerics and Middle Eastern Regimes" (PhD diss., UCLA, 2004); Tamir Moustafa, "Conflict and Cooperation between the State and Religious Institutions in Contemporary Egypt," *International Journal of Middle East Studies* 32, no. 1 (February 2000): 3–22; Hesham al-Awadi, *In Pursuit of Legitimacy: The Muslim Brotherhood and Mubarak, 1982–2000* (London: I. B. Tauris, 2004).

30. "Egypt to Bolster Islamic call against imported ideologies," *Foreign Broadcast Information Service,* NES-LD070911, 12/8/1979, D3–4, NewsBank, Stamford, CT, 1979–1980.

31. The opportunity was mostly military. Saddam and his advisers believed the fall of the shah made a military victory easy, which could also mean the ability to defeat an ancient enemy and redress territorial disputes. While the domestic threat from Iran's export of the revolution was a serious concern, Saddam was also worried that Arab states would become complacent about the threat of Iran. Furthermore, Iran's claim of Islamic leadership challenged Iraq's efforts on pan-Arab unity and prestige. See Kevin M. Woods and Michael R. Pease, *The Mother of All Battles: Saddam Hussein's Strategic Plan for the Persian Gulf* (Annapolis: United States Naval Institute, 2008), 36–40. F. Gregory Gause III argues that threat was the more important factor in "Iraq's decision to go to war in 1980 and 1990," *Middle East Journal* 56, no. 1 (Winter 2002): 47–70; and Gause, *International Relations of the Persian Gulf,* 59. Other accounts tend to favor the idea that opportunity was the biggest driver. Saddam and his advisers felt the fall of the shah would make a military victory easy.

32. "Ghali States Egypt Will Arm Gulf If Asked," *Foreign Broadcast Information Service,* NES 3/7/1979, LD061015, D3–4, NewsBank, Stamford, CT, 1979–1980. There were numerous statements made about Egypt's military commitments to the Gulf including security cooperation.

33. David B. Ottaway, "Egyptians Indicate Limited Readiness to Aid Iraq in War; Concern about Iran's Success Prompts New Role for Cairo," *Washington Post,* May 21, 1982. These soldiers were mostly drawn from the 250,000 Egyptian laborers working in Iraq. This commitment occurred at a time when Iran had turned the tide of the war and was able to enter Iraqi territory. The fear was quite pronounced.

34. Internal factors caused this shift because continued praise of Iran's revolution might have appeared as a choice of transnational loyalty over Egyptian national identity. For more on this change, see Rudi Matthee, "Egyptian Opposition on the Iranian Revolution," in *Shi'ism and Social Protest,* ed. Juan R. Cole and Nikki Keddie (New Haven: Yale University Press, 1986), 247–274.

35. Many Islamic extremists may have admired the Iranian Revolution from a political perspective but they found Khomeini's views to be a distortion of Islam and any association with it a distortion of their vision. For more on Al-Jihad's views see Sivan, "Sunni Radicals," 26.

36. Ramazani, *Revolutionary Iran,* 87–88.

37. Ibid., 87. Ramazani claims it was because of a legacy of Saudi-Iranian accommodation.

38. Ibid., 88.

39. Ibid., 89.

40. For the argument that Saudi Arabia tried to hide their fear see Jacob Goldberg, "Saudi Arabia and the Iranian Revolution," in *The Iranian Revolution in the Muslim World,* ed. David Menashri (San Francisco: Westview Press, 1990), 160. Ramazani leaves the question open of what caused initial Saudi policy but he seems to lean

toward the idea that played the differences down to try to continue cooperation. Interestingly, Ramazani also notes the regime publicly downplayed any fear of contagion effects from the revolution. See Ramazani, *Revolutionary Iran*, 88–89.

41. Cited in Quandt, *Saudi Arabia in the 1980s*, 39.

42. Ibid.

43. See Goldberg, "Saudi Arabia and the Iranian Revolution," 162.

44. Ibid., 159.

45. For example, during the violent clashes of 1981, King Khalid accused the Iranian pilgrims of chanting "God is great, Khomeini is great" and "God is one, Khomeini is one" in the Great Mosque. Martin Kramer, *Arab Awakening and Islamic Revival* (New Brunswick, NJ: Transaction, 1996), 169. Kramer relates that King Khalid's accusation, which was based on an intentional or unintentional linguistic mistake, implied that the Iranian pilgrims granted Khomeini divine leadership status. In addition to the distribution and challenge to the Saudi regime, the charges was that they failed to respect the sanctity of the Great Mosque and that their version of Islam was parochial and not accommodative for all Muslims.

46. Saudi Arabia responded by restricting the number of Iranian pilgrims in subsequent years. But the damage was done. Although Saudi Arabia may have quelled this violent protest and spun it as Iranian extremism, this provocation damaged Saudi Arabia's image. The Guardian of the Holy Shrines was not only challenged; it shed blood in a sacred space.

47. James Piscatori, "Managing God's Guests," in *Monarchies and Nations: Globalization and Identity in the Arab States of the Gulf*, ed. Paul Dresch and James Piscatori (New York: I. B. Tauris, 2005), 222. Piscatori relates three interrelated claims the Saudi state makes about itself related to the Hajj: the provision of security, Saudi munificence, and the House of Saud's intense devotion to Islamic causes, which forms the basis of legitimacy.

48. For selected works on how the al-Saud family governs, see F. Gregory Gause III, *Oil Monarchies: Domestic and Security Challenges in the Arab Gulf States* (New York: Council on Foreign Relations, 1994); Steffen Hertog, *Princes, Brokers and Bureaucrats: Oil and the State in Saudi Arabia* (Ithaca: Cornell University Press, 2011); Michael Herb, *All in the Family: Absolutism, Revolution, and Democracy in the Middle Eastern Monarchies* (New York: State University of New York Press, 1999).

49. Madawi Al-Rasheed, *A History of Saudi Arabia* (Cambridge: Cambridge University Press, 2002), 18–20.

50. Ibid.

51. Gause, *Oil Monarchies*, 24.

52. Iran's domestic motivations are beyond the scope of this study. For more on this, see Ramazani, *Revolutionary Iran*, chap. 2.

53. James Buchan, "Secular and Religious Opposition in Saudi Arabia," in *State, Society, and Economy in Saudi Arabia*, ed. Tim Niblock (New York: St. Martin's, 1982), 119.

54. Ibid., 119.

55. Many scholars have commented on the reasons for the uprising. Buchan argues that it was because of the Shi'a exclusion from the dividends of the oil boom due to discriminatory hiring practices and lack of state investment in infrastructure. Herb claims says rioting can be explained as a product of contagion and opportunism since they based their acquiescence to political authority on stability. See Michael Herb, "Iran and the Shi'a of the Arab States of the Gulf," in *Ethnic Conflict and International Politics in the Middle East*, ed. Leonard Binder (Gainesville: University Press of Florida, 1999), 162.

56. Toby Jones, "Rebellion on the Saudi Periphery: Modernity, Modernization, and the Shia Uprising of 1979," *International Journal of Middle East Studies* 38, no. 2 (2006): 215–216.

57. Ibid.

58. Ibid., 224.

59. Jones argues that there was not coordination as there was in the Iranian revolution, implying that had there been there may have been even greater social unrest.

60. According to Trofimov, French Special Forces were the ones who carried out many parts of the mission.

61. Joseph A. Kechician, "The Role of the Ulama in the Politics of an Islamic State," *International Journal of Middle East Studies* 18, no. 1 (February 1986): 62.

62. Trofimov, *Siege of Mecca*, 169–170.

63. Ibid.

64. Lacroix, *Awakening Islam*, 103.

65. The figure of $30 billion appears with frequency although there is a wide range of estimates. Most estimates are not very specific about what the amounts do and do not include. Of course, there is also no way to know how much unreported aid was given. Fürtig details some of the aid. Saudi Arabia gave $6 billion to Iraq in civilian and military aid until April 1981. From May to December 1981, Riyadh gave an additional $4 billion. Saudi Arabia increased this aid even further as a result of the coup attempt in Bahrain in late 1981 and the Iranian military successes in the spring and summer of 1982, which increased the possibility of an Iraqi collapse. Fürtig also notes that by the end of 1982, Saudi Arabia provided $27 billion. However, the sources he cites seem questionable, it is unclear what that aid included, and this number seems out of proportion from the total aid. See Henner Fürtig, *Iran's Rivalry with Saudi Arabia between the Gulf Wars* (Ithaca: Ithaca Press, 2002), 64.

66. R. K. Ramazani, *The Gulf Cooperation Council* (Charlottesville: University of Virginia Press, 1988), 6. He argues that the war was at best a catalyst. The formation of the GCC allowed Saudi Arabia to realize its historic goal of extending control over other Gulf monarchies for protective power.

67. Statement from: http://www.country-data.com/cgi-bin/query/r-11675.html, accessed August 1, 2012.

68. Jacob Goldberg maintains that the leadership devoted the greatest attention to this aspect of its battle with Iran see Goldberg, "Saudi Arabia and the Iranian Revolution," 162.

69. Ibid.

70. Okruhlik, "Empowering Civility through Nationalism: Reformist Islam and Belonging in Saudi Arabia," in Robert W. Hefner, ed., *Remaking Muslim Politics: Pluralism, Contestation, Democratization* (Princeton, NJ: Princeton University Press, 2005), 194.

71. Toby Jones, "The Clerics, the Sahwa, and the Saudi State," *Strategic Insights* 4, no. 3 (2005), http://calhoun.nps.edu/public/handle/10945/11229, accessed September 2, 2013. In a sense, the regime "outbid" its religious critics by providing a more austere message and empowering state-managed religious institutions that enforced the strict religious codes. One example of this was the expansion of the *mutawwa*'s (religious police) role and jurisdiction in society.

72. Tim Niblock, *Saudi Arabia: Power, Legitimacy, and Survival* (New York: Routledge, 2006), 84. Allocation for religious activities was 1.26 billion Saudi Riyal from 1975 to 1980 and 9.04 billion SR from 1980 to 1985.

73. The Sawha benefited from this state largesse. Lacroix, *Awakening Islam*, 143.

74. Madawi Al-Rasheed, *Contesting the Saudi State*, 105.

75. Hegghammer, *Jihad in Saudi Arabia*, 24–28.

76. Calbrese, *Revolutionary Horizons*, 135.

77. "Tehran's commitment hardly matched its rhetoric." Ali Jalali, "A Historical Perspective on Iran-Afghan Relations," in *Iran and Eurasia*, ed. Ali Mohammadi and Anoushiravan Ehtehshami (Ithaca: Ithaca Press, 2007), 144.

78. Ibid.

79. Fürtig, *Iran's Rivalry*, 164.

Chapter 4

1. Tareq Y. Ismael, *The UAR in Africa: Egypt's Policy under Nasser* (Evanston: Northwestern University Press, 1971), 4.

2. Ibid.

3. See Gabriel Warburg, *Islam, Sectarianism and Politics in Sudan since the Mahdiyya* (London: C. Hurst, 2003).

4. Ibid.

5. James Janowski, *Nasser's Egypt, Arab Nationalism, and the United Arab Republic* (Boulder, CO: Lynne Rienner, 2002), 42.

6. Author interview with Professor Aboul Enein, Director of the African Studies Center, Cairo University, Cairo, December 12, 2007.

7. Ibid.

8. The following year Sudan and Egypt signed another agreement to establish a united political command.

9. Steven R. David, *Choosing Sides: Alignment and Realignment in the Third World* (Baltimore: Johns Hopkins University Press, 1991), 177.

10. Ann Mosley Lesch, *Sudan: Contested Nationalities* (Indianapolis: Indiana University Press, 1998), 61.

11. Gamal Nkrumah, "Abdur-Rahman Sawar al-Dhahab: The Good Field Marshall, One Arab-African Statesman Who Kept His Word," *Al-Ahram Weekly* 685 (April 8–14, 2004), http://weekly.ahram.org.eg/2004/685/profile.htm, accessed September 2, 2013.

12. Ibid.

13. Lesch, *Sudan*, 61.

14. Thomas W. Lippman, "Egypt, Sudan Cement Anti-Leftist Alliance; Joint Parliamentary Session," *Washington Post*, October 25, 1977.

15. Ibid.

16. "Sudan: In Brief; Praise for President Numayri," *BBC Summary of World Broadcasts*, October 4, 1983.

17. As an indicator of the tension, there was not much progress on integration agreements during this period and Cairo refused to extradite Numeiri. See Haim Shaked and Yehudit Ronen, "The Republic of Sudan," in *Middle East Contemporary Survey*, vol 11: 1987 , eds. Itamar Rabinovich and Haim Shaked (Boulder, CO: Westview Press, 1989), 137–138.

18. Egypt and the United States' refusal of military aid also motivated Khartoum to turn to Libya, Egypt's long-standing foe, for assistance. Egypt became "infuriated" by Sudan's improved relationship with Libya and saw it as a threat to Egypt's national security even though this move had started under al-Dhahab. Gamal Nkrumah, "Abdur-Rahman Sawar al-Dhahab: The Good Field Marshall," *Al-Ahram Weekly* 685 (April 8–14, 2004). Also see Neil Henry, "U.S. Takes Cautious Look at New Regime in Sudan," *Washington Post*, July 9, 1989, A22.

19. Author interview with Professor Ibrahim Nur al-Din, Cairo, Egypt, April 4, 2008. See also Yehudit Ronen, "Sudan and Egypt: The Swing of the Pendulum (1989–2001)," *Middle East Studies* 39, no. 3 (2003): 82. Ronen points out that Egypt wanted to secure and possibly increase the flow of the Nile.

20. Neil Henry, "U.S. Takes a Cautious Look at New Regime in Sudan," *Washington Post*, July 9, 1989, A22.

21. Burr and Collins, *Revolutionary Sudan*, 26; "New Sudanese Leader No Stranger to Egypt," *UPI*, July 1, 1989; Michael Ross, "New Sudan Leader Purges Military Most Top Generals Fired; Peace Talk Resumption Pledged," *Los Angeles Times*, July 2, 1989, 5; Henry, "U.S. Takes a Cautious Look at New Regime in Sudan," A22.

22. Professor Ibrahim Nur al-Din, American University of Cairo, interview with author, Cairo, Egypt, April 4, 2008.

23. Owen L. Sirrs, *A History of the Egyptian Intelligence Service* (New York: Routledge, 2011), 160.

24. Professor Mohammed Aboul Enein, interview with author, Cairo, Egypt, December 10, 2007.

25. "The Wooing and Wobbling of Sudan," *The Economist*, June 8, 1985.

26. "Sudanese New Leader to Visit Saudi Arabia," *Xinhua General Overseas News Service*, July 28, 1989.

27. "Sudan in Brief; Bashir Praises Saudi Action in Executing Kuwaiti Shi'is," *BBC Summary of World Broadcasts*, September 29, 1989.

28. "Saudi Arabia to Fund Khartoum–Port Sudan road," *BBC Summary of World Broadcasts*, February 27, 1990; "Sudan, Bashir Promised Economic Assistance during Visit to Saudi Arabia," *BBC Summary of World Broadcasts*, July 26, 1990.

29. "Sudanese Politicians Join 'Holy War' Call in Gulf," *UPI*, September 19, 1990.

30. Jeffrey Ulbrich, "'Betrayed' Saudi Arabia Expected To Be a More Assertive Mideast Player," *Associated Press*, March 10, 1991.

31. "Naif Says Muslim Brotherhood Cause of Most Arab Problems," *Arab News*, November 28, 2002, http://www.arabnews.com/node/226291, accessed December 24, 2013.

32. Ibid.

33. Fürtig, *Iran's Rivalry*, 168.

34. Yehudit Ronen, "Sudan," in *Middle East Contemporary Survey*, vol. 14, 1990, ed. Ami Ayalon (Boulder, CO: Westview Press, 1992), 636.

35. Ibid.; Gabriel Warburg, *Islam, Sectarianism and Politics in Sudan since the Mahdiyya* (Madison: University of Wisconsin Press, 2003), 210.

36. Warburg, *Islam, Sectarianism and Politics in Sudan*, 210. See also Lesch, *Sudan*, 134.

37. Warburg, *Islam, Sectarianism, and Politics in Sudan*, 210.

38. Ibid.; Peter Woodward, "Islamic Radicals in Power," in *Political Islam, Radicalism, Revolution, or Reform*, ed. John Esposito (Boulder, CO: Lynne Rienner, 1997), 101. Plans for this fighting force came from within the NIF before Bashir took power: "Sudan Rebel Radio Calls New Sudanese Militia an 'Islamic Defense Force,'" *BBC Summary of World Broadcasts*, November 10, 1989.

39. Burr and Collins, *Revolutionary Sudan*, 17.

40. Abdel Sitar Amin Azz al-Din, Advisor to the Prime Minister, *Alaqat misr ma'a al-Sudan fi itar natharaha mustaqbaliyya shamila* [Egypt's relations with Sudan in a comprehensive future outlook], unpublished report submitted to Parliament, 1992, 52.

41. Lesch, *Sudan: Contested Identities*, 113.

42. Hassan al-Turabi, "Islam as a Pan-National Movement," *Royal Society of Arts Journal* (August/September 1992): 609.

43. This idea has come to mean patriotism or loyalty to a state as a territorial and political unit.

44. This is the term used by Abdel Wahab el-Affendi, *Turabi's Revolution: Islam and Power in the Sudan* (London: Grey Seal, 1991), 178.

45. Turabi, "Islam as a Pan-National Movement," 614.

46. Judith Miller, "Global Islamic Awakening or Sudanese Nightmare?" in *Spokesmen for the Despised: Fundamentalist Leaders of the Middle East*, ed. Scott Appleby (Chicago: University of Chicago Press, 1996), 194.

47. The popular belief is that a leader will arise in every century to revitalize Islam to defend the traditions (Sunna) of Islam and purify it against innovations (bid'a). See

R. Hrair Dekmejian, *Islam in Revolution* (Syracuse: Syracuse University Press, 1995), 60.

48. Ibid., 188.

49. Dekmejian characterizes Turabi as part of a Murshid type of Islamic leadership and Mohammed Ahmed al-Mahdi as Mahdist to illustrate some fundamental points about their leadership. However, he does not argue that these characteristics and categories are exclusive. Turabi advocated the role of *ijtihad* to revitalize and defend Islam. See Dekmejian's "Typologies of Islamist Leadership," in *Islam in Revolution*, 57–68.

50. Judith Miller, "Global Islamic Awakening or Sudanese Nightmare?" in *Spokesmen for the Despised: Fundamentalist Leaders of the Middle East*, ed. Scott Appleby (Chicago: University of Chicago Press, 1996), 198.

51. Madawi Al-Rasheed, *A History of Saudi Arabia* (Cambridge: Cambridge University Press, 2002), 164.

52. Al-Rasheed, *A History of Saudi Arabia*, 164.

53. Ibid., 167

54. Lawrence Wright, *The Looming Tower: Al-Qaeda and the Road to 9/11* (New York: Alfred A. Knopf, 2006), 179.

55. Bin Laden's fatwa is directly in response to the peace process but also mentions the betrayal in the Gulf war. See Bruce Lawrence, *Messages to the World: The Statement of Osama bin Laden* (New York: Verso, 2005).

56. Following a courtship period that began in 1990 when the government of Sudan sent a formal letter of invitation followed by a visit from Sudanese intelligence officers to discuss details. Wright, *Looming Tower*, 186.

57. The 9/11 Commission report claims Turabi urged Osama bin Laden to come to Sudan and bring his supporters to help fight the war in the South against Christian separatists and help with infrastructure projects (road building). In exchange, bin Laden would be able to use Sudan as a base for worldwide business operations and to wage jihad (see page 57 of the 9/11 Commission Report: http://www.9-11commission.gov/report/911Report.pdf). Many other accounts of Turabi's invitation occur later than when the 9/11 Commission claims. Saad al-Faqih, a major Saudi opposition leader in exile, does not believe bin Laden was involved at all with the war in the south. See Mahan Abedin, "The Essence of Al Qaeda: An Interview with Saad al-Faqih," *Spotlight on Terror*, 2:2, February 5, 2004; interview took place, January 23, 2004, http://www.jamestown.org/single/?no_cache=1&tx_ttnews[tt_news]=26273), accessed June 15, 2008.

58. Wright, *Looming Tower*, 187–191.

59. Thomas Hegghammer, *Jihad in Saudi Arabia* (Cambridge: Cambridge University Press, 2010).

60. "Sudan in Brief; INA Reports Saudi Envoy Summoned on 'Interference' in Sudanese Affairs," *BBC Summary of World Broadcasts, Iraqi News Agency in Arabic*, September 22, 1990.

61. Stephane Lacroix, *Awakening Islam* (Cambridge, MA: Harvard University Press, 2011), 173.

62. Ibid. It should be noted that conservative Sahwis attacked Turabi for his "rationalism." Lacroix mentions that Safar al-Hawali's dissertation contains attacks against Turabi, see endote 122 in *Awakening Islam*, 320.

63. Burr and Collins, *Revolutionary Sudan*, 27.

64. "Gadhafi Expected in Cairo to Restore Egyptian-Sudanese Link," *UPI*, July 1, 1991.

65. Youssef Ibrahim, "War in the Gulf: Egypt; Tensions Rise between Cairo and Pro-Iraqi Sudanese," *New York Times*, January 31, 1991, A18.

66. "Egyptian Authorities Report Discovery of 'Secret Iraqi Terrorist Scheme,'" *BBC Summary of World Broadcasts*, February 11, 1991.

67. Turabi reported that he traveled to Baghdad to secure the release of Islamic activists. Alan Cowell, "Confrontation in the Gulf: Islam's Influence Weighed Differently since Crisis," *New York Times*, October 4, 1990, A14.

68. Naturally, this ignores Saddam's brutal repression of its own Islamists. Many in the region attacked Turabi for his hypocrisy and tried to undermine his credibility this way.

69. Ann M. Lesch, "Contrasting Reactions to the Persian Gulf Crisis: Egypt, Syria, and the Palestinians," *Middle East Journal* 45:1 (Winter 1991): 30–50. See also James Piscatori, "Religion and Realpolitik: Islamic Responses to the Gulf War," in *Islamic Fundamentalisms and the Gulf Crisis*, ed. Piscatori (Chicago: American Academy of Arts and Sciences, 1992), 1–25.

70. "Sudanese Leader Concludes Visit to Iran," *BBC Summary of World Broadcasts*, December 14, 1990. But Burr and Collins claim that Ali Osman Mohamad Taha and Mahdi Ibrahim had secret meetings with President Hashemi Rafsanjani and the Iranian Minister of Interior before November 1989; see J. Millard Burr and Robert O. Collins, *Sudan in Turmoil: Hasan al-Turabi and the Islamist State* (Princeton, NJ: Markus Weiner, 2010), 32.

71. Iran promised oil and military hardware and Revolutionary guard officers. See Ronen, *Middle East Contemporary Survey, 1990*, 16:643.

72. Chris Hedges, "Sudan and Iran Smuggling Arms," *Guardian*, December 28, 1994.

73. See *Al-Wafd*, December 5, 1992. The source was the opposition.

74. Abdel Al-Sitar, *Egypt's Relations*, 42–54.

75. Youssef M. Ibrahim, "Cutting Back in Lebanon, Iran Is Shifting to Sudan," *New York Times*, December 13, 1991, A7.

76. Klaus Knorr, "Threat Perception," in *Historical Dimensions of National Security Problems*, ed. Knorr (Lawrence: University Press of Kansas, 1976).

77. Abdel al-Sitar, *Egypt's Relations*, 43.

78. Ibid., 49.

79. "Sudan's Leader Begins Visit to Iran and Says Sudan Can Learn from Iran's Example," *Voice of the Islamic Republic of Iran* (Tehran), *BBC Summary of World Broadcasts*, December 12, 1990.

80. Ibid.

81. Ronen, *Middle East Contemporary Survey, 1990,* 16: 644.

82. "Al-Akhbar Editorial Denounces Sudanese Regime," *Foreign Broadcast Information Service,* Near East Section-92–237, December 9, 1992.

83. Burr and Collins, *Revolutionary Sudan,* 32. However, the Sudanese delegation was also cautious not to go into too much depth about their own (Sunni) beliefs because they might offend their Shi'a hosts.

84. John Calabrese, *Revolutionary Horizons* (New York: St. Martin's Press, 1994), 158. Calabrese also notes that the Egyptian paper *al-Wafd* reported 10,000 Iranian soldiers.

85. Secular terrorist organizations also had offices in Sudan, including Abu Nidal. Some of the religious terrorist organizations included: al-Qaeda, Abu Nidal Organization, Hizballah, Palestine Islamic Jihad, Egyptian Al-Jihad, Egyptian Islamic Group, Hamas, Armed Islamic Group (Algeria).

86. Ann Mosley Lesch, "Osama bin Laden's 'Business' in Sudan," *Current History* 101, no. 655 (May 2002): 203.

87. "Sudan in Brief; Egyptian Concern over Reported Fundamentalist Training in Sudan," *BBC Summary of World Broadcasts,* May 4, 1990.

88. Ambassador General Basem Abdel Aziz, interview with author, Cairo, Egypt, December 13, 2007.

89. Nahman Tal, *Radical Islam in Egypt and Jordan* (Portland: Sussex Academic Press, 2005), 142.

90. Ronen, "Sudan," 272.

91. Ambassador General Basem Abdel Aziz, interview with author, Cairo, Egypt, December 13, 2007.

92. "Alfi Says Muslim Brotherhood Has Links with Turabi and 'Terrorist Groups' Abroad," *BBC Summary of World Broadcasts,* August 29, 1995.

93. Publicity surrounding Egypt's denial to allow them to attend a PAIC conference exposed the connection. It is unclear to what extent the Muslim Brotherhood as a whole looked to Sudan as a model and Turabi as a leader, but mostly likely, their attitude was not the same as the way Egyptian officials attempted to portray it. While the Brotherhood shares similar goals, the offshoot of the Brotherhood, the NIF, was the first to establish a Sunni version of an Islamic state. There were a few possibilities for their differences. First, toward the middle or late 1990s, many Islamists increasingly resented Turabi's claim of leadership. The Egyptian Muslim Brotherhood, with its own long history, clearly did not see Turabi as its leader. Second, the Egyptian Brotherhood did not see Sudan and the NIF, with its violent rebellion and economic malaise, as a shining example of an Islamic state. Third, after the assassination attempt on Mubarak many more were likely opposed to such a violent action, even if they harbored extreme ill will. Fourth, Salafi trends in the Egyptian Brotherhood likely opposed Turabi's progressive stand on women's issues. Despite the fact that Turabi came from the Sudanese Muslim Brotherhood, there had been historic tensions between the two branches for some time.

94. Hesham al-Awadi, *In Pursuit of Legitimacy: The Muslim Brothers and Mubarak*, 112.

95. Gabriel Warburg, "The Muslim Brotherhood in Sudan: From Reforms to Radicalism" (August 2006), http://www.e-prism.org/images/Muslim_BROTHERS. PRISM.pdf, accessed December 24, 2013.

96. Turabi borrowed the name of the PAIC from the Iraqi People's Islamic Conference, when the latter had ceased to function, taking advantage of the sympathy for Saddam Hussein in the Muslim world during the Gulf Crisis. Gilles Kepel, *Jihad: Trail of Political Islam* (Cambridge, MA: Harvard University Press, 2002), 211.

97. Kepel, *Jihad*, 211–212.

98. Ibid.

99. Anonymous, *Through Our Enemies' Eyes: Osama Bin Laden, Radical Islam, and the Future of America* (Washington, DC: Bracey's, 2002), 129. The author is Michael Scheuer.

100. Burr and Collins, *Revolutionary Sudan*, 57. Yossef Bodansky details one such operation in "'The Mubarak Assassination Attempt Takes the Islamists' War to Centre Stage," *Defense and Foreign Affairs' Strategic Policy* (July/August 1995).

101. Burr and Collins, *Revolutionary Sudan*, 57.

102. "Islamic Mediator," *The Economist*, December 11, 1993, 48.

103. J. Miller, "Global Islamic Awakening or Sudanese Nightmare," 199.

104. "Alfi Says Muslim Brotherhood Has Links with Turabi and 'Terrorist Groups' Abroad," *BBC Summary of World Broadcasts*, August 29, 1995.

105. Ibid.

106. Ibid.

107. "Egypt Says Sudan Mediating between Rival Egyptian Radicals," *UPI*, August 27, 1995.

108. Former Egyptian Ambassador for Africa Affairs, interview with author, Cairo, Egypt, April 10, 2008. A good example of the state's use of the media is an article titled "'The Cloak and Dagger Policy in Sudan: Where To?" by Samir Rajab, the chief editor of the pro-regime paper, *Mayu*. He says no one supports Turabi and his leadership has destroyed the country. See "Egyptian Newspaper Editor Accuses Sudan of Support for Terrorism," *BBC Summary of World Broadcasts*, September 1, 1994.

109. This is referred to as Eudaemonic legitimacy, meaning legitimacy of rule based on the leader's ability to increase the flow of goods to the consumer. See al-Awadi, *In Search of Legitimacy*, 9–10.

110. Jalal Du'edar, "The Jackal and the Wolf's Greed" (in Arabic), *Al-Akhbar*, August 30, 1992.

111. "Mubarak, Military Discuss 'Alternatives,'" *UPI*, July 22, 1995.

112. Mamoun Fandy, *Saudi Arabia and the Politics of Dissent* (New York: St. Martin's Press, 1999), 102.

113. Lacroix, *Awakening Islam*, 161.

114. Ibid.

115. Ibid.

116. In an article published many years later, "What Is between al-Qusaibi and al-Turabi: The Tempest Blew Twice," the author criticizes both al-Qusaibi and al-Turabi for different reasons and reconfirms a few important things about how the Saudi regime viewed Turabi. See Mashari al-Dha'edi, "Ma bayna al-Qusaibi wal Turabi: al-'asifa tahib maratein," *Asharq Al-Awsat*, March 28, 2006, http://www.aawsat.com/leader.asp?section=3&article=355310&issueno=9982, accessed June 1, 2008.

117. Abdullah Hamudha, "al-Gama'a al-Islamiyya al-Misriyya tatabana muhawilah arghtiyal mubarak" (Egyptian Islamic group claims responsibility for the assassination attempt on Mubarak), *Al-Sharq Al-Awsat*, July 5, 1995.

118. "Reaction to Border Incidents; Sudan's Interior Ministry Says Egyptian Attack Part of 'Conspiracy' against Sudan," *BBC Summary of World Broadcasts*, July 1, 1995.

119. "Misr Tahdhur al-Turabi" [Egypt warns Turabi], *Asharq Al-Awsat*, July 3, 1995.

120. See *Asharq al-Awsat*, July 6, 1995.

121. Ibid.

122. Ibid.

123. James Piscatori, "The Rushdie Affair and the Politics of Ambiguity," *International Affairs* 66, no. 4 (1990): 773–774.

124. Lesch, *Contested Identities*, 119.

125. Ronen, *Middle East Contemporary Survey* (1995), 91. "Turabi Accuses Garang of Attempting to Damage Relations with Egypt," *BBC Summary of World Broadcasts*, December 16, 1997.

126. "Turabi Accuses Garang of Attempting to Damage Relations with Egypt," *BBC Summary of World Broadcasts*, December 16, 1997.

127. "Egyptian Foreign Minister Says His Country Opposed to Partitioning of Sudan," *BBC Summary of World Broadcasts*, February 5, 1997.

128. Susan Severeid, "Sudan Coup May End Turabi's Dream," *Associated Press Online*, December 15, 1999. See also Karl Vick, "Sudanese Leader Moves against Rival; Bashir Dissolves Parliament, Dismisses Former Mentor Who Challenged Him," *Washington Post*, December 15, 1999.

129. "President Bashir Leaves for Saudi Arabia to Perform Hajj," *BBC Summary of World Broadcasts*, April 26, 1996.

130. "Sudan Hails Saudi Leadership Role in Promoting Islam," *Agence France Presse*, December 1, 1996. The Originalization department was the body in charge of Islamization. I have carried the literal translation that is found in other English sources. The name of the new presidential adviser was former Minister of Higher Education and Scientific Research Dr. Ibrahim Ahmad Umar.

131. "Egypt, Saudi Arabia Opposed to Division of Sudan," *Agence France Presse*, January 25, 1997.

132. Ibid.

133. Mohamed Hassanein Heikal, "Egyptian Foreign Policy," *Foreign Affairs* (July 1978): 714–727.

134. US Embassy Official, interview with author, Cairo, Egypt, December 23, 2008. The reason why Egypt does care about having a non-hostile government in Khartoum and avoiding a scenario of partition was not that they were about diversion as an existential threat, but that it would be more costly for the state.

135. Kepel, *Jihad*, 184.

136. Sitar, *Egypt's Relations*, 26.

137. John Esposito, *Islam and Politics* (Syracuse: Syracuse University Press, 1984), 236.

138. "Army Lines Up behind Islamisation in Sudan," *Arabia* 33 (May 1984): 22–24.

139. In the end, the parliament suspended the vote. See "On the Road to an Islamic Republic," *Africa Now* (October 1984): 87.

140. Former Egyptian Ambassador and Director of Africa Affairs, interview with author, Cairo, Egypt, April 10, 2008.

141. The security services were aware of a proposed ceasefire by the Islamic Group by at least 1996 and the nonviolence initiative was announced in 1997 and later signed by the historic leadership in 1999. See Lisa Blaydes and Lawrence Rubin, "Ideological Reorientation and Counter Terrorism: Confronting Militant Islam in Egypt," *Terrorism and Political Violence* 20, no. 4 (Fall 2008): 461–479.

Chapter 5

1. John Kifner, "Amid Frenzy, Iranians Bury the Ayatollah," *New York Times*, July 7, 1989.

2. Bruce Maddy-Weitzman, "Inter-Arab Relations," in *Middle East Contemporary Survey*, vol. 16, *1992*, ed. Ami Ayalon (Boulder, CO: Westview Press, 1995), 165.

3. Ibid.

4. Ibid.

5. David Hurst, "Mullahs Take to the Warpath in a New Campaign of Terror," *The Guardian*, November 28, 1992.

6. See Jalal Du'edar, "The Jackal and Wolf's Ambitions," *al-Akhbar*, August 30, 1992. The author opines that Iran's takeover of Abu Tunbs is part of a slow takeover of Arab lands under the veil of Islam (author's translation).

7. Jeremy Sharp, "Egypt–United States Relations," *Congress Research Service Report for Congress*, updated June 15, 2005, 4.

8. "Iran la yurid salaam" [Iran doesn't want peace], *Al-Jumhuriyya*, March 11, 1993, 3.

9. Ibid.

10. See Tareq Ismael, *The U.A.R. and Africa* (1971), 26.

11. "Al-Akhbar Editorial Denounces Sudanese Regime," *Foreign Broadcast Information Service*, NES-92-237, Dec. 9,1992.

12. Abdel Sitar Amin Azz al-Din, Advisor to the Prime Minister, *Alaqat misr ma'a al-Sudan fi itar natharaha mustaqbaliyya shamila* [Egypt's relations with Sudan in a comprehensive outlook], unpublished report submitted to Parliament, 1992, 43 (author's translation).

13. Abdel al-Sitar, *Egypt's Relations*, 43.

14. Nafee quoted in Youssef M. Ibrahim, "Anxious Arabs Accuse Iran," *New York Times*, December 21, 1992.

15. Ibid.

16. Joseph Bodensky, "Egyptians Claim Iran Link with Arrested Terrorists," *Defense and Foreign Affairs' Strategy Policy*, October 31, 1996.

17. "Fadlallah Criticizes Egypt's Anti-Shiite Campaign," *Foreign Broadcast Information Service TOT-97-001-L*, April 14, 1996.

18. John Kifner, "Final Tirade Heard as Throngs Mourn Khomeini," *New York Times*, June 6, 1989, http://www.nytimes.com/1989/06/06/world/final-tirade-heard-as-throngs-mourn-khomeini.html, accessed January 3, 2014.

19. Christopher Walker, "Arab Moderates Are Attacked in Bitter Khomeini Testament; Death of Ayatollah Khomeini," *The Times (London)*, June 6, 1989.

20. Anoushiravan Ehtehshami, *After Khomeini* (New York: Routledge, 1995), 145.

21. Dr. Hassan Al-Ansari, Editor-in-Chief of the *Qatar Tribune* and Advisor Amiri Diwan, interview with author, Abu Dhabi, U.A.E., April 1, 2008.

22. Joshua Teitelbaum, "Saudi Arabia," in *Middle East Contemporary Survey*, vol. 22, *1998*, ed. Bruce Maddy-Weitzman (Boulder, CO: Westview Press, 2001), 22: 529. The Comprehensive Cooperation Agreement of May 1998 dealt with economics, culture, and sports.

23. Ehtehshami, *After Khomeini*, 145.

24. Ibid.

25. Reinhard Schulze, "Forgotten Honor of Islam," in *Middle East Contemporary Survey*, vol. 13, *1989*, ed. Ami Ayalon (Boulder, CO: Westview Press, 1991), 13:175.

26. Ibid., 13:179.

27. Ibid. Schulze claims that in the Saudi media, the Rushdie affair disappeared despite the fact that it was brought up at the beginning of the conference.

28. Ibid., 13:177.

29. Ibid., 13:179. Iran boycotted ICO in Kuwait in 1987 and sent a foreign ministry official instead of the foreign minister in 1988.

30. Dr. Hassan Al-Ansari, Editor-in-Chief of the *Qatar Tribune* and Advisor Amiri Diwan, interview with author, Abu Dhabi, UAE, April 1, 2008. The official motivation for establishing this regime was to enhance Islamic values and cooperation. See OIC's charter: http://www.oic-oci.org/is11/english/Charter-en.pdf, accessed September 1, 2012.

31. Furtig, *Iran's Rivalry with Saudi Arabia*, 226.

32. Martin Kramer, "The Global Village of Islam," *Middle East Contemporary Survey* 16 (1992): 202.

33. Furtig, *Iran's Rivalry with Saudi Arabia*, 226; John Calabrese, *Revolutionary Horizons: Regional Foreign Policy in Post-Khomeini Iran* (London: St. Martins, 19941), 64.

34. Dr. Hassan Al-Ansari (Editor-in-Chief, *Qatar Tribune* and Advisor Amiri Diwan), interview with author, Abu Dhabi, UAE, April 1, 2008.

35. Shahram Chubin and Charles Tripp, *Iran-Saudi Arabia Relations and Regional Order*, Adelphi Paper 304 (London: Oxford University Press, 1996), 58.

36. "Madrid Conference Great Injustice, Iran's Khamanei Says," *Japan Economic Newswire*, October 30, 1991.

37. "Iran Mohtashemi Says the Blood of Madrid Participants 'Must be Shed,'" *BBC World News Service*, October 30, 1991.

38. Chubin and Tripp, *Iran-Saudi Arabia Relations*, 58.

39. Kramer, "Global Village of Islam," 203.

40. Chubin and Tripp, *Iran-Saudi Arabia Relations*, 59.

41. Ibid., 60.

42. Ibid.

43. Esther Webman, "Islamic Politics-Between Dialogue and Conflict," in *Middle East Contemporary Survey*, vol.29 1995 ed. Bruce Maddy-Weitzman (Boulder, CO: Westview Press, 1997), 123.

44. Ibid.

45. The origins of this movement and Saudi Islamism more generally can be traced to the immigration of Muslim Brotherhood refugees escaping from Arab republics such as Egypt and Syria during the 1950s and 1960s. The religious activism in the 1970s and 1980s on Saudi campuses brought this movement to life as a political force. See Kepel, *Jihad*, 23–80.

46. Stephane Lacroix, *Awakening Islam*, 3. Other categories of individuals who played a role in the Sahwi protest movement were some traditional Wahhabi *ulama* from the religious establishment and Sahwi intellectuals. See Lacroix, *Awakening Islam*, 165–175.

47. The first petition, signed by a number of prominent clerics and intellectuals, was issued in May 1991 as a letter to the King that sought to influence the King's decision about political reform, affect public opinion, and counter liberals' political demands. In September 1992, Islamists took a more defiant step and criticized the government's domestic and foreign policies in a letter to Sheikh Ibn Baz titled "The Memorandum of Advice." See Richard Dekmejian, "The Rise of Saudi Islamism," *Middle East Journal* (1994) 631–632.

48. Lacroix, *Awakening Islam*, 164.

49. Ibid., 167

50. Ibid.

51. Ibid., 211–225.

52. The Iranian-sponsored publication *Risalat al-Haramain*, published in Beirut from 1990 to 1995 in Arabic, is an example. This journal overtly appeals to Shi'a sympathies but also attacks the regime as being dominated by Najdi instead of Hedjazi

identity. The articles also attack the regime with the common themes of Wahhabi dominance of the holy sites and its corrupt friendship with the United States and Israel.

53. LaCroix, *Awakening Islam*, 173.

54. "Egypt: Cairo Paper on 'Significant Change in Iranian Policy,'" *Daily Report*, December 16, 1997, FBIS-NES-97–350.

55. "Egypt Iran Official on Arab Ties, Iran's Missiles," Cairo MENA, August 4, 1998, FBIS-NES-98–217.

56. "Iran and Saudi Arabia: The Best of Buddies," *The Economist*, April 4, 1998, 52. *The Economist* takes a cautious view to not see this event as a major breakthrough.

57. Osama el Baz ruled out a return of Egyptian-Iranian relations in the near future; see "Egypt's al-Baz on Ties with Iran, Sudan, Israel," Cairo MENA, July 20, 1999, FBIS-NES-1999–0720.

58. Interview with Dr. Mohammed Abdel Salam, Al-Ahram Center for Strategic Studies, Cairo, Egypt, December 23, 2008.

59. Gause, *International Relations of the Persian Gulf*, 183.

60. WIKILEAKS, http://www.nytimes.com/interactive/2010/11/28/world/20101128–cables-viewer.html#report/egypt-09CAIRO604.

61. Author interviews with Saudi officials, July 2006, Washington, DC.

62. In King Abdullah's most famous statement just before the first Iraqi elections, he claimed "a Shiite crescent" extending from Iran to Lebanon could "alter the traditional balance of power between the two main Islamic sects, and pose new challenges to U.S. interests and allies." Robin Wright and Peter Baker, "Iraq, Jordan See Threat to Election From Iran," *Washington Post*, December 8, 2004, A1.

63. Media Advisor to HRH Prince Turki al-Faisal, in discussion with the author, Washington, DC, July 2006.

64. Transcript in Arabic: http://www.alarabiya.net/Articles/2006/04/08/22686.htm#, accessed August 15, 2007.

65. Interview with President Hosni Mubarak, *al-Musawwar*, No. 4251, March 30, 2006, 5. One can point to the constant reference of preserving the "Arab character of Iraq" when Arab League representatives talk about Iraq around the time of the first Iraqi elections. See also news reports such as "Aruba fi khatar" [Arabism in Danger], *Al-Sharq Al-Awsat*, December 23, 2004, http://www.asharqalawsat.com/default.asp?myday=23&mymonth=12&myyear=2004&goSearch2.x=18&goSearch2.y=9. See also *Al-Ahram*, December 23, 2004.

66. "Palestinian PM Says Iran Pledges $250 Million in Aid," *Reuters*, December 11, 2006; http://uk.reuters.com/article/2006/12/11/us-iran-palestinians-aid-idUKL1123249320061211.

67. Michael Slackman, "Iran Gives Hamas Enthusiastic Support but Discreetly Just in Case," *New York Times*, January 12, 2009.

68. Abigail Hauslohner, "In the Siege of Gaza, Egypt Walks a Delicate Line," *Time*, January 11, 2010.

69. Ibid.

70. "Ahmadinejad's Letter to Saudi Arabia," January 15, 2009, http://edition. presstv.ir/detail/82432.html, accessed September 15, 2013.

71. Slackman, "Iran Gives Hamas Enthusiastic Support," A10.

72. Lawrence Pintak, "Arab Media Wars," *Columbia Journalism Review*, January 23, 2009, http://www.cjr.org/campaign_desk/arab_media_wars.php?page=all, accessed June 1, 2010; Wayne Hunt, "The Gaza War, Theater, and the Big Interview," *Arab Media and Society* 10 (Spring 2010), http://www.arabmediasociety.com/index. php?article=742&printarticle, accessed December 24, 2013; Ian Black, "Al-Jazeera Sees of Satellite Rivals," *The Guardian*, December 30, 2008, http://www.guardian. co.uk/world/2008/dec/31/israelandthepalestinians-middleeast1, accessed December 1, 2013.

73. Tareq al-Homayed, *Asharq al-Awsat*, 2006.

74. Thomas Erdbrink, "Hamas Leader Thanks Iran for Support during Regional Tour," *Washington Post*, February 3, 2009, A10.

75. Hassan M. Fatah, "Militia Rebuked by Some Arab Countries," *New York Times*, July 17, 2006, http://www.nytimes.com/2006/07/17/world/middleeast/17arab. html?_r=2&oref=slogin.

76. Faiza Saleh Ambah, "Arab Leaders, Unlike Much of Public, Uneasy about Hezbollah," *Washington Post*, July 24, 2006, A12.

77. Issued July 14, 2006, the official statement can be found here, http://www.spa. gov.sa/English/details.php?id=375383.

78. Fatah, "Militia Rebuked by Some Arab Countries."

79. Ambah, "Arab Leaders, Unlike Much of Public, Uneasy About Hezbollah."

80. Ibid.

81. See Dan Murphy, "In War's Dust, a New Arab 'Lion' Emerges: Hizballah's Nasrallah Is Hailed as a Regional Hero," *Christian Science Monitor*, August 29, 2006; Rachel Shabi, "Palestinians See Nasrallah as New Hero," August 13, 2006, http://www. aljazeera.com/archive/2006/08/2008410163335528724.html, accessed June 15, 2013; Khaled Abu Toameh, "Hizballah 'Victory' Boosts Extremists," *Jerusalem Post*, August 13, 2006.

82. "Egypt: Muslim Brotherhood Guide Slams Arab Leaders, Calls for Israel's Expulsion," Asharq Al-Awsat, August 21, 2006, http://www.aawsat.net/2006/08/article55265579, accessed December 25, 2013.

83. Murphy, "In War's Dust." See Arab Opinion Polls conducted by Zogby International and Professor Shibley Telhami,. specifically 2002, 2004, 2005, 2006, 2010.

84. Andrew McGregor, "Support for Hezbollah in Egypt Threatens Mubarak's Stability," *Terrorism Focus* 3, no. 34, September 7, 2006, http://www.jamestown.org/ single/?no_cache=1&tx_ttnews[tt_news]=888, accessed September 1, 2012.

85. See "After Threats of Shi'a Proselytizing in Arab Capitals . . . Sunni-Shi'a Clashes at the Cairo International Book Exhibition" (in Arabic), January 31, 2007, http://www.almesryoon.com/ShowDetails.asp?NewID=29893&Page=1, accessed August 1, 2008.

86. See *al-Hayat*, January 1, 2007, http://www.daralhayat.com/arab_news/01–2007/Item-20070121–46330ade-c0a8–10ed-009d-421b1b652f38/story.html, accessed August 1, 2007.

87. Abdullah Kamal, "Egypt's Anesthetization" (in Arabic), *Ruz Al-Yusuf*, December 12, 2006.

88. Egyptian foreign policy adviser and academic, in discussion with the author, Cairo, Egypt, December 19, 2008.

89. Dr. Christian Koch (Director of International Studies, Gulf Research Center), interview with author, Dubai, UAE, April 2, 2008. See also Syad Qamar Hasan, "GCC Calls for a Nuclear Free Middle East," *Arab News*, December 20, 2005, http://www.arabnews.com/node/277642 accessed April 1, 2014.

90. "Egypt Unveils Nuclear Power Plan," BBC, September 25, 2006, http://news.bbc.co.uk/2/hi/middle_east/5376860.stm, accessed August 1, 2008; Michael Slackman and Mona El-Naggar, "Mubarak's Son Proposes Nuclear Program," *New York Times*, September 20, 2006, A14.

91. Chemi Shalev, "Saudi King Vowed to Obtain Nuclear Bomb after Iran," *Haaretz*, May 30, 2012, http://www.haaretz.com/news/diplomacy-defense/dennis-ross-saudi-king-vowed-to-obtain-nuclear-bomb-after-iran-1.433294, accessed September 15, 2013.

92. Senior diplomat, Embassy of Saudi Arabia, in discussion with the author, Washington, DC, July 2006.

93. The extent of Iranian involvement beyond diplomatic support is unclear.

94. F. Gregory Gause III, "Saudi Arabia: Iraq, Iran, the Regional Balance of Power, and the Sectarian Question," *Strategic Insights* 6, no. 2 (March 2007), https://www.hsdl.org/?view&did=471343, accessed December 26, 2013.

95. Anoushiravan Ehteshami, *After Khomeini: The Iranian Second Republic* (New York: Routledge, 1995), 145. Ehteshami argues the turning point was 1988 because of the string of Iranian military defeats and the acceptance of the ceasefire to end the Iran-Iraq War.

Chapter 6

1. F. Gregory Gause III, "Why Middle East Studies Missed the Arab Spring: The Myth of Authoritarian Stability," *Foreign Affairs* 90, no. 4 (2011): 81–90.

2. Marc Lynch, *The Arab Uprisings* (New York: Public Affairs, 2012), 7.

3. Marina Ottaway and Marwan Muasher, "Arab Monarchies: Chance for Reform, Yet Unmet," Carnegie Papers, Middle East December 2011, http://carnegieendowment.org/files/arab_monarchies1.pdf, accessed December 25, 2013. For an explanation of why Arab monarchies fared better, see F. Gregory Gause III and Sean Yom, Resilient Royalties: How Arab Monarchies Hang On," *Journal of Democracy* (October 2012): 74–78.

4. Meris Lutz, "Iran's Supreme Leader Calls Uprising an 'Islamic Awakening,'" *Los Angeles Times*, February 4, 2011, http://articles.latimes.com/2011/feb/04/world/la-fg-khamenei-iran-egypt-20110205, accessed March 1, 2013.

5. Jason Burke, "Al-Qaeda Leaders Welcome Arab Uprisings, Cleric Says," *The Guardian*, March 13, 2011, http://www.theguardian.com/world/2011/mar/31/alqaida-leaders-welcome-arab-uprisings, accessed December 25, 2013.

6. Jonathan Lis, "Netanyahu: Egypt Could Fall into Hands of Radical Islamists," *Haaretz*, February 7, 2011. For a good overview, see Daniel Byman, "Israel's Pessimistic View of the Arab Spring," *Washington Quarterly* (Summer 2011): 123–136, http://csis.org/files/publication/twq11summerbyman.pdf.

7. "Saudi King Expresses Support for Mubarak," Reuters, January 29, 2011, http://www.reuters.com/article/2011/01/29/idININDia-54501220110129, accessed December 25, 2013.

8. Ethan Bronner and Michael Slackman, "Saudi Troops Enter Bahrain to Help Put Down Unrest," *New York Times*, March 14, 2011, http://www.nytimes.com/2011/03/15/world/middleeast/15bahrain.html?pagewanted=all&_r=0, accessed December 25, 2013.

9. Glen Carey, "Saudi King Counters Dissent with $36 Billion as Clerics Scold Protesters," *Bloomberg News*, March 11, 2011, http://www.bloomberg.com/news/2011–03–11/saudi-king-counters-protests-with-36–billion-as-tension-mounts.html, accessed December 25, 2013.

10. Ulf Laessing and Jason Benham, "Analysis: Saudi Rulers Aid Allies against Iran, Arab Revolts," *Reuters*, June 2, 2011, http://www.reuters.com/article/2011/06/02/us-saudi-mideast-idUSTRE7512LP20110602, accessed December 25, 2013.

11. Sara Hamdan "Gulf Council Reaches Out to Morocco and Jordan," *New York Times*, May 25, 2011.

12. Adam Makary, "Shoes Hurled at Iranian President Ahmadinejad during Trip to Cairo," February 7, 2013, http://www.cnn.com/2013/02/06/world/meast/egypt-ahmadinejad-shoe-attack, accessed December 25, 2013.

13. "Dubai Police Chief Warns of Muslim Brotherhood Threat," *Reuters*, July 26, 2012, http://www.reuters.com/article/2012/07/26/us-emirates-police-brotherhood-idUSBRE86P10420120726, accessed September 15, 2013.

14. Ibid.

15. Abdel Bari Atwan, "The War on the Muslim Brotherhood Divides the Gulf," January 16, 2013, see http://www.middleeastmonitor.com/articles/middle-east/5007–the-war-on-the-muslim-brotherhood-divides-the-gulf, accessed December 25, 2013.

16. David Hearst, "Why Saudi Arabia Is Taking a Risk by Backing the Egyptian Coup," *The Guardian*, August 20, 2013, http://www.theguardian.com/commentis-free/2013/aug/20/saudi-arabia-coup-egypt, accessed December 25, 2013.

17. Tariq Almohayed, "Opinion: King Abdullah's Egypt Speech Was Like a Surgeon's Scalpel," *Asharq Al-Awsat*, August 19, 2013, http://www.aawsat.net/2013/08/article55314019, accessed December 25, 2013. The Arabic version appeared under a different title but with the same content.

18. Shibley Telhami, "The 2011 Arab Public Opinion Poll," Brookings Report, November 11, 2011, http://www.brookings.edu/research/reports/2011/11/21–arab-public-opinion-telhami, accessed December 25, 2013.

19. Hugh Pope, "Erdogan's Decade," *Cairo Review of Global Affairs*, http://www.aucegypt.edu/gapp/cairoreview/pages/articleDetails.aspx?aid=149, accessed January 3, 2014.

20. Author Interview with U.S. State Department official, December 18, 2008, Cairo, Egypt.

21. "A Talk with the Ennahda Movement's Rachid Ghannouchi," December 26, 2011, *Asharq Al-Awsat*, http://www.aawsat.net/2011/12/article55243841, accessed December 25, 2013.

22. Pietr Zalewski, "Egypt Turkish Democratic Model Loses Favour," *The National*, December 8, 2011, http://www.thenational.ae/news/world/europe/egypt-turkish-democratic-model-loses-favour, August 15, 2013. For more indications of a decline, see Alastair Macdonald and Tarek Amara, "Erdogan: From 'Rock Star' to Mixed Reviews from Arabs," Reuters, June 12, 2013, http://www.reuters.com/article/2013/06/12/us-turkey-protests-arabs-idUSBRE95B17L20130612, accessed August 15, 2013.

23. An article in *Asharq Al-Awsat* (Arabic) discussed the wording here, http://aawsat.com/details.asp?section=4&issueno=11979&article=640456&feature=#.UiS-5NryE690, accessed December 25, 2013. For the argument that it was misunderstood (or misinterpreted), see Cumali Onal, "Muslim Brotherhood Did Not Understand Erdogan's Message on Secularism," *Today's Zaman*, November 6, 2011, http://www.todayszaman.com/columnists-261991–muslim-brotherhood-did-not-understand-erdogans-message-on-secularism.html, accessed January 3, 2014.

24. "Egypt's Muslim Brotherhood Criticizes Erdogan's Call for a Secular State," *Al Arabiya News*, September 14, 2011, http://www.alarabiya.net/articles/2011/09/14/166814.html, accessed December 25, 2013; "Egypt's Islamists Warn Turkish PM over Regional Role," Reuters, September 14, 2011, http://www.reuters.com/article/2011/09/14/us-turkey-egypt-idUSTRE78D2TD20110914, accessed January 2, 2014.

25. "Turkey's Erdogan Says Morsi Is 'My President' in Egypt," July 14, 2013, *Daily News Egypt*, http://www.dailynewsegypt.com/2013/07/14/turkeys-erdogan-says-morsi-my-president-in-egypt/ accessed January 3, 2014.

26. "Turkey's Erdogan Sees Israel's Hand in Egyptian Overthrow," Reuters, August 20, 2013, http://www.reuters.com/article/2013/08/20/us-turkey-egypt-israel-idUSBRE97J0IK20130820, accessed January 3, 2014.

27. Author interviews with Yemeni government officials and analysts, June–August 2004, Sanaa, Yemen.

28. For how this type is a contribution to realism, see F. Gregory Gause III, "Balancing What? Threat Perception and Alliance Choice in the Gulf," *Security Studies* 13, no. 2 (Winter 2003/2004): 275.

Bibliography

Al-Awadi, Hesham. *In Pursuit of Legitimacy: The Muslim Brothers and Mubarak, 1982–2000*. New York: Tauris Academic Studies, 2004.

al-Din, Abdel Sitar Amin Azz. *Alaqat Misr Ma'a Al-Sudan Fi Itar Natharaha Mustaqbaliyya Shamila*. Cairo: n.p., 1992.

al-Duri, Abd al-Aziz. *Al-Alaqat Al-Arabiyah Al-Iraniyah: Al-Itijahat Al-Rahinah Wa-Afaq Al-Mustaqbal*. Beirut: Markaz Dirasat al-Waḥdah al-Arabiyah, 1996.

Al-Rasheed, Madawi. *Contesting the Saudi State: Islamic Voices from a New Generation*. Boston: Cambridge University Press, 2007.

———. *A History of Saudi Arabia*. Boston: Cambridge University Press, 2002.

al-Qusaibi, Ghazi Abdel Rahman. *Hatta La Takuna Fitnah: Majmu'at Rasail*, 1991.

Anderson, Benedict. *Imagined Communities*. New York: Verso, 1983.

Anonymous (Michael Scheuer). *Through Our Enemies' Eyes: Osama Bin Laden, Radical Islam, and the Future of America*. Washington, DC: Brassey's, 2002.

Appleby, Scott. *Spokesmen for the Despised: Fundamentalist Leaders of the Middle East*. Chicago: University of Chicago Press, 1997.

Ayoob, Mohammed. "National-Security in the Third-World: The Management of Internal and External Threats." *World Politics* 43, no. 2 (1991): 257–283.

———. "Unraveling the Concept: National Secuirty in the Third World." In *The Many Faces of National Security in the Arab World*. Ed. Bahgat Korany, Paul Noble, and Rex Brynen. New York: St. Martin's Press, 1993.

Badeeb, Saeed M. *Saudi-Iranian Relations 1932–1982*. London: Center for Arab and Iranian Studies, 1993.

Barnett, Michael. *Dialogues in Arab Politics: Negotiations in Regional Order*. New York: Columbia University Press, 1998.

———. "Identity and Alliances in the Middle East." In *The Culture of National Security:*

Norms and Identity in World Politics, ed. Peter Katzenstein. New York: Columbia University Press, 1996.

Barnett, Michael, and Raymond Duvall. "Power in International Politics." *International Organization* 59, no. 1 (2005): 39–75.

Benford, Robert. "Frame Disputes within the Nuclear Disarmament Movement." *Social Forces* 71 (1992): 677.

Benford, Robert, and David Snow. "Framing Processes and Social Movements: An Overview and Assessment." *Annual Review of Sociology* 26, no. 1 (2000): 611–639.

Bianchi, Robert. *Unruly Corporatism: Associational Life in 20th Century Egypt* New York: Oxford University Press, 1994. Print.

Binder, Leonard. *Ethnic Conflict and International Politics in the Middle East.* Gainesville: University Press of Florida, 1999.

———. *Islamic Liberalism: A Critique of Development Ideologies.* Chicago: University Of Chicago Press, 1988.

———. "The Middle East as a Subordinate International System." *World Politics: A Quarterly Journal of International Relations* 10, no. 3 (1958): 408–429.

Blaydes, Lisa. *Elections and Distributive Politics in Mubarak's Egypt.* New York: Cambridge University Press, 2011.

Blaydes, Lisa, and Lawrence Rubin. "Ideological Reorientation and Counterterrorism: Confronting Militant Islam in Egypt." *Terrorism and Political Violence* 20, no. 4 (2008): 461–479.

Bloom, Mia. *Dying to Kill: The Allure of Suicide Terror.* New York: Columbia University Press, 2007.

Brown, Carl L. *Religion and State: The Muslim Approach to Politics.* New York: Columbia University Press, 2000.

Brynen, Rex, and Bassel F. Salloukh. "Pondering Permeability." In *Persistent Permeability? Regionalism, Localism, and Globalization in the Middle East*, ed. Rex Brynen and Bassel F. Salloukh. London: Ashgate, 2004.

Boulding, Kenneth E. *Conflict and Defense: A General Theory.* New York: Harper, 1962.

Buchan, James. "Secular and Religious Opposition in Saudi Arabia." In *State, Society and Economy in Saudi Arabia*, ed. Tim Niblock. New York: St. Martin's, 1982.

Burr, Milton, and Robert Collins. *Revolutionary Sudan: Hasan Al-Turabi and the Islamist State, 1989–2000.* Leiden: Brill, 2003.

Buzan, Barry, and Ole Wæver. *Regions and Powers: The Structure of International Security.* Cambridge Studies in International Relations 91. New York: Cambridge University Press, 2003.

Buzan, Barry, Ole Wæver, and Jaap de Wilde. *Security: A New Framework for Analysis.* Boulder, CO: Lynne Rienner, 1998.

Byman, Daniel. "Israel's Pessimistic View of the Arab Spring." *Washington Quarterly* (2011): 123–136.

Calabrese, John. *Revolutionary Horizons: Regional Foreign Policy in Post-Khomeini Iran.* New York: St. Martin's, 1994.

Carney, Timothy. "The Sudan: Political Islam and Terrorism." In *Battling Terrorism in the Horn of Africa*. ed. Robert Rotberg. Cambridge: Brookings Institutions Press, 2005.

Chubin, Shahram, and Charles Tripp. *Iran-Saudi Arabia Relations and Regional Order*. London: Oxford University Press for the International Institute for Strategic Studies, 1996.

Chwe, Michael. *Rational Ritual: Culture, Coordination, and Common Knowledge*. Princeton: Princeton University Press, 2003.

Clark, Janine A. "Islamist Women in Yemen." In *Islamic Activism: A Social Movement Theory Approach*, ed. Quintan Wiktorowicz. Bloomington: Indiana University Press, 2004.

Cohen, Raymond. *Threat Perception in International Crisis*. Madison: University of Wisconsin Press, 1979.

Cole, Juan, and Nikki Keddie. *Shi'ism and Social Protest*. New Haven: Yale University Press, 1986.

Cronin, Audrey, and James Ludes. *Attacking Terrorism: Elements of a Grand Strategy*. Washington, DC: Georgetown University Press, 2004.

Dahl, Robert. "The Concept of Power." *Behavioral Science* 2, no. 3 (1957): 201–215.

David, Steven. *Choosing Sides: Alignment and Realignment in the Third World*. Baltimore: Johns Hopkins University Press, 1991.

Dekmejian, Richard H. *Islam in Revolution: Fundamentalism in the Arab World*. Syracuse: Syracuse University Press, 1995.

Dekmejian, Richard H., and Margaret Wyszomirski. "Charismatic Leadership in Islam: The Mahdi of the Sudan." *Comparative Studies in Society and History* 14, no. 2 (1972): 193–214.

Desch, Michael. "Culture Clash: Assessing the Importance of Ideas in Security Studies." *International Security* 23, no. 1 (1998): 141–170.

Dresch, Paul, and James Piscatori. *Monarchies and Nations: Globalisation and Identity in the Arab States of the Gulf*. New York: I. B. Tauris, 2005.

Edelman, Murray. *The Symbolic Uses of Politics*. Bloomington: University of Illinois Press, 1985.

Ehteshami, Anoushirivan. *After Khomeini: The Iranian Second Republic*. New York: Routledge, 1995.

Eickelman, Dale, and James Piscatori. *Muslim Politics*. Princeton: Princeton University Press, 1996.

Elwey, Mostafa. "Al-Tahdid Al-Irani L'il Imn Al-Qaumi Al-Misri" (The Iranian Threat to Egyptian National Security). *Al-Ba'ath Al-Arabi* (October–December 1987): n.p.

Entessar, Nader. "The Lion and the Sphinx: Iranian-Egyptian Relations in Perspective." In *Iran and the Arab World*, ed. Hooshang Amirahmadi and Nader Entessar. New York: St. Martin's Press, 1993.

Esposito, John. *Political Islam: Revolution, Radicalism, or Reform?* Boulder, CO: Lynne Rienner, 1997.

Fandy, Mamoun. *(Un) Civil War of Words: Media and Politics in the Arab World*. Westport, CT: Praeger Security International, 2007.

Farnham, Barbara. "The Theory of Democratic Peace and Threat Perception." *International Studies Quarterly* 47 (2003): 395–415.

Ferguson, Chaka. "The Strategic Use of Soft Balancing: The Normative Dimensions of the Chinese-Russian 'Strategic Partnership.'" *Journal of Strategic Studies* 35, no. 2 (2012): 197–222.

Fox, Jonathan. "Religion as an Overlooked Element of International Relations." *International Studies Review* 3, no. 3 (2001): 53–73.

Fox, Jonathan, and Shmuel Sandler. *Bringing Religion into International Relations.* New York: Palgrave Macmillan, 2004.

Fuller, Graham. *The Center of the Universe: The Geopolitics of Iran.* Boulder, CO: Westview, 1991.

Fürtig, Henner. *Iran's Rivalry with Saudi Arabia between the Gulf Wars.* Ithaca: Ithaca Press, 2002.

Gause, F. Gregory III. "Balancing What? Threat Perception and Alliance Choice in the Gulf." *Security Studies* 13, no. 2 (2003): 273–305.

———. *The International Relations of the Persian Gulf.* Cambridge: Cambridge University Press, 2010.

———. "Iraq's Decision to Go to War in 1980 and 1990." *Middle East Journal* 56, no. 1 (2002): 47–70.

———. *Oil Monarchies: Domestic and Security Challenges in the Arab Gulf States.* Washington, DC: Council on Foreign Relations, 1994.

———. "Saudi Arabia: Iraq, Iran, the Regional Balance of Power, and the Sectarian Question." *Strategic Insights* 6, no. 2 (2007).

———. "Systemic Approaches to Middle East International Relations." *International Studies Review* 1, no. 1 (1999).

———. "Why Middle East Studies Missed the Arab Spring: The Myth of Authoritarian Stability." *Foreign Affairs* 90, no. 4 (2011): 81–90.

George, Alexander. "Case Studies and Theory Development: The Method of Structured, Focused Comparison." In *Diplomacy: New Approaches in History, Theory, and Policy*, ed. Paul Gordon Lauren. New York: Free Press, 1979.

Gerring, Jason, and John Seawright. "Case Selection Techniques in Case Study Research: A Menu of Qualitative and Quantitative Options." *Political Research Quarterly* 61, no. 2 (2008): 294–308.

Glaser, C. L. "The Security Dilemma Revisited." *World Politics* 50 1 (1997): 171–201.

Gleditsch, Kristian, and Michael Ward. "Diffusion and the International Context of Democratization." *International Organization* 60, no. 4 (2006): 911–933.

Goemans, Hein. *War and Punishment: The Causes of War Termination and the First World War.* Princeton: Princeton University Press, 2000.

Goffman, Erving. *Frame Analysis: An Essay on the Organization of Experience.* New York: Harper & Row, 1974.

Goldberg, Jacob. "Saudi Arabia and the Iranian Revolution: The Religious Dimension." In *The Iranian Revolution and the Muslim World*, ed. David Menashri. San Francisco: Westview, 1990.

Gould-Davies, Nigel. "Rethinking the Role of Ideology in International Politics during the Cold War." *Journal of Cold War Studies* 1, no. 1 (1999): 90–109.

Haas, Mark L. *The Ideological Origins of Great Power Politics, 1789–1989.* Cornell Studies in Security Affairs. Ithaca: Cornell University Press, 2005.

Hall, Rodney Bruce. "Moral Authority as a Power Resource." *International Organization* 51, no. 4 (1997): 591–622.

Hassner, Ron E. *War on Sacred Grounds.* Ithaca: Cornell University Press, 2009.

Hegghammer, Thomas. *Jihad in Saudi Arabia: Violence and Pan-Islamism since 1979.* Cambridge Middle East Studies. New York: Cambridge University Press, 2010.

Hegghammer, T., and S. Lacroix. "Rejectionist Islamism in Saudi Arabia: The Story of Juhayman Al-[Ain] Utaybi Revisited." *International Journal of Middle East Studies* 39, no. 1 (2007): 103–122.

Herb, Michael. *All in the Family: Absolutism, Revolution, and Democracy in the Middle Eastern Monarchies.* New York: State University of New York Press, 1999.

———. "Iran and the Shi'a of the Arab States of the Gulf." In *Ethnic Conflict and International Politics in the Middle East,* ed. Leonard Binder. Gainesville: University Press of Florida, 1999.

Hertog, Steffen. *Princes, Brokers, and Bureaucrats: Oil and the State in Saudi Arabia.* Ithaca: Cornell University Press, 2011.

Herz, John. *Political Realism and Political Idealism* Chicago: University of Chicago Press, 1951.

Hirschkind, Charles. *The Ethical Soundscape: Cassette Sermons and Islamic Counterpublics.* New York: Columbia University Press, 2006.

Hoffman, Bruce. *Inside Terrorism.* New York: Columbia University Press, 2006.

Hopf, Ted. *Social Construction of International Politics: Identities and Foreign Policies, Moscow, 1955 and 1999.* Ithaca: Cornell University Press, 2002.

Horgan, John. *The Psychology of Terrorism.* New York: Routledge, 2005.

Houghton, David. "Reinvigorating the Study of Foreign Policy Decision Making: Toward a Constructivist Approach." *Foreign Policy Analysis* 3, no. 1 (2007): 24–45.

Hudson, Michael. *Arab Politics: The Search for Legitimacy.* New Haven: Yale University Press, 1979.

Huntington, Samuel. "The Clash of Civilizations?" *Foreign Affairs* 72, no. 3 (1993): 22–49.

———. "If Not Civilizations, What? Samuel Huntington Responds to His Critics." *Foreign Affairs* 72, no. 4 (1993): 186–194.

Israeli, Raphael. "The Role of Islam in President Sadat's Throught." *Jerusalem Journal of International Relations* 4, no. 4 (1980): 1–12.

Jalali, Ali. "A Historical Perspective on Iran-Afghan Relations." In *Iran and Eurasia,* ed. Ali Mohammadi and Anoushiravan Ehtehshami. Ithaca: Cornell University Press, 2007.

Jankowski, James. *Nasser's Egypt, Arab Nationalism, and the United Arab Republic.* Boulder, CO: Lynne Rienner, 2001.

Jervis, Robert. *The Logic of Images in International Relations*. Princeton: Princeton University Press, 1970.

———. *Perception and Misperception in International Politics*. Princeton: Princeton University Press, 1976.

Jones, Toby. "The Clerics, the Sahwa and the Saudi State." *Strategic Insights* 4, no. 3 (2005), http://calhoun.nps.edu/public/handle/10945/11229.

———. "Rebellion on the Saudi Periphery: Modernity, Marginalization, and the Shia Uprising of 1979." *International Journal of Middle East Studies* 38, no. 2 (2006): 213–233.

Kaplan, Robert. *Balkan Ghosts: A Journey through History*. New York: Picador, 2005.

Karpat, Kemal. *The Politicization of Islam: Reconstructing Identity, State, Faith, and Community in the Late Ottoman State*. New York: Oxford University Press, 2001.

Kaufman, Stuart. "Symbolic Politics or Rational Choice? Testing Theories of Extreme Ethnic Violence." *International Security* 34, no. 4 (2006): 45–86.

Keohane, Robert, Gary King, and Sidney Verba. *Designing Social Inquiry: Scientific Inference in Qualitative Research*. Princeton: Princeton University Press, 1994.

Kepel, Gilles. *Jihad: The Trail of Political Islam*. Cambridge, MA: Harvard University Press, 2002.

———. *Muslim Extremism in Egypt: The Prophet and Pharoah*. Berkeley: University of California Press, 1993.

Knorr, Klaus. "Threat Perception." In *Historical Dimensions of National Security Problems*. ed. Knorr. Lawrence: University Press of Kansas, 1976.

Korany, Bahgat, Paul Noble, and Rex Brynen. "The Analysis of National Security in the Arab Context: Restating the State of the Art." In *The Many Faces of National Security in the Arab World*. ed. Bahgat Korany, Paul Noble, and Rex Brynen. New York: St. Martin's Press, 1993.

Kramer, Martin. *Arab Awakening and Islamic Revival: The Politics of Ideas in the Middle East*. New Brunswick, NJ: Transaction, 1996.

———. "The Global Village of Islam." *Middle East Contemporary Survey*. Vol. 16, 1992. Boulder, CO, and Oxford: Westview, 1994, 193–226.

Kuran, Timur. *Private Truths, Public Lies: The Social Consequences of Preference Falsification*. Cambridge, MA: Harvard University Press, 1997.

———. "Sparks and Prairie Fires: A Theory of Unanticipated Political Revolution." *Public Choice* 61, no. 1 (1989): 41–74.

Kurlantzick, Joshua. *Charm Offensive: How China's Soft Power Is Transforming the World*. New Haven: Yale University Press, 2007.

Lacroix, Stéphane. *Awakening Islam: The Politics of Religious Dissent in Contemporary Saudi Arabia*. Cambridge, MA: Harvard University Press, 2011.

Lankina, Tomila, and Lullit Getachew. "A Geographic Incremental Theory of Democratization: Territory, Aid, and Democracy in Postcommunist Regions." *World Politics* 58, no. 4 (2006): 536–582.

Larson, Deborah Welch. *Anatomy of Mistrust: U.S.-Soviet Relations during the Cold War*. Cornell Studies in Security Affairs. Ithaca: Cornell University Press, 1997.

Lasswell, Harold, and Abraham Kaplan. *Power and Society: A Framework for Political Inquiry*. New Haven: Yale University Press, 1950.

Lawrence, Bruce, and James Howarth. *Messages to the World: The Statements of Osama Bin Laden*. New York: Verso, 2005.

Lee, Robert. *Overcoming Tradition and Modernity: The Search for Islamic Authenticity*. Boulder, CO: Westview, 1997.

Lesch, Ann Mosley. *Sudan: Contested Nationalities*. Indianapolis: Indiana University Press, 1998.

Lewis, Bernard. *The Political Language of Islam*. Chicago: University of Chicago Press, 1991.

Lijphart, Arend. "Comparative Politics and the Comparative Method." *American Political Science Review* 65, no. 3 (1971): 682–693.

Lobell, Steven, Norman Ripsman, and Jeffrey Taliaferro. *Neoclassical Realism, the State, and Foreign Policy*. Cambridge: Cambridge University Press, 2009.

Lohmann, Susanne. "The Dynamics of Informational Cascades." *World Politics* 47, no. 1 (1994): 42–101.

Louër, Laurence. *Transnational Shia Politics: Religious and Political Networks in the Gulf*. New York: Columbia University Press, 2009.

Lynch, Marc. *The Arab Uprising: The Unfinished Revolutions of the New Middle East*. 1st ed. New York: Public Affairs, 2012.

———. *State Interests and Public Spheres: The International Politics of Jordan's Identity*. New York: Columbia University Press, 1999.

———. *Voices of the New Arab Public: Iraq, Al-Jazeera, and Middle East Politics Today*. New York: Columbia University Press, 2006.

Mach, Zdzislaw. *Symbols, Conflict, and Identity: Essays in Political Anthropology*. Albany: State University of New York Press, 1993.

Maddy-Weitzman, Bruce. "Inter-Arab Relations." *Middle East Contemporary Survey*. Vol. 16, *1992*, ed. Ami Ayalon. Boulder, CO: Westview, 1995.

Malek, Alia. "Al-Alam's Game." *Columbia Journalism Review* (2007), http://www.cjr.org/feature/alalams_game.php, accessed September 2, 2009.

Mandaville, Peter. *Global Political Islam*. New York: Routledge, 2007.

Matthee, Rudi. "Egyptian Opposition on the Iranian Revolution." In *Shi'ism and Social Protest*, ed. Nikki Keddie and Juan R. Cole, 247–274. New Haven: Yale University Press, 1986.

McAdam, Doug, and Dieter Rucht. "The Cross-National Diffusion of Movement Ideas." *Annals of the American Academy of Political and Social Science* 528 (1993): 56–71.

Middle East Contemporary Survey. Vols. 14, 15, 19, 20 (*1990, 1991, 1995, 1996*). Boulder, CO: Westview, 1990, 1991, 1995, 1996.

Miles, Hugh. *The Inside Story of the Arab News Channel That Is Challenging the West*. New York: Grove Press, 2005.

Miller, Judith. "Global Islamic Awakening or Sudanese Nightmare?" In *Spokesmen for the Despised: Fundamentalist Leaders of the Middle East*, ed. Scott Appleby. Chicago: University of Chicago Press, 1996.

Mitzen, Jennifer. "Ontological Security in World Politics: State Identity and the Security Dilemma." *European Journal of International Relations* 12, no. 3 (2006): 341–370.

Mufti, Malik. *Sovereign Creations and the Political Order in Syria and Iraq.* Ithaca: Cornell University Press, 1996.

Nahas, Maridi. "State-Systems and Revolutionary Challenge: Nasser, Khomeini, and the Middle East." *International Journal of Middle East Studies* 17, no. 4 (1985): 507–527.

Nasr, Vali. *The Shia Revival: How Conflicts within Islam Will Shape the Future.* New York: Norton, 2006.

Niblock, Tim. *Saudi Arabia: Power, Legitimacy and Survival.* New York: Routledge, 2006.

Noble, Paul. "The Arab System: Pressures, Constraints, and Opportunities." In *The Foreign Policies of Arab States,* ed. Bahgat Korany and A. Hillal Dessouki. Boulder, CO: Westview, 1991.

———, Rex Brynen, and Baghat Korany. "Conclusion." In *The Many Faces of National Security in the Arab World,* ed. Korany, Noble, and Brynen. New York: St. Martin's Press, 1993.

Nye, Joseph. *Bound to Lead: The Changing Nature of American Power.* New York: Basic Books, 1990.

———. *Soft Power: The Means to Success in World Politics.* New York: Public Affairs, 2004.

Okruhlik, Gwenn. "Saudi Arabian-Iranian Relations: External Rapprochement and Internal Consolidation." *Middle East Policy* 10, no. 2 (2003): 113–125.

———. "Empowering Civility through Nationalism: Reformist Islam and Belonging in Saudi Arabia." In Robert W. Hefner, ed., *Remaking Muslim Politics: Pluralism, Contestation, Democratization),* 189–212. Princeton, NJ: Princeton University Press, 2005.

O'Neill, Barry. *Honor, Symbols, and War.* Ann Arbor: University of Michigan Press, 1999.

Ottaway, Marina, and Marwan Muasher. *Arab Monarchies: Chance for Reform, Yet Unmet.* Carnegie Endowment for International Peace, December 2011. Washington, DC: Carnegie Endowment, 2011, http://carnegieendowment.org/files/arab_monarchies1.pdf.

Parsi, Trita. *Treacherous Alliance: The Secret Dealings of Israel, Iran, and the United States.* New Haven: Yale University Press, 2007.

Pease, Kevin M., and Michael R. Woods. *The Mother of All Battles: Saddam Hussein's Strategic Plan for the Persian Gulf.* Annapolis: United States Naval Institute, 2008.

Piscatori, James. "Managing God's Guests." In *Monarchies and Nations: Globalization and Identity in the Arab States of the Gulf,* ed. James Piscatori and Paul Dresch. New York: I. B. Tauris, 2005.

———. "Religion and Realpolitik: Islamic Responses to the Gulf War." In *Islamic*

Fundamentalisms and the Gulf Crisis, ed. James Piscatori, 1–25. Chicago: American Academy of Arts and Sciences, 1992.

———. "The Rushdie Affair and the Politics of Ambiguity." *International Affairs* 66, no. 4 (1990): 767–789.

Pope, Hugh. "Erdogan's Decade." *Cairo Review of Global Affairs* (2012), http://www.aucegypt.edu/gapp/cairoreview/pages/articleDetails.aspx?aid=149, accessed September 2, 2013.

Quandt, William. *Saudi Arabia in the 1980s: Foreign Policy, Security, and Oil.* Washington, DC: Brookings Institution Press, 1981.

Rabinovich, Itamar, and Haim Shaked. *Middle East Contemporary Survey.* Boulder, CO: Westview Press, 1989.

Rahman, Fazlur. *Islam and Modernity.* Chicago: University of Chicago Press, 1982.

Ramazani, R. K. *The Gulf Cooperation Council: Record and Analysis.* Charlottesville: University of Virginia Press, 1988.

———. *Revolutionary Iran: Challenge and Response in the Middle East.* Baltimore: Johns Hopkins University Press, 1986.

Rapoport, David. "Four Waves of Terrorism." In *Attacking Terrorism: Elements of Grand Strategy*, ed. Audrey Kurth Cronin and James M. Ludes, 46–73. Washington, DC: Georgetown University Press, 2004.

———. "The Fourth Wave: September 11 in the History of Terrorism." *Current History* 100, no. 650 (2001): 419–424.

Rekhess, Elie. "The Iranian Impact on the Islamic Jihad Movement in the Gaza Strip." In *Iranian Revolution and the Muslim World*, ed. David Menashri. San Francisco: Westview Press, 1990.

Ronen, Yehudit. "Sudan and Egypt: The Swing of the Pendulum (1989–2001)." *Middle Eastern Studies* 39, no. 3 (2003): 81–98.

Ronen, Yehudit, and Haim Shaked. "The Republic of Sudan." *Middle East Contemporary Survey.* Vol. 11, *1984–1985*, ed. Itamar Rabinovich. Boulder, CO: Westview Press, 1985.

Rothenbuhler, E. W. *Ritual Communication: From Everyday Conversation to Mediated Ceremony.* Thousand Oaks, CA: Sage, 1998.

Roy, Olivier. *The Failure of Political Islam.* Cambridge, MA: Harvard University Press, 1994.

Ryan, Curtis R. *Inter-Arab Alliances: Regime Security and Jordanian Foreign Policy.* Governance and International Relations in the Middle East. Gainesville: University Press of Florida, 2009.

Sadat, Anwar. *In Search of Identity.* New York: Harper & Row, 1977.

Sadowski, Yahya. "Political Islam: Asking the Wrong Questions?" *Annual Review of Political Science* (2006): 215–240.

Sageman, Marc. *Leaderless Jihad: Terror Networks in the Twenty-First Century.* Philadelphia: University of Pennsylvania Press, 2008.

Sakr, Naomi. *Arab Television Today.* London: I. B. Tauris, 2007.

Schelling, Thomas. *The Strategy of Conflict*. Cambridge, MA: Harvard University Press, 1960.

Schulze, Reinhard. "The Forgotten Honor of Islam." *Middle East Contemporary Survey*. Vol. 13, *1989*, ed. Ami Ayalon. Boulder, CO: Westview, 1991.

Schweller, Randall. "Unanswered Threats: A Neoclassical Realist Theory of Underbalancing." *International Security* 29, no. 2 (2004): 159–201.

Shaffer, Brenda. *The Limits of Culture: Islam and Foreign Policy*. Cambridge, MA: MIT Press, 2006.

Sharp, Jeremy. "Egypt-United States Relations." http://www.fas.org/sgp/crs/mideast/IB93087.pdf. 2005, accessed November 1, 2009.

Sirrs, Owen L. *A History of the Egyptian Intelligence Service*. New York: Routledge, 2011.

Singer, J. David. "Threat-Perception and the Armament-Tension Dilemma." *Journal of Conflict Resolution* 2 (1958): 90–105.

Singerman, Diane. *Avenues of Participation*. Princeton: Princeton University Press, 1995.

Sivan, Emmanuel. *Radical Islam: Medieval Theology and Modern Politics*. New Haven: Yale University Press, 1990.

———. "Sunni Radicalism in the Middle East and the Iranian Revolution." *International Journal of Middle East Studies* 21, no. 1 (1989): 1–30.

Siverson, Randgold, and Harvey Starr. "Regime Change and the Restructuring of Alliances." *American Journal of Political Science* 38, no. 1 (1994):145–161.

Smith, Anthony. *National Identity*. Reno: University of Nevada Press, 1993.

Snow, David, and Robert Benford. "Clarifying the Relationship between Framing and Ideology." *Frames of Protest: Social Movements and the Framing Perspective* (2005): 205.

———. "Ideology, Frame Resonance, and Participant Mobilization." *International Social Movement Research* 1 (1988): 197–217.

Snyder, Jack, ed. *Religion and International Relations Theory*. New York: Columbia University Press, 2011.

Solingen, Etel. *Nuclear Logics: Contrasting Paths in East Asia and the Middle East*. Princeton: Princeton University Press, 2007.

Sprinzak, Ehud. "The Process of Delegitimation: Towards a Linkage Theory of Political Terrorism." *Terrorism and Political Violence* 3, no. 1 (1991): 50–68.

Steele, Brent J. *Ontological Security in International Relations*. London and New York: Routledge, 2008.

Swidler, Ann. "Culture in Action: Symbols and Strategies." *American Sociological Review* 51, no. 2 (1986): 273–286.

Tal, Nahman. *Radical Islam in Egypt and Jordan*. Portland: Sussex Academic Press, 2005.

Tang, S. P. "The Security Dilemma: A Conceptual Analysis." *Security Studies* 18, no. 3 (2009): 587–623.

Tarrow, Sidney. *The New Transnational Activism*. Cambridge: Cambridge University Press, 2005.

Taylor, Julie. "Prophet Sharing: Strategic Interaction between Islamic Clerics and Middle Eastern Regimes." Unpublished PhD diss., UCLA, 2004.

Teitelbaum, Joshua. "Saud Arabia." *Middle East Contemporary Survey*. Vol. 22, *1998*, ed. Bruce Maddy-Weitzman. Boulder, CO: Westview, 2001.

Telhami, Shibley. "Power, Legitimacy, and Peace-Making in Arab Coalitions." In *Ethnic Conflict and International Politics in the Middle East*, ed. Leonard Binder. Gainesville: University Press of Florida, 1999.

Telhami, Shibley, and Michael Barnett. *Identity and Foreign Policy in the Middle East*. Ithaca: Cornell University Press, 2002.

Toft, Monica Duffy. "Getting Religion? The Puzzling Case of Islam and Civil War." *International Security* 31, no. 4 (2007): 97–131.

Treverton, Gregory, and Seth Jones. *Measuring National Power*. Washington, DC: RAND Corporation, 2005.

Trofimov, Yaroslav. *The Siege of Mecca: The Forgotten Uprising in Islam's Holiest Shrine and the Birth of Al-Qaeda*. New York: Doubleday, 2009.

Turner, Victor. *The Ritual Process: Structure and Anti-Structure*. Chicago: Aldine, 1995.

Valbjorn, M., and A. Bank. "The New Arab Cold War: Rediscovering the Arab Dimension of Middle East Regional Politics." *Review of International Studies* 38, no. 1 (2012): 3–24.

Van Evera, Stephen. *Guide to Methods for Students of Political Science*. Ithaca: Cornell University Press, 1997.

Walt, Stephen M. *The Origins of Alliances*. Cornell Studies in Security Affairs. Ithaca: Cornell University Press, 1987.

———. *Revolution and War*. Cornell Studies in Security Affairs. Ithaca: Cornell University Press, 1996.

Waltz, Kenneth Neal. *Theory of International Politics*. Addison-Wesley Series in Political Science. Reading, MA: Addison-Wesley, 1979.

Warburg, Gabriel. *Islam, Sectarianism and Politics in Sudan since the Mahdiyya*. Madison: University of Wisconsin Press, 2003.

Webb, Kieran. "The Continued Importance of Geographic Distance and Boulding's Loss of Strength Gradient." *Comparative Strategy* 26 (2010): 295–310.

Wedeen, Lisa. "Acting 'As If': Symbolic Politics and Social Control in Syria." *Comparative Studies in Society and History* 40, no. 3 (2004): 503–523.

Wehrey, Frederic, et al. *Saudi-Iranian Relations since the Fall of Saddam*. Washington, DC: Storming Media/RAND Corporation, 2009.

Wendt, Alexander. *Social Theory of International Politics*. Cambridge: Cambridge University Press, 1999.

Wiktorowicz, Quintan. ed. "Introduction: Islamic Activism and Social Movement Theory." In *Islamic Activism: A Social Movement Theory Approach*. Bloomington: Indiana University Press, 2004.

———. *Islamic Activism: A Social Movement Theory Approach*. Bloomington: Indiana University Press, 2004.

———. *The Management of Islamic Activism: Salafis, the Muslim Brotherhood, and State Power in Jordan.* Albany: State University of New York Press, 2001.

Wohlforth, William. *The Elusive Balance: Power and Perceptions during the Cold War.* Ithaca: Cornell University Press, 1993.

Woodward, Peter. "Sudan: Islamic Radicals in Power." In *Political Islam: Revolution, Radicalism or Reform.* ed. John Esposito. Boulder: Lynne Rienner, 1997.

Wright, Lawrence. *The Looming Tower: Al-Qaeda and the Road to 9/11.* New York: Knopf, 2006.

Yom, Sean, and F. Gregory Gause III. "Resilient Royalties: How Arab Monarchies Hang On." *Journal of Democracy* (2012): 74–88.

Other sources cited

Agence France Presse
Al-Ahram (Arabic)
Al-Ahram Weekly
Al-Arabiyya *(Arabic)*
Al-Jazeera satellite *(Arabic)*
Al-Jumhuriyya *(Arabic)*
Al-Wafd *(Arabic)*
Arab News
Ashraq al-Awsat (Arabic)
BBC World Service
CNN
The Economist
Foreign Broadcast Information Service (FBIS)
Haaretz
Los Angeles Times
Newsweek
New York Times
Reuters
Ruz al-Yusuf (Arabic)
Today's Zaman
UPI
Washington Post

Index